PASTOR
PAUL

THEOLOGICAL
EXPLORATIONS
for the
CHURCH
CATHOLIC

PASTOR PAUL

NURTURING A CULTURE
OF CHRISTOFORMITY IN THE CHURCH

SCOT McKNIGHT

BrazosPress

a division of Baker Publishing Group
Grand Rapids, Michigan

Published by Brazos Press
a division of Baker Publishing Group
PO Box 6287, Grand Rapids, MI 49516-6287
www.brazospress.com

Printed in the United States of America

Library of Congress Cataloging-in-Publication Data
Names: McKnight, Scot, author.
Title: Pastor Paul : nurturing a culture of Christoformity in the Church / Scot McKnight.
Description: Grand Rapids : Brazos Press, a division of Baker Publishing Group, 2019. | Series: Theological explorations for the Church Catholic | Includes bibliographical references and index.
Identifiers: LCCN 2018053563 | ISBN 9781587434266 (cloth : alk. paper)
Subjects: LCSH: Pastoral theology. | Bible. Epistles of Paul—Criticism, interpretation, etc.
Classification: LCC BV4011.3 .M425 2019 | DDC 253—dc23
LC record available athttps://lccn.loc.gov/2018053563

19 20 21 22 23 24 25   7 6 5 4 3 2 1

For Jay, Amanda,
and Stephanie

I left the Château at mid-day, and had to start at once for Dombasle. On my way back I stopped on the fringe of the wood from which one has a view of wide flat country, long scarcely visible slopes which trail slowly downwards to the sea. I had bought some bread and butter in the village and I ate it hungrily. The kind of torpor had come over me which I feel after every decisive moment, every real trial in my life: a not unpleasant dullness of thought bringing with it a strange sensation of lightness, of joy. What sort of joy? I can find no word. A shapeless joy. That which had to be, has been and is no longer—no more than that. I got back home very late and met old Clovis on the road. He gave me a small packet from Mme la Comtesse. I could not make up my mind to open it, and yet I *knew* what was inside. It was the little empty medallion, strung at the end of its broken chain. There was also a letter. Here it is. A curious letter:

"Monsieur le Curé, I don't suppose you can imagine my state of mind when you left me, since all such questions of psychology probably mean nothing at all to you. What can I say to you? I have lived in the most horrible solitude, alone with the desperate memory of a child. And it seems to me that another child has brought me to life again. I hope you won't be annoyed with me for regarding you as a child. Because you are! May God keep you one for ever! . . .

I wanted you to know all this to-night. I had to tell you. And don't let's mention it ever again. Never again. How peaceful that sounds! Never. I'm saying it under my breath as I write—and it seems to express miraculously, ineffably, the peace you've given me."

Georges Bernanos, *The Diary of a Country Priest*

Paul never spoke other than as a pastor.

J. D. G. Dunn, *The Theology of Paul the Apostle*

He was a pastor, and a pastor's pastor.

N. T. Wright, *Paul and the Faithfulness of God*

They [the pastors] were the stewards of ultimate things.

Marilynne Robinson, *Home*

Contents

Series Preface   ix
Preface   xi
Abbreviations   xv

1. Pastors as Culture Makers   1
2. A Culture of Friendship   31
3. A Culture of Siblings   57
4. A Culture of Generosity   79
5. A Culture of Storytellers   103
6. A Culture of Witness   127
7. A Culture of World Subversion   147
8. A Culture of Wisdom   169
   Final Thoughts: Nurturing Christoformity   191

Notes   197
Bibliography   225
Scripture and Ancient Writings Index   247

Series Preface

Long before Brian McLaren began speaking about a "generous ortho-doxy," John Wesley attempted to carry out his ministry and engage in theological conversations with what he called a "catholic spirit." Although he tried to remain "united by the tenderest and closest ties to one particular congregation"[1] (i.e., Anglicanism) all his life, he also made it clear that he was committed to the orthodox Christianity of the ancient creeds, and his library included books from a variety of theological traditions within the church catholic. We at Nazarene Theological Seminary (NTS) remain committed to the theological tradition associated with Wesley but, like Wesley himself, are very conscious of the generous gifts we have received from a variety of theological traditions. One specific place this happens in the ongoing life of our community is in the public lectures funded by the generosity of various donors. It is from those lectures that the contributions to this series arise.

The books in this series are expanded forms of public lectures presented at NTS as installments in two ongoing, endowed lectureships: the Earle Lectures on Biblical Literature and the Grider-Winget Lectures in Theology. The Earle Lecture series is named in honor of the first professor of New Testament at NTS, Ralph Earle. Initiated in 1949 with W. F. Albright for the purpose of "stimulating further research in biblical literature," this series has brought outstanding biblical scholars to NTS, including F. F. Bruce, I. Howard Marshall, Walter Bruegge-mann, and Richard Hays. The Grider-Winget Lecture series is named in honor of J. Kenneth Grider, longtime professor of theology at NTS, and in memory of Dr. Wilfred L. Winget, a student of Dr. Grider and the son of Mabel Fransen Winget, who founded the series. The lecture-ship was initiated in 1991 with Thomas Langford for the purpose of "bringing outstanding guest theologians to NTS." Presenters for this lectureship have included Theodore Runyon, Donald Bloesch, and Jür-gen Moltmann.

The title of this monograph series indicates how we understand its character and purpose. First, even though the lectureships are geared toward biblical literature *and* systematic theology, we believe that the language of "theological explorations" is as appropriate to an engage-ment with Scripture as it is to an engagement with contemporary sys-tematic theology. Though it is legitimate to approach at least some biblical texts with nontheological questions, we do not believe that doing so is to approach them *as Scripture*. Old and New Testament texts are not inert containers from which to draw theological insights; they are already witnesses to a serious theological engagement with particular historical, social, and political situations. Hence, biblical texts should be approached *on their own terms* through asking theological questions. Our intent, then, is that this series will be characterized by theological explorations from the fields of biblical studies and systematic theology.

Second, the word *explorations* is appropriate since we ask the lectur-ers to explore the cutting edge of their current interests and thinking. With the obvious time limitations of three public lectures, even their expanded versions will generally result not in long, detailed mono-graphs but rather in shorter, suggestive treatments of a given topic— that is, explorations.

Finally, with the language of "the church catholic," we intend to con-vey our hope that these volumes should be *pro ecclesia* in the broadest sense—given by lecturers representing a variety of theological tradi-tions for the benefit of the whole church of Jesus Christ. We at NTS have been generously gifted by those who fund these two lectureships. Our hope and prayer is that this series will become a generous gift to the church catholic, one means of equipping the people of God for participation in the *missio Dei*.

Andy Johnson
Lectures Coordinator
Nazarene Theological Seminary
Kansas City, Missouri

Preface

Curiosity about the topic of this book arrived while I was pondering a lecture on the Corinthian correspondence for students, many of them pastors with gripping realities to sift what I and Paul had to say, at Northern Seminary. As I was reading 1 Corinthians 1–4, I was taken aback by Paul's sarcasm, his lack of pastoral sensitivity, and his profound theological subversion of the ways of the Corinthians. Our session made for an adventurous conversation and confusion about how to implement Paul's pastoral ways. That first lecture led to others with ever-new branchings out. In pondering those chapters in 1 Corinthians, then, I branched out to two other sections of Paul's letters that silently requested time in the classroom too: 2 Corinthians 2:12–7:16 and Colossians 1:24–2:5, two passages I consider more pastoral than even the Pastoral Letters. I was baffled and excited about how to explain Paul's pastoral strategies to pastors or those training to be pastors. My first formal opportunity to do so was in a gathering of church planters and pastors connected to the Anglican Church of North America (Christ Church, Plano, Texas, where I met David Roseberry). My second opportunity was in nearby Dallas, at a Churches of Christ pastors network headed up by Pat Bills (Highland Oaks Church of Christ). The third opportunity was with Pat Bills's network again, where I began to explore what is now in chapter 2 ("A Culture of Friendship").

When Andy Johnson at Nazarene Theological Seminary invited me to give the Ralph Earle Lectures on Biblical Literature for Pastors Day, I knew my topic and was delighted Andy agreed. Since that day, now nearly two years ago, I have been constantly pondering Pastor Paul, studying the texts in context, and finding great joy reading pastors writing about pastoring. I am grateful to Andy for the invitation, and as one now old enough to remember using the word studies done by Ralph Earle, I am doubly honored. Invitations such as these come with administrative care, so I express thanks to Dana Preusch, director of the Center for Pastoral Leadership, for her efficiency in handling the details of the event.

Since the invitation from Andy I have lectured and preached and discussed Paul as pastor in a number of settings, each of which deserves to be mentioned and thanked. I give thanks to my classes at Northern Seminary; to Trinity College Bristol (Justin Stratis), where I gave a lecture in J. I. Packer's old office (!); to Westminster Theological Centre (Nick and Lucy Peppiatt Crawley) and to Woodlands Church Bristol (Dave Mitchell); to Greg Mamula and Robin Stoop for the invitation to speak to the American Baptist Pastors of Nebraska; and especially also to Regent College Vancouver for giving me a full week to teach on the topic in the summer of 2017 as a warm-up to the whole set of lectures now published here. In February 2018 I spoke about these themes to Nelson Searcy's Renegade Conference in Orlando, Florida, a nice place to be in the midst of a Chicago winter. "Memory," Mary Karr once shrewdly observed, "is a pinball in a machine."[1] I appeal to her image of a memory bouncing around from bumper to bumper if I have forgotten anyone or any of the bumpers where the lights went off for something in this book.

I have mentioned my students at Northern, but now I must express my thanks to the president, Bill Shiell, for his enthusiasm for this study of Pastor Paul and to the board of trustees for their generosity and protection of professors' time and schedules. Because Paul has been on my mind and in my writing since I've been at Northern Seminary, my conversations with colleagues have often wandered into Paul, or my colleagues' comments have made me wander into Paul, so I thank—in the order of our offices—Jason Gile, Robert Price, Cherith Fee Nord-ling, David Fitch, Sam Hamstra, and Geoff Holsclaw.

I am grateful, too, to those who have read portions of this manu-script and offered feedback: Josh Casey, Sven Soderlund, Tara Beth Leach, and Becky Castle Miller, the last of whom read several versions of several chapters and made many suggestions. The book is better for her comments and I want to thank her for her sharp mind and no-nonsense approach to writing. An early conversation with Amanda Holm Rosengren spun out into the first chapter in several versions and her suggestions refined where I ended up. More than anyone else, Jay Greener's pastoring at Church of the Redeemer has inspired this book. He probably knows, but has not said so, that my occasional scribblings during his sermons are as often as not "notes to self" for this book. Jay—and this comes from the first chapter—pastors people. So does Stephanie, who has a rambunctious bundle of children and moms and dads to pastor.

Editors at Baker: Bob Hosack and the others. An editor, someone has said, is someone who knows more about writing than writers but somehow has managed to escape the compulsion to write. I haven't, they have, and I am grateful they have.

All my books end up as discussions in our home, and my wife, Kris, found this book's topic a welcome change from a recent, more controversial book. The chapter on Paul and friendship became a series of short talks I gave to a tour group through Pauline sites in Turkey and Greece. Those talks gave Kris a special interest in the subject and motivated her to keep me motivated to get this book sent off to Baker.

Scot McKnight
Lent 2018

Abbreviations

English Bible Versions

ASV	American Standard Version	KJV	King James Version
CEB	Common English Bible	NIV	New International Version
ESV	English Standard Version	NRSV	New Revised Standard Version

Old Testament

Gen.	Genesis	Song	Song of Songs
Exod.	Exodus	Isa.	Isaiah
Lev.	Leviticus	Jer.	Jeremiah
Num.	Numbers	Lam.	Lamentations
Deut.	Deuteronomy	Ezek.	Ezekiel
Josh.	Joshua	Dan.	Daniel
Judg.	Judges	Hosea	Hosea
Ruth	Ruth	Joel	Joel
1–2 Sam.	1–2 Samuel	Amos	Amos
1–2 Kings	1–2 Kings	Obad.	Obadiah
1–2 Chron.	1–2 Chronicles	Jon.	Jonah
Ezra	Ezra	Mic.	Micah
Neh.	Nehemiah	Nah.	Nahum
Esther	Esther	Hab.	Habakkuk
Job	Job	Zeph.	Zephaniah
Ps./Pss.	Psalm/Psalms	Hag.	Haggai
Prov.	Proverbs	Zech.	Zechariah
Eccles.	Ecclesiastes	Mal.	Malachi

New Testament

Matt.	Matthew	Acts	Acts
Mark	Mark	Rom.	Romans
Luke	Luke	1–2 Cor.	1–2 Corinthians
John	John	Gal.	Galatians

Eph.	Ephesians	Heb.	Hebrews
Phil.	Philippians	James	James
Col.	Colossians	1–2 Pet.	1–2 Peter
1–2 Thess.	1–2 Thessalonians	1–3 John	1–3 John
1–2 Tim.	1–2 Timothy	Jude	Jude
Titus	Titus	Rev.	Revelation
Philem.	Philemon		

Deuterocanonical Books

Sir.   Sirach

Dead Sea Scrolls

| CD | Cairo Genizah copy of the Damascus Document | 1QM | War Scroll |
| | | 1QS | Rule of the Community |

Mishnah

m. Avot   Mishnah Avot

Secondary Sources

ABRL	Anchor Bible Reference Library	ICC	International Critical Commentary
BBR	*Bulletin for Biblical Research*	*IG*	*Inscriptiones Graecae*
BDAG	Bauer, Walter, Frederick W. Danker, William F. Arndt, and F. Wilbur Gingrich. *Greek-English Lexicon of the New Testament and Other Early Christian Literature*. 3rd ed. Chicago: University of Chicago Press, 2000	*JBL*	*Journal of Biblical Literature*
		JSNT	*Journal for the Study of the New Testament*
		JSNTSup	Journal for the Study of the New Testament Supplement Series
		JSOTSup	Journal for the Study of the Old Testament Supplement Series
BNTC	Black's New Testament Commentaries	*JTI*	*Journal of Theological Interpretation*
CBET	Contributions to Biblical Exegesis and Theology	LCL	Loeb Classical Library. London: Heinemann; New York: Putnam's Sons, 1922
CBQ	*Catholic Biblical Quarterly*		
CurBR	*Currents in Biblical Research* (formerly *Currents in Research: Biblical Studies*)	LNTS	The Library of New Testament Studies
DPL	*Dictionary of Paul and His Letters*. Edited by Gerald F. Hawthorne and Ralph P. Martin. Downers Grove, IL: InterVarsity, 1993	*NewDocs*	*New Documents Illustrating Early Christianity*. Edited by Greg H. R. Horsley and Stephen Llewelyn. North Ryde, NSW: The Ancient History

Documentary Research Centre, Macquarie University, 1981–

NICNT   New International Commentary on the New Testament

NIGTC   New International Greek Testament Commentary

NovT   *Novum Testamentum*

NovTSup Supplements to Novum Testamentum

NPNF¹ *The Nicene and Post-Nicene Fathers*, Series 1. Edited by Philip Schaff. 1886–89. 14 vols. Repr., Peabody, MA: Hendrickson, 1994

NTS   *New Testament Studies*

OBT   Overtures to Biblical Theology

SBT   Studies in Biblical Theology

SNTSMS Society for New Testament Studies Monograph Series

SNTW   Studies of the New Testament and Its World

TLNT   C. Spicq. *Theological Lexicon of the New Testament.* Translated and edited by J. D. Ernest. 3 vols. Peabody, MA: Hendrickson, 1994

TynBul *Tyndale Bulletin*

WBC   Word Biblical Commentary

WUNT   Wissenschaftliche Untersuchungen zum Neuen Testament

Other Abbreviations

AD   *anno Domini*, in the year of our Lord

BC   before Christ

ca.   *circa*/about

cf.   confer/compare

esp.   especially

1

Pastors as Culture Makers

I am a professor who loves the church, but I am not a pastor and I know it. When I start to think I comprehend pastoring or when I consider a special angle on pastoring, a conversation with a pastor reminds me that I'm a professor. I believe the pastoral calling is noble, and at times I envy the pastoral calling, but I am a professor, and so I am fascinated by how the New Testament talks (or does not talk) about the pastoral calling. Our theme will be how Paul pastored, and I will explore seven illustrations of a single theme, but first I want to speak to the general themes of pastoral theology. (If I occasionally use the first-person plural—"we," for those who have forgotten or would like to forget their days of beginning Greek—forgive me the transgression of identifying with you and the apostle Paul.)

The Complication of the Pastoral Life

Pastoring is a complicated calling, but at least we know where it begins: with spiritual formation.[1] Eugene Peterson, the dean of pastoral theology for many, once opined on the inadequacy of the typical form of education by professors—in other words, people like me—in seminaries and how ineffective the normal preparation is for ministry, landing at this spot when he was done opining: "The more I worked with people at or near the centers of their lives where God and the human, faith and the absurd, love and indifference were tangled in daily traffic jams, the less it seemed that the way I had been going about teaching made much difference, and the more that teaching them to pray did."[2] Or, as he said in another context, the three pastoral acts are "praying, reading Scripture, and giving spiritual direction."[3]

Formation, then, is the core, but then the complications begin, leading even the most accomplished pastor to wonder if it is beyond anyone's ability. No wonder Paul called himself a "clay pot" (2 Cor. 4:7 CEB). Ordinary pastors often wonder if what they are doing matters, and they doubt sometimes (or more often than not) if they are called, and they end some days with a sigh and wake up with shards of hope, though even that hope weakens in some seasons. On some days the pockets of parsons are filled with ambiguity and rebellions against pragmatic certainties.[4] I believe this is all part of the calling and not a sign of weakness or even a lack of the calling. People wear pastors down because they expect so much and need what the pastor often can't provide, and any pastor worth her salt cares and emotes and does what she can, and it's never enough. But it's complicated.

Pastors are, to use a medical analogy, general practitioners rather than specialists. They are, to switch images, teachers in a one-room schoolhouse on the prairie. The complexity of the human person— heart, soul, mind, and body—is why the pastoral calling is so engagingly and endlessly complicated. One never knows what pastoral care a person might need or what discernment the pastor might discover. A day accompanying Jesus or Paul or Peter or John would have revealed the same unpredictable, wild complication at the heart of the pastoral calling. That's what pastoring is. Over a decade a pastor accumulates more stories of goodness and nonsense than anyone in society, and that fund of experience penetrates behind the walls of wisdom in ways that amaze me as a professor. This means the pastor's calling is multiple, or, to use the words of Paul, it is the calling to "become all things to all people" (1 Cor. 9:22). That's the complication I'm talking about, and it's the pastor I admire for entering into its mysteries.

Some people who want to pastor think pastoring is about preaching sermons and studying all week, but what I mean by *pastor* is *the parson who pastors people*. The average size of a church in the US is about seventy-five, and I want to speak directly to the pastor of churches of that size as well as to pastors of larger churches. Why? Because the pastor of an average-size church *pastors*. We live in an age of specialization, and that has meant that some pastors get to be preachers, and others counselors, and yet others administrators, and even others focus on Bible studies and teaching. But most pastors do it all, and that means (to this professor) that they pastor. Pastor A once started talking about Pastor B, who was "on campus" only on Sunday mornings when he preached to big audiences on TV. Pastor A told me Pastor B, when asked, didn't even know if the church had a Sunday school program or a discipleship program. We both got a good laugh, but it was also a sad story for me: the Sunday morning big-show personality preacher is not a pastor if he or she is not pastoring people during the week. Pastor B was not, and I'm not telling you who Pastor A is because I don't know if he pastors either.

The genius of pastoring is only discovered over time and only by those who enter into the fullness of the complexity of pastoring. Karl Barth, reflecting later in his life on his contemporaries who had been pastors for four decades, said this of the pastoral calling: "I can visualize what it means to spend forty years in giving instruction to first communicants, in seeking the right spiritual word at a graveside or for young married couples, in being pastor to every conceivable kind of folk, and above all in expounding the Gospel Sunday by Sunday and proclaiming the Word of salvation for the community and world of to-day, in face of all kinds of afflictions, irritations and hostilities, of the suspicion of the times and (not least, but above all) of all one's own unbelief."[5]

Barth lived in a time when the pastor's calling was far less complicated. Add four more sentences to Barth and you approximate the life of the pastor today. Except of course in Kansas or Iowa. I think one of the pastors in Marilynne Robinson's novels about Gilead, Iowa—perhaps John Ames—said he liked to go to church when the people weren't there. People, however, are what make it a church, and pastors and people belong together. And when pastors and people get together, the complications show up. I calculate that pastoring is between ten and twelve times more complicated than professoring, which is why some pastors would like to be professors. Professors who want to be pastors often don't know what they're getting themselves into. (Just in case you are wondering, I have no statistical basis for that "ten or twelve," but it sounds about right.)

Pastor as Culture Maker

Now to the theme of this book: *The pastor is called to nurture a culture of Christoformity*. One of this generation's best scholars on the apostle Paul, Michael Gorman, has made the word *cruciformity* popular, and I've learned much from him. So, my use of *Christoformity* stands on his shoulders, and by it I mean that we are called to be conformed to Christ. Pastors are nurturers of Christoformity in this sense: we are formed by his life, by his death, and by his resurrection and ascension. We are not only to believe the gospel but also to embody it. To use the Greek and Latin terms no one uses, *bio*-formity, *cruci*-formity, and *anastasi*-formity. Add those together and you get Christoformity, but the way we become Christoform is through participation in Christ: through baptism, through faith, through indwelling and being indwelled by Christ, through the Spirit, through being clothed with Christ, through fellowship, through transformation, and through sharing all the events in Christ's life.[6]

Christoformity is rooted in Jesus's own words and life. Hence Jesus said,

> A disciple is not above the teacher, nor a slave above the master; it is enough for the disciple to be like the teacher, and the slave like the master. If they have called the master of the house Beelzebul, how much more will they malign those of his household! (Matt. 10:24–25).
>
> For the Son of Man came not to be served but to serve, and to give his life a ransom for many (Mark 10:45).

If we take the second text first, we see that the mission of Jesus was to serve and give himself for others. The first text says it's enough for us to be like Jesus. That's Christoformity. If the Christian life is about Christoformity, then pastoring is about nurturing Christoformity in ourselves and in others.[7] In his summary of Paul as a pastor, Paul Barnett concludes, "In topic after topic, issue after issue Paul . . . relentlessly taught the Corinthians to reproduce the character of Christ in their community."[8]

To take a step back, this is the *mission of God*. Graham Buxton, a pastor and professor of pastors, calls us to see what ministry actually is—participation in what God is doing in Christ through the Spirit. "Only Christ," he presses on his readers, "is able to make God known to us. . . . Our response is a willing participation in God's self-revelation. That is our privilege and our calling as coworkers with Christ in God's ongoing ministry in the world."[9] Pastors are not so much on mission *for* God as they are participating in the mission *of God*, which means that it is the mission God is carrying out and that pastors enter into God's own work.[10] Pastoring, then, is participation in what God is doing, and what God is doing is rescuing all creation from its enslavement and liberating it. Which means it is participating in the ongoing work of Christ through the Spirit in the world. Take, for instance, how Paul understands his own ministry in Romans 15:18–19: "For I will not venture to speak of anything *except what Christ has accomplished through me* to win obedience from the Gentiles, by word and deed, by the power of signs and wonders, *by the power of the Spirit of God*, so that from Jerusalem and as far around as Illyricum I have fully proclaimed the good news of Christ."

It is not Paul's ministry or mission so much as it is Christ's ministry and mission through the Spirit (1 Thess. 1:5–6; 2:13; 4:3–9, 19–21).[11] To the Colossians Paul speaks of his ministry by appealing to the work of Christ in himself: "the energy that he powerfully inspires within me" (Col. 1:29).[12] Thus Paul is only participating in what God—Father, Son, Spirit—is doing: "My little children, for whom I am again in the pain of childbirth until Christ is formed in you . . ." (Gal. 4:19). James Thompson, who has labored over the Pauline texts in order to comprehend Paul's pastoral theology, says it well: "*Ministry is participation in God's work of transforming the community of faith until it is 'blameless' at the coming of Christ.*"[13]

The ultimate end of Christoformity, then, is participation in the rule of Christ over all creation to the glory of God.[14] Paul makes this clear in Romans 8:18–30 by connecting glory in verse 18 with conformity to Christ in verse 29 in a grand sweep that completes cosmic redemption.

That is, the divine intention in creating human beings in Genesis 1–2 will be realized in the new heavens and new earth. Christoformity, then, is more than cruciformity, but the cross is central to all Christoformity. Christoformity is as complex as the pastoral calling is complicated. Pastors don't create Christoformity—that's done by God in Christ through the Spirit. But they are called to nurture it, to plant and to water and to weed and to protect and to provide. Christoformity is complex and is, as Duke New Testament professor C. Kavin Rowe speaks of it, "a narrative way of life."[15] His colleague at Duke, Will Willimon, professor of the practice of Christian ministry, describes this narrative way of life as a "culture."[16] To Rowe's and Willimon's thoughts, I add some from C. S. Lewis:

> May I come back to what I said before? This is the whole of Christianity. There is nothing else. . . . In the same way the Church exists for nothing else but to draw men into Christ, to make them little Christs. If they are not doing that, all the cathedrals, clergy, missions, sermons, even the Bible itself, are simply a waste of time. God became Man for no other purpose. It is even doubtful, you know, whether the whole universe was created for any other purpose. It says in the Bible that the whole universe was made for Christ and that everything is to be gathered together in Him.[17]

I add together these thoughts from Christian leaders to say a pastor nurtures a Christoform culture. As culture makers, pastors nurture Christoformity.

Peggy Noonan, in the Oval Office to interview President George W. Bush while researching for her beautiful biography of Ronald Reagan, coaxed Bush into ruminating on Reagan. What Bush said about presidents can, I suggest, be said about pastors as well: "But if you really think about it a president's job is to define the spirit of the nation. And to help define the soul."[18] I believe this: one of the pastor's jobs is to nurture the spirit and soul of a local church. Emmanuel Lartey, a Ghanaian who studied in England and has taught and pastored in Africa, the UK, and the US, claims that "pastoral theologians . . . are on a journey of creatively imagining a different kind of world community."[19] That community is marked by Christoformity. To imagine such is to nurture it.

Forming a Christoform Culture in a Church: Four Elements

We must ask, *How do we nurture a culture?* A church culture emerges from four separate but integrated elements.[20] Think of this as a diamond where the four points are (A) the pastor (or pastors) and leaders; (B) the congregation; (C) the relationship among the pastor (or pastors), leaders, and the congregation; and (D) the policies, structures, and systems that govern A, B, and C.

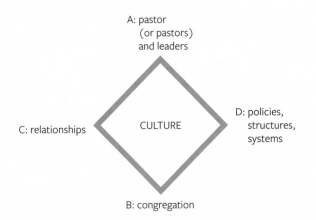

A: pastor
(or pastors)
and leaders

C: relationships   CULTURE   D: policies,
structures,
systems

B: congregation

   It would take a specialist to explain all this and it surely requires both a full book and someone else to do it, but I'd like us to think of pastors as culture makers in terms of this diamond. Pastors and congregations together form the culture as A, B, C, and D mutually indwell one another. It is not just A and not just B. The more charismatic or domineering the pastor is, the more influence he or she has on culture formation. Pastors are called to be influential in the formation of a church culture. A good pastor and a bad congregation form into a mixture of cultures while a bad pastor and a good congregation will lead often to the same mixture. Good pastors and good congregations help each other just as bad pastors and bad congregations fight each other. The relationships that form between A and B cannot be emphasized enough. But I want to stress that the less contact A actually has with B leads to a persona formation for the pastor and persona culture for the pastor's relationship with the congregation. This means that a persona, the public presentation of a person, can become false and fraudulent and be powerfully influential in the formation of a corrupted culture. Yet, and I have seen this over and over in my own life, genuinely good relationships between A and B can form C: flourishing and good relationships. The culture that forms in a church is determined by the kind of relationships between A and B. The structures, policies, and systems that churches establish and then indwell are not removed from these relationships; they are expressions of A, B, and C. In the middle of the diamond a culture emerges out of A and B, as well as out of relationships and structures involved. Culture emerges out of what happens between these elements; cultures are not intentionally created as much as they emerge from existent realities.

For a church culture to flourish as God wants, *goodness* is required on the part of the pastor, pastors, and leaders, as well as on the part of the congregation. No church culture is completely *good* because it emerges from human beings who are not completely good. Yet the gospel's power transforms what could be a bad culture into good at some level, so churches have at least some small chance of emerging as a culture of (some) goodness. Finally, in this book, goodness culture will be called Christoformity. For a Christoform culture to emerge in a church requires Christoformity in A and in B, with C formed in Christoform relationships and D becoming structural expressions of Christoformity. My last observation repeats what has been said: the pastor, with pastors and other leaders, are called to nurture Christoformity so that a culture of Christoformity emerges in their local church. (I must repeat: no church will be completely Christoform, but having a goal of Christoformity sets us all in the right direction.)

The Complicated Culture Called "Church"

I now turn to sketch briefly ten elements of a Christoform culture that the pastor can nurture.

A Culture of People

My go-to definition of pastoring is this: a pastor pastors people. People will occasionally ask if I think they are called to pastor, and my go-to answer is a twofold question: Are you presently pastoring anyone? And who sees you as their pastor? Pastoring is not a job one gets when one graduates from seminary, the way one gets a job as an engineer, but is a calling on one's life that grabs hold and turns a person into a parson. The parson's way of life is pastoring.

To *pastor* means to nurture Christoformity in both individuals and congregations. Pastors are designed for what used to be called the "cure of souls" and what Eugene Peterson once called the "ministry of small talk"[21] about ordinary life. In another context, he wrote about Paul and said, "Pastoral theology, as Paul lives and writes it, is relational— persons are involved as persons-in-relationship."[22] Many today, such as Margaret Whipp, define pastoral theology as a theology of care.[23] To do so opens the aperture to see that pastoring is about pastoring people in each person's specific realities. The irony of pastoring today emerged in the recent Barna Group study called *The State of Pastors*. When pastors were asked what they like to do most, 66 percent said preaching and teaching. "There is a big drop-off from there," Barna concludes. "One in 10 says 'developing other leaders' is their most enjoyable task (10%), and one in 12 prefers 'discipling believers' (8%). 'Evangelizing' (6%) and 'pastoral care' (5%) bring the most joy to smaller proportions of pastors, and a mere 2 percent say they enjoy 'organizing church events, meetings or ministries.'"[24]

How unlike Paul.[25] He calls pastoring a "daily pressure" and speaks of his "anxiety for all the churches" (2 Cor. 11:28).[26] When he leaves the church at Ephesus, which I consider his favorite church, he says he has been warning everyone "with tears" (Acts 20:31). So concerned is he over the response of the Christians of Corinth, which I consider his least favorite church, that he tells them his "mind could not rest" and he has to avoid a golden opportunity for ministry (2 Cor. 2:12–13). He pleads with them to "make room" in their "hearts" for him (7:2). When he gets the good news from Titus of their positive response to his message, he says it is God who "consoled" and that Paul "rejoiced" (7:7). One senses here the heart of Pastor Paul: his emotions are shaped by how his churches are responding and growing in Christlikeness.

To the Thessalonians Paul writes that he treated them as a mother (1 Thess. 2:7) and a father (2:11): "As you know, we dealt with each one of you like a father with his children, urging and encouraging you and pleading that you lead a life worthy of God, who calls you into his own kingdom and glory" (vv. 11–12). He even says the Thessalonians had received his teaching as if it was God's very word (v. 13). Perhaps the most revealing pastoral moment in this splendid little unity in the middle of the letter is that for him and his companions to be separated from them was like being "made orphans" and that he and Silvanus and Timothy "longed with great eagerness to see [them] face to face" (v. 17). When the separation was too much, he sent his good friend Timothy (3:1–2; see 3:5). And the loving pastor knows exactly what Paul means when he says, after hearing good news upon Timothy's return, "For we now live"—under what conditions?—"if you continue to stand firm in the Lord" (3:8). Paul pastored God's people.[27] Henri Nouwen, in his classic book on pastoring called *The Wounded Healer*, describes pastoring in those very terms: pastors are wounded healers. They are themselves wounded; they are themselves finding healing; and as ministers they are wounded by the sufferings of the world and their people; and they are called to minister the graces of healing.[28] So the first element is that pastors nurture a culture of people, and people— not programs and pews and plans—are the focus.

The complications of individuals become the complications of con- gregations, and I must emphasize here that by *people* I don't just mean individuals but congregations. Paul's theology of ministry was for churches, *and therefore individuals*, to be nurtured into Christoformity. Not just individuals, which is the downside of too many books today on spiritual formation. That is, spiritual formation is understood as "me and God" and "intimacy with God" and "how to pray" or "practicing solitude." I'm not against any of these, and I'm all for each of them, but formation in the Bible is first about being formed as a community, as a church, as a fellowship. Through that, formation becomes personal and individual. The fundamental and primary formation virtue in the New Testament is *love*, love for God (individual) and love for others (communal). Love, in fact, is never alone: love is for the other. James Thompson gets this exactly right when he observes that for the Pauline Christians "the test of their progress will be their capacity to exist as a family within the community of faith."[29]

And so does Michael B. Thompson, who comes from a context simi- lar to that of James Thompson:

> I have often thought it curious how many churches in the country of my birth (the US) have in their names the word "Independent." By that

they are emphasizing that they are not part of any larger denomination, membership in which they see as a disadvantage. Indeed, the notion of "independence" is a cultural fundamental in America because of our history. But the danger of Christian "independence" is an unhelpful isolation and a profound susceptibility to error (as well as a poor witness to the wider love of Christ). . . . If anything, Paul would have wanted the Corinthians to be known as a "Dependent" church—dependent upon Christ and the rest of his people to whom they belonged.[30]

Pastoring, then, is nurturing Christoformity in persons. Formation deserves a deeper look.

A Culture of Formation

The pastor is a Christian more than a person performing a role, a task, a sermon.[31] Barbara Brown Taylor, distinguishing between our office and our vocation, said it this way: "My office, then, is in the church. . . . But my vocation is to God's person in the world, and that makes me the same as those among whom I serve."[32] The pastor's first responsibility is to nurture and to be nurtured into spiritual formation. One of the great Hebrew words in the Bible is *dabaq*, which is often rendered "cleave to" or "hold fast to" or "cling to." The Bible uses this term for Adam cleaving to Eve (Gen. 2:24), but it is a common word for one's relationship to God as well:

> You shall fear the LORD your God; him alone you shall worship; to him *you shall hold fast*, and by his name you shall swear (Deut. 10:20).
>
> If you will diligently observe this entire commandment that I am commanding you, loving the LORD your God, walking in all his ways, and *holding fast to him* . . . (11:22).
>
> The LORD your God you shall follow, him alone you shall fear, his commandments you shall keep, his voice you shall obey, him you shall serve, and to him *you shall hold fast* (13:4).
>
> . . . loving the LORD your God, obeying him, and *holding fast to him*; for that means life to you and length of days, so that you may live in the land that the LORD swore to give to your ancestors, to Abraham, to Isaac, and to Jacob (30:20).[33]

The term takes on the sense of following closely or pursuing (1 Sam. 14:22) and describes close attachment, as in Job 41:17: "They [sections of Leviathan's armor] are joined one to another; / they clasp each other and cannot be separated." Perhaps the most evocative of all uses is found in Jeremiah 13:11: "For as the loincloth *clings* to one's loins, so I made the whole house of Israel and the whole house of Judah *cling* to me, says the LORD, in order that they might be for me a people, a name, a praise, and a glory. But they would not listen." This is the idea I want to call to your attention: the pastor's responsibility is to cling to the Lord in love, adoration, worship, obedience, and faithfulness. As a man loves his wife, as soldiers pursue, and as—yes, this—underwear clings to one's body, so the pastor is to cling to God.

Unfortunately, clinging to God is not seen by enough as the first step in the pastoral life. Nouwen said it well: "Most . . . are used to thinking in terms of large-scale organization, getting people together in churches, schools and hospitals, and running the show as a circus director."[34] Too often pastoring is fashioned today by theories of business leaders instead of dipping into the spiritual masters such as Saint Macrina, Saint Bonaventure, Teresa of Ávila, Rebecca Protten, Evelyn Underhill, Alexander Schmemann, or Robert Mulholland. These and many others, like A. W. Tozer, pastored out of a heart ablaze with the presence of God in the inward journey.

What are the marks of spiritual formation, and, thus, what are the marks of the pastor's spiritual formation? Whatever the answer is finds its way into expectations for the pastor and in most cases in the pastor's own desires for himself or herself. We could list the Beatitudes as virtues or look to the fruit of the Spirit or make some composite macro-list from one passage after another. Rather than piling on and piling up, I suggest we look at the following list of cardinal virtues in the New Testament. Without defining each of these at length, we can say,

A pastor is loving,
a pastor is holy,
a pastor is just and embodies justice,
a pastor is a peacemaker,
and a pastor is wise.

How? By being a Spirit-filled person, by being a person who prays and reads the Bible and kneels before God for grace and power to fulfill the impossible calling. In the Jewish world of Jesus and the apostles this would mean being a *hasid* (a devout pastor) and a *hakam* (a sage).[35] This is what churches want from their pastor or pastors, and these are the sorts of virtues pastors ought to strive for. In the history of the church these are the virtues held up as marks of distinction among pastors, and in the history of spiritual formation this character is the focus.

Pope Gregory the Great, in one of the most important books ever written on the pastoral life (*The Book of Pastoral Rule*), puts into words the expectations of most people in a church, and, perhaps more importantly, what he says is both tradition in the church and no longer popular. So, let me begin with his opening claim: "The conduct of a prelate [= bishop] should so far surpass the conduct of the people, as the life of a pastor sets him apart from the flock." Many don't like this, and I know that, but I want to continue anyway. "For one who is so regarded that the people are called his flock, must carefully consider how necessary it is for him to maintain a life of rectitude." And of what does such a life of rectitude consist? He answers: "It is necessary, therefore, that he should be pure in thought, exemplary in conduct, discreet in keeping silence, profitable in speech, in sympathy a near neighbour to everyone, in contemplation exalted above all others, a humble companion to those who lead good lives, erect in his zeal for righteousness against the vices of sinners."[36]

If that is not enough, Gregory adds the tension of pastoring people: "One must not be remiss in the care for the inner life by preoccupation with the external; nor must one, in solicitude for what is internal, fail to give attention to the external."[37] This can, of course, sound like perfectionism, but it need not be.

The importance of personal spiritual formation for the pastor's pastoring of people into Christoformity cannot be overestimated. In her wonderful book about the pastor as moral theologian, Sondra Wheeler contends that pastors are not just moral theologians; beyond that, "because ministers will continually be preaching by behavior and teaching by example, they must also become certain kinds of people." What might that kind of people be? "Not only people who possess certain knowledge and techniques but also people whose character is shaped in particular ways."[38] Victor Copan's *Saint Paul as Spiritual Director* explains why. Spiritual direction, which I'm using for the moment to refer to pastoring people, often gets wrapped into programs and techniques, but Copan digs deeper with two points: "It is my contention . . . that the total shape of the life of the director is a key factor—if not the key factor—in the success of spiritual direction; [and] effectiveness in spiritual direction is not to be found primarily in technique, but in the character and lifestyle of the one providing the direction."[39]

His point is that behind the program of discipleship and behind the techniques and disciplines is the person, and the personal formation of the pastor matters. One should not be a pastor if one doesn't shoulder the responsibility of being an example, because being an example is what the pastor is whether she knows it or not. That is, people will imitate the pastor, and what Paul would have experienced (in being an example) was common to the world of Paul: Jewish, Greek, and Roman.[40] Imitation, in fact, is the first principle of all forms of education: children imitate parents, and students imitate that parental relationship with their teachers. Hence, the congregant and the pastor are in a similar relationship: people need an embodied example to follow, and they will follow the embodied example—good or bad. To be sure, what some in a church will know of a pastor will be a projected image, the persona of the pastor as presented in sermons and various leadership roles. Hence, some will be "imitating" a false persona, but this illustrates the influence of even a persona. I could go on, but my point is that the pastor's personal formation is important to pastoring people.

One must also consider that congregants follow the pastor not because they know in advance that the pastor is like Christ. Rather, the order is the reverse: they come to love the pastor or admire the pastor as an exemplar, and that becomes their image of Christ. The pastor inevitably is understood to display what true godliness in the way of Christ is like, so people, not least new converts, follow the pastor because they think he is patterning before them the way of Christ. Douglas Campbell, professor of New Testament at Duke Divinity School, in his splendid new book on Paul, proposes that churches are to be learning communities shaped not by programs but by imitation of exemplary Christians: "The $64,000 question is not, should we have elites? But what sort of elites should we have? The answer for Christian communities is that we should have Christian leaders who are characterized by the relational qualities that we want everyone else to copy. Appropriate churches will be arranged as learning communities with leaders and followers or disciples (sound familiar?)."[41]

Each of the Pauline texts on imitation (1 Cor. 10:32–11:1; Phil. 3:17; 4:9; 1 Thess. 1:6) has specific resonance for a specific church, but one can't dispute the sweeping kind of exhortations Paul gives, not least in Philippians 4:9: "Keep on doing the things that you have learned and received and heard and seen in me, and the God of peace will be with you." And he ties this all to Christ in 1 Corinthians 11:1 when he says, "Be imitators of me, as I am of Christ." Wisdom, education, formation—choose your term—each occurred then, as they do most effectively now, in the context of embodied examples investing life in those who need to be formed.

The pastor nurtures a culture of spiritual formation in the direction of Christoformity. Not long ago I read Georges Bernanos's *The Diary of a Country Priest*.[42] My biggest impression of the book was this: unknown to all around him, the priest of a rural French church was dying of cancer, but his own suffering did not stop the petty demands of his parishioners, nor did it stop him from making the daily rounds of visitation and pastoring people. I grew annoyed with the people as the priest's condition was clarified, and my admiration of the priest grew as his own humility and suffering grew. "Monks," he said, "suffer for souls, our *pain* is on behalf of souls."[43] Very few novels capture Christoformity better than what we see in this priest. His story reminded me of pastors I know who faithfully serve their congregations in the midst of intense personal anguish—their own struggles in marriage, the anxious nights of concern over their children, divorces in the family and in the parish, physical suffering and disease, and, on top of it all and running right through it all, doubts about one's success and a consciousness of failure. The priest in Bernanos's novel asks a question that pastors commonly ask: "Am I where Our Lord would have me be? Twenty times a day I ask this question. For the Master whom we serve not only judges our life but also shares it, takes it upon Himself. It would be far easier to satisfy a geometrical and moralistic God."[44] Precisely.

A Culture of Listening

Pastors are preachers and teachers, and this section in my book was originally called "A Culture of the Word." Pastors talk, and some too much. In this dimension of ministry pastors see themselves as people who stand behind a pulpit and preach, and who also sit for hours in their offices poring over books and outlining sermons . . . and everywhere they go, they think about sermons.[45] So I bristle at James Thompson when he says, "Preaching is the central activity for creating a corporate consciousness."[46] Never mind that "corporate consciousness" is language drawn from social ideologists (and it means forming Christians into a fellowship); I am unconvinced that preaching is *the* central activity. Only someone who loves to preach says such things. Some preachers are blowhards, and some talk so much they don't learn to listen; they merely pretend silence until they can get in their next word. No matter how much I value preaching and teaching, preaching and teaching are not *the* central activities that will nurture Christoformity. They are both vital, but Christoformity is nurtured in numerous ways, not all of them even directly connected to preaching. A Christoform culture, then, is not first a culture of talking but of listening.[47] Listening to God, to Scripture, to the Eucharist . . . I could go on, but our immediate focus is preaching.

A Christoform culture begins well before the sermon or the instruction. As a preacher, the pastor nurtures both for herself and for the congregation the habit of listening to God speak in Scripture. This gives preaching more than a subtle shift. Here's one of my favorite test questions: Do you read or study the Bible only for the sermon? If so, I doubt you are listening to Scripture. Mandy Smith illustrates this perfectly when she writes about preaching, nay, confesses, "I thought it was my job to create a beautiful product, divorced from the messiness of life. But preaching forces me to become part of the product, always in the mess—my own and others'." She recognizes that preaching is not preaching until she herself gets involved in listening to God—listening so well it becomes personal: "Instead of imparting otherworldly enlightenment to me in my quiet study, God seeks embodiment, wants to use my life as the testing ground for each sermon." Then she asks the right question: "If I expect each individual in the congregation to find some connection between life and text that week, why shouldn't I expect the same of myself?"[48] Pastors won't create a culture that nurtures Christoformity through preaching and teaching until they themselves—daily, weekly, always—listen to God speak person-to-parson in the Scriptures.

Listening leads to speaking, and the one who listens is most able to speak or preach or teach as a pastor. It is this listening alone that qualifies the pastor to have a word for the congregation. The word preached, then, is to be the word heard first. Seminary training has importantly focused always on mentoring future preachers, and more than a few theories of preaching rise to the surface. My point here is not to square up with one theory—narrative preaching, expository preaching, seeker-friendly preaching, theological preaching[49]—but to contend that preaching and teaching derive from listening to God in Scripture and inspire a congregation to listen to God in the Word, both read and preached.

Listening means knowing one's congregation, and that means Christo-form preaching to people in a real church requires pastoral sensitivity. I turn to Frederick Buechner. In his beautiful book *Telling the Truth*, originally delivered as the Lyman Beecher Lectures at Yale, Buechner speaks of every people-oriented sermon in these words:

> There is the one who can't stop thinking about suicide. The one who experiences his own sexuality as a guilt of which he can never be absolved. The one whose fear of death is only a screen behind which lies his deeper fear of life. The one who is in a way crippled by her own beauty because it has meant that she has never had to be loving or human to be loved but only beautiful. And the angry one. The lonely one. For the preacher to be relevant to the staggering problems of history is to risk being irrelevant to the staggering problems of the ones who sit there listening out of their own histories. To deal with the problems to which there is a possible solution can be a way of avoiding the problems to which humanly speaking there is no solution.[50]

The concern in this book is to ground pastoral theology in the pastoral praxis of the apostle Paul, and I will devote two chapters (chaps. 5 and 6) to the theme of storytelling. So here I'll recommend looking at Romans 9–11, then skipping to Romans 15, and then skimming through the rest of Paul's letters, watching how your Bible clues you in to the quotations from the Old Testament in Paul's letters. Then develop an ear for what scholars such as Richard Hays and Ross Wagner call "echoes" and "allusions,"[51] and before long you'll know that Paul could never have done what he did without indwelling and demonstrating a culture of listening to God's voice in the words of Scripture. Alongside his listening to God was his listening to those in his churches. A Christoform culture develops ears to hear God and others, and so pastors nurture that kind of Christoformity.

A Culture of Prophecy

In nurturing Christoformity in a congregation sometimes the pastor teaches and sometimes preaches, and sometimes the pastor's communications are prompted by the Spirit in such a manner that we must say the words are prophetic. When that prophetic word is embodied it becomes prophetic action, which means the pastor or congregation or congregants become an embodied message that speaks from God to a community and often enough against the ways of the community. Yes, Christoformity is sometimes prophetic.

What is a prophet? What does it mean to be prophetic? Ellen Davis, in her baccalaureate address at Duke Divinity School in 2011, looked at pastoral ministry through the lens of Mount Elijah, that is, through the life of Elijah. In the course of her address she defines a prophet like this:

> So, class of 2011, standing on Mount Elijah and looking toward Zarephath, what do we learn about ministry that might be called prophetic? This: you have to trust in God's ability to create out of the most unpromising raw material a community of mutual caring. Like Elijah, you have to be willing to be called into a desperate situation, with no clue as to how to improve it. Like him, you have to go among strangers, as needy as you and even more clueless, with nothing more substantial to offer than a word that you trust is from God. Like Elijah, you have to go to people who don't seem to know God at all, and risk everything on God's ability to speak into their profound deafness— the deafness not just of individuals but of a whole culture. You have to trust that God's Word and Spirit can awaken in them a capacity for generous and faithful action, so they will make your work fruitful in that unpromising place.[52]

That's a beautiful sketch of a prophet, but for many today a prophet is someone who criticizes social injustices and systemic sins, and who, often enough, becomes a social activist. In other words, someone who has a blog or a Twitter handle. This reduces the prophetic calling. To be prophetic in a biblical sense requires a claim of inspiration from God for a particular vision and message. There is a Spirit-promptedness to the gift of prophecy that must be respected and present before it can be called prophetic—which is not the same as being passionate about something. The pastor at times, as a result of communion with God, of Scripture study, of theological vision, and of Spirit-promptedness, has something prophetic to proclaim to her congregation, and the pastor must have the courage to speak forth. I have never worshiped with a congregation for any length of time that didn't at times show the presence of this gift, though in some of those cases I know the pastor-preacher-expositor would have been wary of making the claim.

Briefly, neither Jesus nor the apostle Paul spent much time dropping comments on websites or lighting up the Twitter world with outlandish claims. Yet they were prophetic to the core: Jesus in his summons to follow him, his offering of grace to the marginalized, his embodiment of the kingdom at the table, and his stunning words about moral corruption. Paul made even fewer direct comments to the authorities in the empire than Jesus did, but everything about Paul's mission, message, and embodied living offered an alternative to the way of Rome. Both Jesus and Paul, then, were prophetic in hearing from God and speaking to the people of God's way. Pastors need to nurture the prophetic gift if the culture is to become Christoform.

A Culture of Presence

Pastors pastor people by becoming a Spirit-prompted presence. Here pastors embed themselves in their own community and seek fresh words for that community. Pastors are then a holistic redemptive presence in and for a specific community. Such pastors—and here is the deeper point—*are seen as the presence of God in the community.* Please understand that this is not some goofy idea, nor is it a subtle attempt to deny the importance of the church itself as God's embodied presence. My colleague David Fitch speaks here of three circles of "faithful presence": first, the pastor and the church are present in a "close" circle (that is, as the church in worship and fellowship); second, they are present in a "dotted" circle (that is, as present in the neighborhood, both one's own neighborhood and that surrounding the church's gathering place); third, they are present in a "half" circle (that is, among the marginalized, where the church must be welcomed in). I contend, with David Fitch, that the pastor and congregation embody the faithful presence of God in Christ through the Spirit, though I will emphasize the pastor-as-presence as a singular instance of the congregation's presence.[53]

Margaret Whipp, in her insightful study of pastoral theology, knows that pastoring is caring and caring is first about being present. She writes, "Pastoral care requires availability. Being there, for and with the other, in the steadfast immanence of covenant love is itself a presencing of the gospel, a tangible expression of the immediacy of God's love and the nearness of his grace, through the extended ministry of incarnation which Christ has entrusted to his Church."[54] I hope that verb *presencing* stood out as much to you as it did to me, because that's my point: pastors are to "presence" the grace of God through the Spirit. To "presence" God is to recognize that pastors—though this is true of each Christian—are to *embody* Christ in their tangible presence.

No pastor is perfect, but every pastor knows what happens when the conversation turns to "What do you do?" and the pastor says, "I'm a pastor [or a priest or a minister]." My favorite story of the importance of a pastor as embodied presence comes from Alec Guinness, known to most of us as Obi-Wan Kenobi in the megahit film *Star Wars Episode IV: A New Hope*. In his autobiography he tells how, during a late-evening shoot while he was acting the role of a priest in *Father Brown* in Burgundy, France, a fair number of local folk, including children, gathered around:

> A room had been put at my disposal in the little station hotel three kilometres away. By the time dusk fell I was bored and, dressed in my priestly black, I climbed the gritty winding road to the village. In the square children were squealing, having mock battles with sticks for swords and dustbin lids for shields; and in a café Peter Finch, Bernard Lee and Robert Hamer were sampling their first Pernod of the evening. I joined them for a modest Kir, then discovering I wouldn't be needed for at least four hours turned back towards the station. By now it was dark.

I hadn't gone far when I heard scampering footsteps and a piping voice calling, "Mon père!" ["My father!"] My hand was seized by a boy of seven or eight, who clutched it tightly, swung it and kept up a non-stop prattle. He was full of excitement, hops, skips and jumps, but never let go of me. I didn't dare speak in case my excruciating French should scare him. Although I was a total stranger he obviously took me for a priest and so to be trusted. Suddenly with a "Bonsoir, mon père," ["Good night, my father"] and a hurried sideways sort of bow, he disappeared through a hole in a hedge. He had had a happy, reassuring walk home, and I was left with an odd calm sense of elation. Continuing my walk I reflected that a Church which could inspire such confidence in a child, making its priests, even when unknown, so easily approachable could not be as scheming and creepy as so often made out. I began to shake off my long-taught, long-absorbed prejudices.[55]

Not many can tell such a story, but such an event contributed to Guinness's conversion as he tells it in his memoir. This story also illustrates not just a former era's respect for the priest but even today's realities. Pastors *are*—they don't choose to be and they can't avoid being—an embodied presence of God in this world.

A Culture of Priesthood

To claim that pastors are to nurture a divine presence entails the undeniable mediatorial responsibility of pastoring. That is, the pastor mediates God to the world and mediates the people of God before God. The pastor in this sense is a priest. Barbara Brown Taylor says the priest is a "representative person . . . who walks the shifting boundary between heaven and earth, representing God to humankind, representing humankind to God, and serving each in the other's name."[56] She's right, and she knows this experientially because she has been a pastor.

To say one of the pastoral responsibilities—even delights—is priestly is to raise an old debate between what Flannery O'Connor is said to have called the "Catlicks" and the Protestants. Four typical observations have been raised against calling the pastor a priest: (1) no church leader is called a priest in the New Testament; rather, (2) Christ alone is the Great High Priest and Mediator for Christians (1 Tim. 2:5; Heb. 5:6; 7:11, 15–17, 20–23; 8:6; 9:15; 10:21; 12:24); but (3) within three centuries Christian pastors were being called "priests"; therefore (4) this was a departure that jumped the rails of consistent apostolic teaching.[57] Ironically, those most suspicious of the term *priest* are often the most insistent on their own mediating roles between God and the church—that is, in knowledge, in piety, in example, and in structural location. They may not use the terms *priest* and *mediator*, but such they are in identity and function. The criticism of pastors-as-priests belongs on the Shelf of Former Ideas. Why? The apostle Paul explicitly depicts himself in priestly terms: "because of the grace given me by God to be a minister [*leitourgon*] of Christ Jesus to the Gentiles in the priestly service [*hierourgounta*] of the gospel of God, so that the offering [*prosphora*] of the Gentiles may be acceptable [*euprosdektos*], sanctified [*hēgiasmenē*] by the Holy Spirit" (Rom. 15:15–16). These five italicized Greek words speak of liturgy, of sacred priestly work, of priestly offerings, of divine acceptance of a priest's offering, and of the Spirit making the offering sacred. One can hardly imagine a more priest-drenched sentence than this. If one attends to 1 Corinthians 9:13's words (*ta hiera*; *thysiastēriō*) as they form the analogy to ministry, one has yet another instance of the pastoral role as priestly. (These two Greek words refer to sacred things and sacrifices on an altar.) There's another reason why this argument against priestly pastoring fails the Bible: we are all priests, as Peter tells us (1 Pet. 2:9), and that means the pastor as a priest represents each of us in her priestly ministry. That we are all priests means that the pastor must see herself *especially* in priestly terms or she will fail to represent us well.

The pastor, whether she wants to or not, whether he is conscious of it or not, has a priestly relation with congregants. I want to say this another way: the pastor is gifted with privilege to be priestly. How so? I suggest four ways, and each works from the essential idea of mediating the presence and grace of God to others: First, the pastor mediates redemption, holiness, and sacred space by preaching and teaching the gospel to the congregation, by working in particular church buildings and within certain organizational structures, and through the active life of the church in the community. Which is to say, one-on-one discipleship, pastoral visitations, and leading the church are each a form of priestly ministry. Second, the pastor mediates knowledge as one called to catechesis, preaching, teaching, (occasionally) writing, and various forms of communication. Third, the pastor mediates between the congregation and God in intercessory prayer, both privately and in directing corporate worship. If the prophet is one who mediates God to the people, the priest in intercession is one who mediates the people to God.[58] Fourth, perhaps the most influential priestly act of the pastor is to mediate the presence of God wherever the pastor is present. Think of who the pastor is and what the pastor does in major moments of life: birth, baptism, confirmation, marriage, loss of jobs, divorce, sickness, and death. In each of these the pastor is called on to be the presence of God in a variety of ways to those in her church.

I add one more because it belongs everywhere. The pastor is a priest in designing and leading worship. Worship involves singing; reading, listening to, and preaching Scripture; confessing of our creed; offering prayers of the people; offering confession and granting absolution; passing the peace; giving offerings; administering Eucharist; thanksgiving; blessing; fellowship; and mission. We stand, sit, (sometimes) kneel, and process forward to receive forgiveness in bread and wine. The pastor as priest teaches, oversees, and embodies these elements of public worship, and in so doing nurtures Christoformity through congregational worship. Eugene Peterson typifies many pastors when he takes up the seriousness of the task: "Every Sunday I look across this congregation and wonder, prayerfully, what is going on. I know most of you pretty well. But there is a lot I don't know. I am here every week with the conviction that this place of worship is the most important place you can be right now, that the scriptures, hymns, prayers, and sermon can enter into your souls, your lives, bringing you into a deeper participation in eternal life."[59]

Sunday worship means more than Sunday services, because all of life is now our worship, as Paul teaches so explicitly in Romans 12:1–2. Whether it is J. R. R. Tolkien's Niggle painting leaves,[60] a public school chemistry teacher explaining the periodic table, an insurance man guiding his business, a retired woman filling her schedule with service and reading and resting, or a professional baseball scout, each of these persons turns labor or work into vocation by offering all that is done as the theater of grace, of witness, of obedience and love. The pastor as priest teaches, oversees, and embodies work as vocation as well.

The pastor is a priest as Peter was an apostle: *primus inter pares* ("first among equals"). Inasmuch as all Christians have a priestly role, the pastor has a responsibility to lead in that priestly role—not so much as one totally unlike all others but as a more concentrated version of the others. If I had to choose one element of the pastoral task most central to what pastors actually do, I would choose the pastor's priestly role. The healthiest pastors both know this and sense its sacred burden in a way that makes the pastor feel unworthy of the task. The pastor's calling is to be the priest who nurtures the presence of God among us in a way that shapes us all into Christoformity.

A Culture of Servanthood

For the next element of a pastor nurturing Christoformity, I begin with a story about John Stott as told by René Padilla:

> The second trait that really impressed me was [John Stott's] humility. I have never forgotten his demonstration of it in Bariloche, a beautiful Argentine city near the Chilean border. We arrived rather late at night, under pouring rain. In order to get to the room where we were to stay overnight, we had to walk a distance. The path was very muddy, and we got our shoes quite dirty. We were tired, so we went to bed right away. Next day I was woken by a sound. When I opened my eyes, I saw John sitting on his bed—brushing my shoes! "John!" I said, "what are you doing?" "My dear Rene," he responded, "Jesus told us to wash one another's feet. Today we do not wash feet the way people did in Jesus' day, but I can clean your shoes." Several times I heard John preach on humility; many times I saw him putting it into practice.[61]

When the pastor acts like this, the church observes that it is here for others, not for itself. By serving others the pastor nurtures a Christoform culture.

Jesus spoke of himself and his mission in terms of servanthood (Mark 10:42–45 // Luke 22:24–27). Paul often speaks of leaders in terms of servanthood (2 Cor. 4:5). With Jesus as the paradigm for the early churches (Phil. 2:6–11), servanthood has taken on a special kind of life with respect to pastoral theology: the combination of servanthood with leadership both jars leadership and sets it free from lording it over others.[62] Any kind of leadership that is soaked in cruciformity will become servant leadership.[63] If with Jesus and Paul, so with pastors today: serving others is the way of Christ.

At times the expression *servant leadership* takes us to the depth of genuine leadership, ecclesial or secular,[64] but at other times it takes on magical-potion powers, as if saying Christian leaders and pastors are servant leaders solves all the problems and releases them from leadership! While it is unwise as well as inaccurate to avoid the service orientation and other-orientation of Christian ministry and leadership, the extensive studies of John Collins have demonstrated that the words used in the Hebrew and Greek Scriptures that are translated by the English term *servant* quite often lost the connotations of servile actions and instead connoted a go-between, an ambassador or a representative. That is, *servant* belongs in the register of pastoral vocabulary with *priest* and *prophet*. The pastor as servant is a go-between, between God and the people and between the people and God. Hence one must at least buffer the sense of *servile* or *menial* in the term *servant* and affirm the dignity of the one called to represent Christ or a bishop or a church.[65] Collins has attracted many proponents, but his point is a bit overcooked.[66] Even if one grants a stronger emphasis of the serving element of *servant leadership*, someone eventually raises a hand to ask this question: When do we move from the term *servant* to the term *leader* and what makes servant leadership *leadership*? This is our next point.

A Culture of Leadership

To pastor people is to be a leader, which for many means extroversion and (as commonly used) *charisma*, which really means "dynamic personality type." But some of the most significant leaders are introverts and are not "born to lead." One of my favorites is Brian Harris, a pastor and seminary president in Perth, Australia, who wrote a book called *The Tortoise Usually Wins*, and it is about what he calls "quiet" leadership.[67]

We must shelve as a period piece the view that the early church was radically egalitarian and democratic and charismatic and pneumatic and utopian and that, instead of being led by hierarchies and powers and authorities, it was only led by the Spirit through spiritual gifts but that, unfortunately, later it became institutionalized, hierarchical, and catholic and so developed offices such as "bishop" and "elder" and "deacon."[68] Quoting Sydney Smith, Joseph Epstein once countered this kind of argument with these words: "The best way of answering a bad argument is not to stop it, but to let it go on its course till it leaps over the boundaries of common sense."[69] This happens often and seems to surface today among critics of pastors—often smeared with the bugaboo word *institutional*—but it has been placed on a no-longer-to-be-used shelf by the best scholarship.[70] The charismatic and the institutional lived happily alongside one another in the world of Paul.[71] So the idea that there were no recognized leaders is the wishful thinking mostly of those who would prefer not to have to listen to their pastor. Wayne Meeks, a pioneer in discerning the social world of the first Christians, was right when he said, "No group can persist for any appreciable time without developing some patterns of leadership, some differentiation of roles among its members, some means of managing conflict, some ways of articulating shared values and norms, and some sanctions to assure acceptable levels of conformity to those norms."[72] I agreed when I first read that fifteen years ago, and I agree now.

Leaders of weight and grace were there from the beginning—starting with the Twelve. Without question, we can see leadership skills in the apostle Paul. A good case has been made that the fundamental term Paul used was *ho proistamenos*, that is, "the one who leads" or "the one who is prominent" or "the one who stands in front" (e.g., Rom. 12:8; 1 Thess. 5:12; 1 Tim. 3:4, 12; 5:17). It is noticeable, too, that Paul avoids many common terms for leaders in the Roman Empire. Why? Paul's terms for leaders were shaped by Pauline needs for Pauline communities, and Pauline churches were house churches, not the public square. A pastor is a leader who, on the basis of either giftedness or position and example, nurtures a Christlike culture, seeking wisdom from appropriate sources and inspiring and motivating congregants by vision, preaching, teaching, and example to participate in that culture.[73] I'll reframe this slightly: pastors have the responsibility of being worthy of being heard, and when they are worthy, they create a culture where leading is nurturing others to follow Christ.

I return to Brian Harris and his book *The Tortoise Usually Wins*. Harris describes the typical profile of a leader and then turns to the quiet leader:

> By contrast we have usually benefited from leaders who work quietly and
> conscientiously to ensure that their organization flourishes and grows.

They include others in their decision-making, but aren't swayed by every voice. They know where they are going and won't be sidetracked. They affirm and recognize others, especially noticing the contribution that each makes and helping ensure that it is both acknowledged and optimized. When the going is tough, they see things through. They always knew they had signed up for the long term, and that even the best years have a range of seasons. They are quiet leaders, and those who follow their lead feel a sense of security in knowing that they are there.[74]

Leadership, especially when of the noisy or hierarchical or authority-wielding sort, can drift well outside the pastoral calling, and I want to turn now to two problems with the pastoral calling in contemporary church life: celebrity and power.

A Culture of Temptation to Celebrity

By focusing here on only two temptations of the pastor I do not mean to say these are the only two temptations. There are, of course, many. Temptations emerge out of character flaws, which means we could circle back to the culture of formation above. Sondra Wheeler does this when she says, "Most pastors who lose their way do so because they lose themselves, in a sense, and grasp at anything (approval, admiration, celebrity, inflated authority, money, sex, or the unhealthy dependency of those they lead) to fill the void they experience."[75]

Nothing is more worldly than a desire for status and honor and money. A negation of this worldliness is an important element of a Christoform culture. The pastor as celebrity, then, is the world at work in the pastor's heart and congregation's soul. Status and honor were the two Roman quests that Paul found to be obstacles to a Christoform culture. Cicero, Rome's vain but accomplished orator, said, "Nature . . . offers nothing more excellent, nothing more desirable than honour, than renown, than distinction, than glory" (*Tusculan Disputations* 2.20.46). Jesus was against glory and the quest for it (Matt. 23:1–12), and Paul's constant battle with the Corinthians was shaped by their worldly yearning for glory and status and honor (1 Cor. 1–4). The city of Rhodes in the first century had some three thousand monuments of glory, and Rhodes was typical for the Roman world. This monument-loving culture was a testimony both to honoring its greats and to the quest for honor among its citizens. It has been said that in ancient Rome, *to be* was all about being seen.

The temptation to celebrity is the temptation of performance. As Will Willimon puts it, "The pastor as performer, as grinning, impersonal personality supersedes the roles of teacher, priest, and leader of the congregation."[76] Mastering the proper gesture, knowing where the camera is for the projected image of the pastor on the screen behind them, knowing the right color to wear, focusing on the most emotive story rather than the Word of God—these are all at work in the celebrity pastor who understands Sunday morning as a performance. That's not pastoring, and it is decidedly non-Christoformity.

I've watched one pastor after another become a celebrity. In so becoming, he worked hard at nurturing his image and reputation and brand and, when his status was in jeopardy, he sought to destroy his critics. He may say he's doing everything—including nurturing his status—for the glory of God. Disagree with him and you may discover the problem. Church historian and pastor Carl Trueman, in the foreword to David Starling's *UnCorinthian Leadership*, has discussed this problem: "Celebrity culture, focused as it is on the charismatic individual, pervades the American evangelical landscape and, as recent years have shown, the conservative, reformed wings of this type of Christianity are saturated in such. Further, the combination of management theory and the emergence of the celebrity CEO in the wider world have also shaped evangelical notions of leadership. It is not only the hipster-chic skinny jean pastors who ape the world; it can also be the sharp-suited, straight-talking strong man."[77]

Pastors are not celebrities; they ought not to pursue fame. Nor do they need acting classes or weekly sun baths to gain the right image. Those bowing before the Lord Jesus ought not to be drawing attention to themselves. Those who follow the Man of Poverty ought not to be seeking dollars.

A Culture of Temptation to Power

In a commencement address at Kenyon College, David Foster Wallace said that we all worship someone or something and that it is in our power what or who it will be. "Worship power," he says in *This Is Water*, and "you will feel weak and afraid, and you will need ever more power over others to keep the fear at bay."[78] He's right, and he could be pointing as much at some pastors as at politicians: it's about power *over* and needing "ever more power," and the reason we need power is to keep "the fear at bay."

Power ruins the capacity of pastors to pastor in a way that creates Christoformity. Not long ago in *The Atlantic* Jerry Useem wrote about power and what it does to the brain of the powerful. Summarizing research he noted that over time unchecked power leads to "manifest contempt for others, loss of contact with reality, restless or reckless actions, and displays of incompetence."[79] Useem quotes Henry Adams, who gives power a potent image: power, Adams says, is "a sort of tumor that ends by killing the victim's sympathies."[80]

This is my last point: a Christoform culture is nurtured not by those seeking power *over* but by those seeking power *for* (God, others). Power in itself is good or at least neutral, so our concern is power *over* versus power *for*. The fear that prompts desire for power *over* is the fear that you might not be in control, so some pastors seize power by the horns and start heaving others into silenced corners in the room. Knowledge, too, is power and authority, especially for the pastor. Pastors are asked questions about God and are expected to have answers about truth with a capital *T*. David Foster Wallace points out the inherent insecurity revealed by how some pursue knowledge or a reputation for knowledge: "Worship your intellect, being seen as smart—you will end up feeling stupid, a fraud, always on the verge of being found out."[81] Knowledge and power are tied into a knot for pastors. Sometimes the two lead the pastor to become a recluse for fear of being found out, but at other times the two can be used as tools to coerce and manipulate.

A local church has a symbiotic relationship at work in power: the pastor and the congregation, or the pastor and the board and the congregation. When the power is shared and is power *for*, power in a church is a good thing. However it works out, there is often some struggle. I could point either at pastors or at the kind of layperson who complains that the pastor is on a power trip but who, ironically, wants control himself. But instead I want to urge us to think of this in terms of a Christoform culture. If the pastor nurtures a Christoform culture, and the way of Christ is the way of other-orientation, then genuine Christoform power is about empowering others to be empowered by God to do what God calls them to do. I don't think Paul always lived up to this, but Jesus did. Paul is at his best when he is at his worst: in his tense relationship with Corinth he both related their criticisms (read 2 Cor. 10–13) and responded with a gospel of the cross, a gospel of Christoformity; but sometimes he preached this gospel in ways that almost betrayed that Christoformity (think of Paul and Peter in Antioch, Paul and Barnabas in Jerusalem, Paul and the Corinthians). But his message got through, and one example is to be found in 2 Corinthians 10:17–18, with which I close the main argument of this chapter: "'Let the one who boasts, boast in the Lord.' For it is not those who commend themselves that are approved, but those whom the Lord commends."[82]

What follows is not a complete pastoral theology or even a complete Pauline pastoral theology. Instead I will take seven samples of how nurturing Christoformity was at the heart of the Pauline mission. The seven themes that illustrate nurturing Christoformity are (1) a culture of friendship, (2) a culture of siblings, (3) a culture of generosity, (4) a culture of storytellers, (5) a culture of witness, (6) a culture of world subversion, and (7) a culture of wisdom. While the first two have a special relationship with each other, the other five stand entirely on their own. It would probably take at least forty such studies to approximate a complete pastoral theology of Paul, so this book is but a sampling of seven studies on a single theme: Christoformity.

2

A Culture of Friendship

An editor once told me, "Never begin with a quotation." Now that I have gotten the quotation of that editor behind me, I turn to the magnificent, and not lacking in confidence, stylist of yesteryear, Edward Gibbon. In *The Decline and Fall of the Roman Empire* he said this about the mentors of the young emperor Alexander Severus as Rome's decline was sputtering along:

> But the most important care of [Julia Avita] Mamaea [his mother] and her wise counselors, was to form the character of the young emperor, on whose personal qualities the happiness or misery of the Roman world must ultimately depend. The fortunate soil assisted, and even prevented, the hand of cultivation. An excellent understanding soon convinced Alexander of the advantages of virtue, the pleasure of knowledge, and the necessity of labour. A natural mildness and moderation of temper preserved him from the assaults of passion, and the allurements of vice. His unalterable regard for his mother, and his esteem for the wise [legal scholar] Ulpian, guarded his inexperienced youth from the poison of flattery.[1]

Alexander's character will determine the happiness or misery of the empire, and one corrupted and corrupting emperor after another—with an occasional man of virtue—is put on display in Gibbon's work

31

of stereotypes. More precisely, the emperor's character shaped the empire from the inside out, and the closer a situation was to the emperor, the more his character mattered. With Gibbon the concern is emperors and empires.

Our concern is pastors and churches.

The implication of Gibbon's wise observation is this: leaders form, shape, nurture, and sustain cultures. Good leaders form and sustain good cultures, and bad leaders form and sustain bad cultures. To alter words of Jesus, "By their culture ye shall know them." Pastors are culture shapers. This is not to say that congregations don't build culture, because congregations both form the culture and help the pastor form the culture. They can also destroy the culture. This is not an either-or. But this book is about a singular theme in pastoral theology, and I want to begin with it: pastors are leaders and leaders nurture culture. Where to begin?

Nurturing friendship, I contend, is the first step pastors can take in nurturing a culture. Pastors are called to nurture a Christoform culture, one where the life, teachings, death, resurrection, and ascension of Jesus are formative, and friendship is quite often the front door into that culture.

Pastors and Friendships

In the previous chapter we discovered that pastors pastor people but that 66 percent of pastors like preaching and teaching far more than working with people! I cite the Barna study again: "There is a big drop-off from there. One in 10 says 'developing other leaders' is their most enjoyable task (10%), and one in 12 prefers 'discipling believers' (8%). 'Evangelizing' (6%) and 'pastoral care' (5%) bring the most joy to smaller proportions of pastors, and a mere 2 percent say they enjoy 'organizing church events, meetings or ministries.'"[2]

This needs to be repeated because many pastors today, for a variety of reasons, are known for *not* having deep friendships.[3] The pastor is often the *solo pastor*. One can spend time pointing fingers, or one can propose an alternative, which is what I want to do in examining Paul's coworkers as a network of friends. The implication for us leaps out before we're ready: pastors today, perhaps more than at any time in history, need to become part of a network of fellow pastors. Many pastors burn out, and at least some of them could have been preserved had they been a part of a network. A few of my pastor friends are in such a network—they meet annually for a retreat, they preach sermons in conjunction with others preaching the same series or texts, and they email prayers and notes to one another in a network of collegial friendships. We need more of this.

Pastors also need more margin in their schedules, because friendship only thrives in the margins of our life. Friendship—like golf or reading for pleasure or wandering on a long walk through the forest to see leaves changing colors—only finds itself in leisure time, and Americans are some of the worst at leisure in the world.[4] More has been said by many about this topic,[5] but I have space here only to observe that friendship, leisure, and margin are soul mates. Perhaps the pastors will now turn to me to ask whether it might be advisable in seminary training for students to become familiar with the history of friendship studies? Yes.[6]

Where would that kind of study take us? To Aristotle, and to him we now go, but before we get there, a brief word: the classical world discussed, debated, and indwelled friendship in ways that are foundational to all studies of friendship. Paul lived in a world that embodied or tried to embody the classical ideals of friendship, so his "theory" of friendship would have interacted with this classical idea. He did not, however, simply assume it; he reframed it as a pastor among pastors.

Friendship in the Classical World

Aristotle developed a theory of friendship rooted in his experience of friendship.[7] The place to begin is with the brilliant study of friendship in Aristotle's *Nicomachean Ethics*,[8] a section worthy of far more reading today than it gets among pastors I know. Other voices, such as Cicero and Plutarch, will be invited to the platform as well. I intend only to sketch what friendship generally looked like in the classical world—roughly from Aristotle to Plutarch and their Roman counterparts. This sketch of major themes about friendship will serve as a point of comparison for the apostle Paul and for pastors' own friendships. All of this is designed to take a first step: pastors are charged with helping to form a church as a culture where friendships flourish, even if in the flow of this book we will see that Paul moves beyond friendship relations.

Definition

First, we need to define *friendship*. I'll begin with Aristotle and move on to Cicero and Plutarch. In *Nicomachean Ethics*, Aristotle writes, "To be friends therefore, persons must (1) feel goodwill for each other, that is, wish each other's good, and (2) be aware of each other's goodwill, and (3) the cause of their goodwill must be one of the lovable qualities mentioned above [namely, what is useful and good and pleasant]" (8.2.4, numbers added).

Centuries after Aristotle's famous definition, Cicero, the Roman jurist and brilliant orator, advanced Aristotle's theory (if that is possible) by focusing on "accord": "For friendship is nothing else than an accord in all things, human and divine, conjoined with mutual goodwill and affection, and I am inclined to think that, with the exception of wisdom, no better thing has been given to man by the immortal gods" (*On Friendship* 6.20).

Friendship begins with clear communication of love. Cicero again:

[Speaking to Atticus] In the true accomplishments of uprightness, integrity, conscientiousness, and scrupulousness, I put neither myself nor anyone else before you, while as for your love toward me, I leave aside my brother's love and that at home, I award you first prize. For I have seen . . . your worries and your joys . . . your congratulations. . . . Now, indeed, when you are absent I most miss not only the advice which is your forte but also our exchange of conversation, which is sweetest of all to me with you. (*Letters to Atticus* 17.5–6)

Mutual goodwill toward each other is both tested and sustained by actions, conversations, and general circumstances. Friendship in action means each person in a friendship contributes to the other and can be relied upon in times of need.

Plutarch, gifted as he was with simple prose, reduced the definition to five (Greek) words: Friendship "is goodwill and grace with virtue" (*On Having Many Friends*, 3, my translation). Friendship, then, is a consensual, committed, caring, and conversational relationship in which persons think well of each other and say so to each other.

Aim of Friendship

The aim of friendship in the classical world is growth in virtue by emulation.[9] Here the classical world presses friendship out of the world of simple pleasure and fun into the world of morality. Plutarch touches on this: "Indeed a peculiar symptom of true progress is found in this feeling of love and affection for the disposition shown by those *whose deeds we try to emulate*, and in the fact that our efforts to *make ourselves like them* are always attended by a goodwill which accords to them a fair meed [reward] of honour." Genuine desire for growth in virtue checks envy and jealousy: "But, on the other hand, if any man is imbued with a spirit of contentiousness and envy towards his betters, let him understand that he is merely chafing with jealousy at another's repute or power, but not honouring or even admiring virtue" (*How a Man May Become Aware of His Progress in Virtue* 14; italics added).

Mutual openness to learning and growth in virtue are noticeable in classical friendship. The teacher was to teach sensitively and frankly just as the student was to learn receptively while also contributing to the teacher's own growth in virtue. Manuals were developed to help people become virtuous. Hence the moral treatises of Plutarch's *Parallel Lives*, the study titled *Characters* by Theophrastus, and the biographies by Suetonius. Morality is learned more by contact with a living embodiment of virtue than by a moral treatise.

For Whom?

The person for whom such friendships are designed, in classical thought, is a person known for virtue. Friendship, then, is meritorious; those of virtue merit one another. Again, I must add that such persons are male and elite, and the scene for celebrating or discussing friendships for such male elites is the symposium, with its love of poetry.[10] While there is some margin for debate, it is conventional to believe in that world that a man and his wife were not "friends" (*philoi*).[11]

Aristotle is an early proponent of connecting virtue to friendship: "Therefore, it is *between good persons* that affection and friendship exist in their fullest and best form"; that is, persons of excellence (*Nicomachean Ethics* 8.3.8). Cicero said this most succinctly: "*Good persons* love and join to themselves other *good persons*, in a union which is almost that of relationship and nature" (*On Friendship* 13.50, italics added; also 5.18). Sounding much like this classical, elitist theory of friendships, the Jewish wisdom text Proverbs says much the same: "Whoever walks with the wise becomes wise, but the companion of fools suffers harm" (13:20). If we but observe that many think the pro-verbialist writer belongs to the ruling elites and understands the life of the sage as available only to the leisured class (Sir. 38:24–25), we see "wise" in a clearer light.[12]

Along the same lines, the relationship of friends in this classical sense is a relation of equals (*isotes*; cf. Aristotle, *Nicomachean Ethics* 8.5), and even if the two are unequal in status, they are to actualize the friendship as equals (Cicero, *On Friendship* 19.69). Their relationship is symmetrical, while an erotic relationship of lovers in the classical world was asymmetrical, one dominant (the male) and one receptive (the female). This kind of asymmetry is also characteristic of same-sex relations: a dominant male with a subordinate male (boy, slave). (The same does not obtain for lesbian relations, about which one reads in Sappho,[13] for it appears these friendships are both often erotic and more symmetrical.) A generalization is typical: male friendship is by nature not an erotic relationship since it is a relationship of equals; same-sex male erotic relationships, then, are not friendships because they are erotic. So this classical sense.

Kinds of Friendships

Aristotle famously broke friendships into three types:[14] friendships of utility, of pleasure, and of virtue (*Nicomachean Ethics* 8.3.1–6).[15] I would encourage pastors to ponder their "friendships" and assign their friends to only one of these categories. How many, it can then be asked, of our friendships are genuinely friendships of virtue? Speaking of classifying kinds of friendship—and just for fun—what kind of friendship or relationship is found in the following illustration? I take it from a story Peggy Noonan tells in her wonderful collection *The Time of Our Lives* about the actor Tony Curtis as a child in Brooklyn, resting his arms on a window and watching the "el" go by each morning:[16]

As a boy he would sit each morning at the window of his parents' apartment and watch the elevated trains. Every morning he'd see a man on the 8 a.m. train sitting in the same seat, wearing a brown hat and reading the *Herald Tribune*. The train would stop, young Tony would glance at the man and the man would glance at Tony. Then he'd go back to reading the paper and the train would roar off. In his seat. Next day he's not there, next week. Then 10 days later he's back in his same seat with the paper and the brown hat. And he glances over at Tony and Tony glances at him. And for once they maintain their gaze. And the man lowers the paper and mouths, "I've been sick!" And the train roars off.

Aristotle knew of such relationships, and so do we, but is this about "friends"? If so, what kind? If not, why not?

We know friendships of utility and of pleasure. We may have the former with someone to whom we speak often because we are doing the same thing they are—say, coaching a youth baseball team or standing and waiting for a child at school—but of whom we think little when we are not with them. With people whose company we enjoy, we can have friendships of pleasure, to which distance does no damage because the friendship exists only in those moments of presence. In one of the most enjoyable books ever written on friendship, Joseph Epstein defines friendship in much the same way as Aristotle defined a friendship of pleasure: "A best friend is that person who gives you the most delight, support, and comfort, often in those realms where family cannot help. A best friend is perhaps the only person to whom you can complain about the difficulties presented by your family."[17]

But utility and pleasure are not virtue. Concerning a friendship of virtue, Cicero famously wrote: "For when persons have conceived a longing for this virtue they bend towards it and move closer to it; so that, by familiar association with that person whom they have begun to love [emulation], they may enjoy that person's character, equal that person in affection, become readier to deserve rather than demand that person's approval, and vie with that person in a rivalry of virtue" (*On Friendship* 9.32). (One catches here a whiff of what it meant for the disciples of Jesus to experience his presence as well as what it must have meant for the friends of Paul to be with him.)

Trust

Trust is foundational to friendship. The Stoic Seneca, tutor to Nero himself, speaks of trust in a letter of his to Lucilius:

> You have sent a letter to me through the hand of a "friend" of yours, as you call him. And in your very next sentence you warn me not to discuss with him all the matters that concern you, saying that even you yourself are not accustomed to do this; in other words, you have in the same letter affirmed and denied that he is your friend. Now if you used this word of ours in the popular sense, and called him "friend" in the same way in which we speak of all candidates for election as "honorable gentlemen," and as we greet all men whom we meet casually, if their names slip us for a moment, with the salutation "my dear sir,"—so be it. *But if you consider any man a friend whom you do not trust as you trust yourself, you are mightily mistaken and you do not sufficiently understand what true friendship means.*
>
> Those persons indeed put last first and confound their duties, who . . . judge a man after they made him their friend, instead of making him their friend after they have judged him. Ponder for a long time whether you shall admit a given person to your friendship; but when you have decided to admit him, welcome him with all your heart and soul. Speak as boldly with him as with yourself. (*Letters to Lucilius* 3.1–2; italics added)

But we are not yet done.

Loyalty

Dio Chrysostom's third oration on kings speaks of the significance of friendship for a king—and in the process Dio brings in trust, *loyalty*, vulnerability, and love as well. For someone to be a friend to a king, of course, stretches the meaning of *friend*, for the friends of a king not only are unequals but also have a strong sense of utility and patronage as well. But there is an idea at work in what Dio says here that applies immediately to the relationships pastors have with "friends" in the church, and I think you will agree:

> *Friendship, moreover, the good king holds to be the fairest and most sacred of his possessions,* believing that the lack of means is not so shameful or perilous for a king as the lack of friends, and that he maintains

his happy state, not so much by means of revenues and armies and his other sources of strength, as by the loyalty of his friends. For no one, of and by himself, is sufficient for a single one of even his own needs; and the more and greater the responsibilities of a king are, the greater is the number of coworkers that he needs, and the greater the loyalty required of them, since he is forced to entrust his greatest and most important interests to others or else to abandon them.

Furthermore, the law protects the private individual from being easily wronged by men with whom he enters into business relations, either by entrusting them with money, or by making them agents of an estate, or by entering into partnership with them in some enterprise; and it does so by punishing the offender. *A king, however, cannot look to the law for protection against betrayal of a trust, but must depend upon loyalty. Naturally, those who stand near the king and help him rule the country are the strongest, and from them he has no other protection than their love.* Consequently, it is not a safe policy for him to share his power carelessly with the first men he meets; but *the stronger he makes his friends, the stronger he becomes himself.* (*Discourses 1–11,* 3.86–90; italics added)

Leaders need friends who are loyal, who can be trusted, and who can support the leader. Our sixth point is tied to a seventh. Leaders need not just loyal friends but honest friends.

Honesty

Honesty is called *frankness* (*parrhēsia*) by the Greeks in the context of friendship, and they also believe in the resolute need to avoid flatterers, who seem always to find their way to leaders. Friends are necessary to leaders but only if they can tell the truth. Here we have a full display of the Aristotelian and classical theory of friendship: if the aim of friendship is that the friends grow in virtue, then a leader's friends must both receive and give. That is, they learn from the leader, but the leader also learns from them.

One of the great themes of the ancient world, which often had its eye on leaders—after all, the texts were written by prominent males— was flattery. Plutarch wrote an entire essay on the theme: *How to Tell a Friend from a Flatterer.* It could be quoted ad nauseam, but the term *flatterer* evokes for most leaders all one needs to hear. Avoid them. In a letter to Antipater, Isocrates commends in glowing terms a man named Diodotus and includes these important lines on his frankness:

> In addition to these good qualities he possesses frankness in the highest degree, not that outspokenness which is objectionable, but that which would rightly be regarded as the surest indication of devotion to his friends. This is the sort of frankness which princes, if they have worthy and fitting greatness of soul, honor as being useful, while those whose natural gifts are weaker than the powers they possess take such frankness ill, as if it forced them to act in some degree contrary to their desires—ignorant as they are that those who dare to speak out most fearlessly in opposition to measures in which expediency is the issue are the very persons who can provide them with more power than others to accomplish what they wish. For it stands to reason that it is because of those who always and by choice speak to please that not only monarchies cannot endure—since monarchies are liable to numerous inevitable dangers—but even constitutional governments as well, though they enjoy greater security: whereas it is owing to those who speak with absolute frankness in favor of what is best that many things are preserved even of those which seemed doomed to destruction. For these reasons it is indeed fitting that in the courts of all monarchies those who declare the truth should be held in greater esteem than those who, though they aim to gratify in all they say, yet say naught that merits gratitude; in fact, however, the former find less favor with some princes. (*Letter 4, To Antipater*, 4–6)

Here then, in summary, are the principal terms about friendship in the classical world: *males, elites, equality, virtue, goodwill, consensus, affection, trust, loyalty*, and *frankness* or *honesty*.[18] While our world differs dramatically from the classical world, and while Paul himself will turn some of this on its head (especially the elitism), if one discounts the first two of the above terms, one can observe that friendship here has its explanation.

Friendship was glue in ancient societies: one made friends in order to seal one's relationships; to love, to learn from, to instruct, and even to rebuke one another; and to enjoy one another. But these purposes do not exclude friendships to strengthen one's power and business and political relations (Aristotle, *Nicomachean Ethics* 9.10), to forge connections in patronage (even among friends of different statuses, and this also extends to other kings, tribes, and countries[19]), and to establish boundaries of power. If pastors are to nurture a culture of Christoformity, and if friendship is the portal into church culture, then these seven themes of friendship deserve our attention. But before we can get there, we turn to Paul.

Paul, Love, and Friendship

Those who read Paul's letters carefully know that Paul had ministry associates, whom he often calls "coworkers" (*synergoi*) and who appeared in the Roman world as "friends" (*philoi, amici*). A list includes Priscilla and Aquila, Urbanus, Timothy, Titus, Epaphroditus, Clement, Jesus called Justus, Philemon, Mark, Aristarchus, Demas, and Luke.[20] The names known to Paul in Romans 16 also indicate the extent of Paul's friends.

Paul inherited a classical theory of friendship that was reimagined through a covenantal understanding of love and friendship and that, as will be seen in the next chapter, reframed friendship.[21] In other words, yes, due to his Greek-Roman education in Tarsus, he could think in terms of *virtue* (a term he does not use), goodwill, accord, and trust. But as a Jew trained as a rabbi, Paul thought in other terms, and it was through these that he approached friendship with his many coworkers. The implication of this difference is that Paul refused to call his coworkers friends.

Paul's choice of *agapē* rather than *philia* to refer to the love he has for his circle of associates provides a clue as to why he does not call his coworkers "friends." To understand one of Paul's favorite terms, *love* (noun, *agapē*; verb, *agapaō*), requires that we dig into the Bible. One of the biggest mistakes made in Christian thinking about "love" is to assume the English (or American) dictionary gives us the meaning. Hence *Merriam-Webster* says the noun *love* means "strong affection for another."[22] Almost all dictionaries do the same, including *Samuel Johnson's Dictionary*, where the number-one definition of the verb *love* is "to regard with passionate affection, as that of one sex to the other."[23] But one of the beginning lessons in Bible studies is to let the Bible's authors define their own terms. Hence, we need to re-ask what the meaning of love is by asking what love meant in the Bible.[24] We need an even deeper beginning: we need to observe how God loves in order to understand what love means.

Covenant

First, the Bible opens up the meaning of love when the creator God becomes the covenant God with Abram/Abraham (e.g., Gen. 12; 15; 17; 22). God loves by entering into the rugged commitment of a covenant, a covenant that finds new expression in the promise to David and discovers a brand-new future in the new covenant prophecy of Jeremiah 31—and each of these before the New Testament's new covenant. God's choice to express his love in terms of covenant defines love as a rugged commitment of one person (God) to another person (Abraham) and to a corporate person (Israel). The famous Hebrew term *hesed*, sometimes translated as "unfailing love" or "loving-kindness," can perhaps be translated even better as God's "loving commitment" (see Ps. 119:41, 64, 76, 88, 124, 149, 159). Our parties, YHWH and Israel, shuttle back and forth in their commitment throughout the Bible, but it is clear that God's rugged covenant commitment remains (this is the point of Rom. 9–11). Hence each person is loved by God, and God's love is not only shown to Israel but also expanded in the story to the body of Christ, the church. Paul's relationship to his friends, those whom he loves (*agapētoi*), is a covenant first and foremost. That is, Paul's love for his coworkers is a rugged commitment to them as persons (see the depiction of Ruth and Naomi in Ruth;[25] 1 Sam. 18:1–4;[26] Ps. 55:13–14).

Presence

Second, biblical love involves a covenant of presence. The central covenant promise can be found in this biblical promise of ongoing presence:[27] "I will be your God and you will be my people" (Jer. 7:23 NIV). How was God *with* humans? God was with Abraham in a smoking pot and with Israel in a pillar of cloud and fire, then in a mobile shrine called a tabernacle and then in the immobile temple, and all along God's presence was known through his leaders, such as kings and priests and prophets. But God's deepest commitment to be "with" is the incarnation, for as Matthew states it in his opening chapter, Jesus was "Immanuel, God *with* us" (Matt. 1:23). Then Jesus sends the Spirit to be *with* us. Finally, the book of Revelation's climactic scene says that "God's dwelling place is now *among* the people [of God], and he will dwell *with* them" (Rev. 21:3).

Pastors pastor people who differ, but pastors often are told by their own people of how God spoke to them or how they have been speaking to God. I know this is true because after sermons people tell me as if I'm their pastor. Pastors with a heart must love these personal stories of knowing God's presence. Recently my wife, Kris, was reading Olympian gold medalist swimmer Missy Franklin's story about finding God and faith in her parochial high school. She learned to speak to God and to listen for God speaking to her, and I got to thinking of the joy her pastor must have to hear someone nurture the presence of God and be present with God as Missy does. Here are some of her words:

> Always, I think about Jesus the same way I think about my good, good friends. I'm not going to grow in my relationship with a friend if I only see her or talk to her for five minutes at the end of each day. I like to keep connected throughout the day, either on an as-needed basis, or just as a way to check in. If I'm in the car and I hear a sad story on the radio, I might just pull over and catch myself saying, "Hey, God, please keep these good people in your prayers. Let them know there are people thinking about them." Then I'll switch the station, find a song I like, turn up the volume, and drive on.
>
> He's with me all the time, and so I talk to him all the time. I don't just reach out to him when I need his sure hand. No, I tell him everything. The good stuff, the bad stuff, the stuff in between. I'll even tell him about stupid, inconsequential stuff, like an amazing new sandwich I tried at Panera Bread, just to keep connected. And do you know what? I hear back from him. I do. Not in the ways you see in movies or on television. I'm a firm believer in the notion that God speaks to us in a variety of ways, through our interactions with others, through the songs that find us on the radio, or the books we're reading, or the colors of a brilliant blue sky.[28]

"He's with me all the time"—that's the line that stood out to me, a line that would be tested later in Missy's own journey. Love in the Bible is God's rugged commitment to be present to and with us, and, therefore, if we love someone it means we have a rugged commitment of presence with that person. This too resonates so often in Paul's letter, not least when Titus's absence torments Paul so much he can't minister (e.g., 2 Cor. 7:5–7's "fears within" resolved by Titus's arrival). One who gets to the heart of presence in friendship is Eugene Peterson, who in a sermon once observed this of friends: "They visit simply for the pleasure of the other's company. Things don't have to get done in a friendship. Friendship is not a way of accomplishing something but a way of being with another in which we become more authentically ourselves."[29] Thoreau comes at this from a different angle, but I have needed to return to his line more than a few times in my own life: "What business have I in the woods, if I am thinking of something out of the woods?"[30]

Advocacy

The third element of a God-shaped covenant love is that love is a rugged commitment of advocacy. To love someone means you are on their side and in their corner and that you've got their back. Again, the Bible emphasizes that in his covenant with us, God promises that he will be our God and that we will be God's people, and a common understanding of this is that God is our advocate, our warrior, our protector. Thus, Exodus 15:3 reads "[YHWH] is a warrior; [YHWH] is his name." God, the "I am who I am," has our back.[31] This corresponds to the classical theory of friendship of goodwill, but relates even more closely to how we see Paul standing alongside and advocating for his friends. Think, for instance, of Timothy or Epaphras.

Direction: Virtue as Christoformity

Finally, once again corresponding in some ways to the classical theory, Paul's theory of love and friendship entailed virtue in a Christian sense. To love someone is to be so committed to them that we yearn for and work for their growth into Christoformity. To remind ourselves of the method, we learn love by watching God love, and God loves, in a rugged covenant commitment, to be with us, to be for us, and he loves us *unto* his perfect design for us. Love in the Bible has a direction, and that direction—to use the theological term—is sanctification, or to use David deSilva's term, "transformation."[32] I prefer here to speak of

Christoformity: to love another is to yearn for mutual Christoformity. This deserves a little expansion. The heart of the Old Testament's "law" is the Shema, and the heart of the Shema is to love God with one's heart, soul, and strength (Jesus adds "mind" in Mark 12:28–32). What is perhaps not noticed is how close love and obedience are in the Bible, not least because the covenant arrangement, after all, is borrowed from the ancient suzerainty treaty.[33] Jon Levenson, in a monumentally important study of God's love, says, "The love [of God and of Israel for God] at issue here is a quasi-political—or, to be more precise, a theopolitical— allegiance. It is a love that becomes real and attains social force in acts of service and homage."[34] To love God then is to obey God, and to obey the God revealed to us in Christ is to be formed into Christoformity.

God loves us and dwells with us in order to make us loving and holy, God-glorifying and other-oriented people in God's kingdom. God loves us in the direction of Christoformity. How does this happen? The personal dynamic at work in God's love for us works like this: God's loving presence transforms us because God's presence is transformative! Our love of others does the same: when we love others, we indwell them and they indwell us, and personal presence makes space for others, and that space now occupied by the one we love influences us to become like them. Genuine friendships, which are two way, are always transformative. To make space for another is to invite change.

Affective

Yet, as I mentioned above, the rugged covenant commitment between God and his people does have an emotive, affective dimension. Covenant, Levenson reminds us, emerges as much from family relations as it does from commercial treaties. Therefore, it is never simply contractual or legal but always first and foremost relational. That is, a covenant is a relational bond between two persons. Love, he says, is both active and affective.[35] God is love, and therefore God determines what love is. And God, the Bible tells us, is one who "set his heart" on Israel (*hashaq*; Deut. 7:7; 10:15; Ps. 91:14; Isa. 38:17),[36] a term that bears close resemblance to the erotic:

> But Hamor spoke with them, saying, "The heart of my son Shechem *longs for* your daughter; please give her to him in marriage." (Gen. 34:8)

> When you go out to war against your enemies, and the LORD your God hands them over to you and you take them captive, suppose you see among the captives a beautiful woman whom *you desire* and want to marry, and so you bring her home to your house: she shall shave her head, pare her nails, discard her captive's garb, and shall remain in your house a full month, mourning for her father and mother; after that you may go in to her and be her husband, and she shall be your wife. But if you are not satisfied with her, you shall let her go free and not sell her for money. You must not treat her as a slave, since you have dishonored her. (Deut. 21:10–14)

Levenson thus says the Bible teaches that God "fell in love" with Israel. We could again go on but won't. To love in the Bible is an affectional, rugged commitment to another person. A crystal-clear example among friends in the Bible is the language used of David and Jonathan: "The soul of Jonathan was bound to the soul of David, and Jonathan loved him as his own soul" (1 Sam. 18:1; cf. Gen. 44:20, 30–31). This is the language of deep affection.

Paul's emotional love for his friends is in his face, on his tongue, in his letters, and everywhere revealed. Paul's coworkers knew Paul's affectional, rugged commitment, his presence (whenever possible), and his advocacy for them, but they knew, too, that his rugged commitment was all shaped toward each of them becoming, along with him, more Christlike. I suspect that Paul did not leave his friends alone, and they did not leave Paul alone. They were committed to one another in a covenant sense, like David and Jonathan were committed in their covenant of friendship (1 Sam. 18:1–4). Paul, then, had many occasions to ponder the famous expression in Deuteronomy, "your most intimate friend," or, as the KJV has it, "thy friend, which is as thine own soul" (Deut. 13:6). Or also Proverbs 17:17's "a friend loves at all times" and 18:24's well-known line about friendship, "but a true friend sticks closer than one's nearest kin."

An Example

What did this look like in the ancient world? I will use a beautiful example from the much later Christian priest-theologian John Chrysostom and his friendship with Basil. I believe that with proper historical adjustments, the friendship between these two leaders (as portrayed in *Treatise on the Priesthood*) was like those of the apostle Paul and his coworker friends. In what follows notice the affection, the commitment, the presence, the advocacy, and the direction of their friendship:

[Book 1.1] I had many genuine and true friends, people who understood the laws of friendship and faithfully observed them; but out of this large number there was one who excelled all the rest in his attachment to me, striving to outstrip them as much as they themselves outstripped ordinary acquaintance. He was one of those who were constantly at my side; for we were engaged in the same studies and employed the same teachers. We had the same eagerness and zeal about the studies at which we worked, and a passionate desire produced by the same circumstances was equally strong in both of us. For not only when we were attending school, but after we had left it, when it became necessary to consider what course of life it would be best for us to adopt, we found ourselves to be of the same mind.

3. But when it became our duty to pursue the blessed life of monks, and the true philosophy, our balance was no longer even, but his scale mounted high, while I, still entangled in the lusts of this world, dragged mine down and kept it low, weighting it with those fancies in which youths are apt to indulge. For the future our friendship indeed remained as firm as it was before, but our intercourse was interrupted; for it was impossible for persons who were not interested about the same things to spend much time together. But as soon as I also began to emerge a little from the flood of worldliness, he received me with open arms; yet not even thus could we maintain our former equality: for having got the start of me in time, and having displayed great earnestness, he rose again above my level, and soared to a great height.

Notice, too, the classical themes intertwined with Christian themes. This kind of exchange between friends, this kind of verbal communication about love for one another, about soul-revealing topics, with life-changing significance, and all tied into salvation itself—this, I believe, was not unusual for Christian leaders in the early church.

Pastors are to nurture a culture of Christoformity, and a church's opening cultural move is to be friendly. Pastors are to be friends and friendly, and they are to nurture a culture of friendship in the context of the local church. What does this mean? Pastors are to nurture relationships with others and among congregants that are shaped by these terms: *commitment*, *affection*, *presence*, *advocacy*, and *direction*. Pastors will help congregants make commitments to one another, show affection for one another, be present with one another, be advocates for one another, and support one another as they grow into Christoformity. This sounds too good to be true because, well, it is.

Friendship can be idealized quickly, and idealized friendship quickly becomes frustration and a source of disillusionment in the church. So, given this sketch of classical friendship in the world Paul inherited, and given his reimagination of that friendship in terms of covenant love, what did Paul's own "friendships" look like? The reality of Paul's own relationships quickly dispels the myths of the ideal and ushers us into rooms of disagreement, discussions, disappointments, and, well, fractures and reconciliations. I turn first to his relationship with John Mark.

Paul and John Mark: A Friendship Marked by Reconciliation

Friendship is a splendid ideal until we have a friend, and then the complications begin. Paul's relationship with the young man John Mark is a story not often told, and we need perhaps to be reminded that Paul was not perfect. He was an ordinary human being with common passions and regular problems and routine tensions with other people, including his best friends.[37] In fact, you may, like many of us, prefer your apostles to walk slightly above the ground and conduct themselves always in sanctified ways. Not so Paul, and we'll just have to get used to it.

Two very close friends in ministry were Barnabas and the young and freshly converted Saul of Tarsus. Barnabas senses a need for Paul in a major city called Antioch, so Paul joins him in a vibrant yearlong mission effort there. About the same time an angel delivers Peter from prison in Jerusalem and leads him to the home of Mary, mother of a young Christian named John Mark. It happens that Barnabas and Paul are in Jerusalem to deliver financial relief to the poor saints of Jerusalem. Done with their mission effort in Jerusalem, Paul and Barnabas—I presume ever vigilant at locating young gifted missionaries—decide to return to Antioch and take along with them the young John Mark.

With John Mark now known as a potential leader for the church, Barnabas and Paul take him with them on Paul's first mission trip. For some reason John Mark decides to return home to Jerusalem. Some time later both Paul and Barnabas return to Jerusalem for the major conference on how to (fully) welcome gentile converts (to circumcise or not?). Once done, they are off again to the mission churches they established on the first mission trip—but Barnabas again wants John Mark to accompany them. Perhaps Barnabas knows that the young man has grown up. Paul will have none of it because John Mark deserted them on the previous mission trip. Their disagreement is fierce enough that Barnabas and John Mark abandon Paul's mission, choosing to do missionary work on the island of Cyprus, and Paul returns to his churches with another mission worker, named Silas.

Here's what we have: sometimes the best of friends—Barnabas and Paul—and sometimes the best of evangelists, missioners, and apostles side against one another. I find this story sad. I confess that I think Paul was just too hard-nosed, and it appears to me that Barnabas— time will prove him more discerning—was the one who was right here. John Mark will learn his lesson. We can be grateful both teams had flourishing ministries, but that doesn't mean Paul was living up to his gospel of reconciliation (Rom. 5:8–11; 2 Cor. 5:16–21).[38]

A time comes when it is clear that Paul, Barnabas, and John Mark are reconciled. When Paul later says, "Is it only Barnabas and I who have no right to refrain from working for a living?" (1 Cor. 9:6), he implies that he and Barnabas are again on the same mission page. The news is the same about John Mark. Three different times in Paul's letters John Mark comes up, and he's become a very close friend and mission worker alongside Paul. I want to quote all three texts briefly:

> Aristarchus my fellow prisoner greets you, as does Mark the cousin of Barnabas, concerning whom you have received instructions—if he comes to you, welcome him (Col. 4:10).
> [Greetings are sent from several . . .] and so do Mark, Aristarchus, Demas, and Luke, my fellow workers (Philem. 24).
> Get Mark and bring him with you, for he is useful in my ministry (2 Tim. 4:11).

I suspect that Paul and Barnabas discussed their break over John Mark and came to terms and agreement and reconciled. In that process Paul acknowledged John Mark as a mature-enough minister, embraced the man, and made him one of his close friends and coworkers (a term of high praise for Paul).

Friendship in the biblical mode is like this: all things will be reconciled, and we are summoned to begin living in that reconciliation now. Friendship is about an affective, rugged commitment, about presence and advocacy, and it is about growing in Christoformity. Paul and John Mark's reconciliation illustrates the Pauline form of friendship.

Paul and Phoebe: A Friendship of Advocacy

Even if social location and the accidents of history have determined who speaks in the Greco-Roman world, it is nonetheless a fact that Aristotle's theory of friendship was designed for male elites. Paul, too, made friends with elites, at least one of whom was a woman. About Phoebe,[39] made known to us in only two verses in the Bible, we read in Romans 16:1–2: "I commend to you our sister Phoebe, a deacon of the church at Cenchreae, so that you may welcome her in the Lord as is fitting for the saints, and help her in whatever she may require from you, for she has been a benefactor of many and of myself as well." She's from Corinth's beautiful port of Cenchreae on the Saronic Gulf, almost certainly active in the body of Christ in Corinth, and most think that her name Phoebe, or "Titaness," indicates that her parents were pagan.

Phoebe belonged to the elite. She is called a *benefactor* (*prostatis*), a term that most now agree refers to her financial capacities and generosities. The term *prostatis*, however, probably says more than "benefactor," and the CEB's translation, "sponsor," is probably closer to the meaning. I suggest it means something like chief patron for Paul's ministry on the Isthmus of Corinth. Paul also says she is worthy to be received in the Lord, an expression that indicates generous hospitality as a form of reciprocating with Paul for his work in spreading the gospel.

In addition to being a financial elite, Phoebe had gifts for ministry and so she is called a *deacon*. Note, she is not a *deaconess*, which often diminishes role of *deacon* to things women can do, such as cleaning up

Communion cups after the Lord's Supper. In Paul's churches deacons are gospel agents,[40] pastors in a local body of Christ, and financial collectors and distributors in the church. What is more, most agree that Phoebe was the courier of this magnificent letter of Paul's to the churches of Rome. Two observations jump ahead of all others: it would have been her responsibility to read the letter publicly to each of the five house churches in Rome, and as well it was her responsibility to respond to questions about the letter. The former involved being coached by the apostle Paul and his many friends, such as Tertius (Rom. 16:22), who contributed to this letter by indicating how to "perform" the letter in the churches, and the latter means Phoebe was responsible for comprehending the theology of the letter as well as clarifying and commenting on the letter.

Paul had friends who were male and female; Paul had friends in low places (think of Onesimus) and high places (such as Erastus and Phoebe); and Paul's friendships involved extending one another's ministries. What I see in this text about Phoebe is that friendship entails advocacy for those who are journeying into Christoformity. Hence Paul thinks she is worthy, and so he advocates for abundant hospitality to be shown to Phoebe. Another observation concerns generosity and reciprocity among friends, very common features of benevolence in the Roman world and characteristic of Paul's own friendships and relationships.[41] She was generous to Paul; Paul expected his churches to be generous to her. Finally, Paul petitioned and benefited from those who were financially capable of supporting his ministries. His solicitation of funds for the saints of Jerusalem is but one instance, and soliciting funds and resources from Phoebe was simply part of the gospel pattern: those who benefit spiritually can expect a material reward (see chap. 4).

Paul and Epaphras: A Friendship Rooted in Trust

It was Seneca who made trust central to friendships, and his form of trust expresses the height of vulnerability and accountability to one another. The apostle himself had that kind of vulnerability as well, as can be seen in his communications with the churches of Corinth through Titus (2 Cor. 2:12–13; 7:2–16). But my example here will be

Paul's friend Epaphras, another one of those coworkers of Paul who are largely ignored (and should not be).[42]

Epaphras was from Colossae in the Lycus Valley along the Meander River, and he was a convert to Jesus Christ through the ministries of the apostle Paul in Ephesus on his second mission trip (ca. AD 49–52), or at least that is the consensus. It was as Paul's associate and friend that Epaphras evangelized the Lycus Valley and planted churches in Colossae, Laodicea, and Hierapolis.

Paul must have known from the start that Epaphras was unusually gifted for ministry, for it was not long after his conversion that Paul seems to have sent the young man into the Lycus Valley. If one dates Colossians, as I do, to about AD 54, it means Epaphras was converted, was apprenticed, was sent, and had established at least three churches all within the space of about four years. Noticeably—in that Paul is totally dependent on Epaphras for all the news about Colossae since Paul himself has never been there (Col. 2:1)—we learn from Epaphras both the great news of the spiritual growth of the Colossians (1:3–8) and the bad news of their philosophical, theological, and mystical dabblings—I like "halakic mystics" as a summary of this group (2:8–9, 16–23 with resonances, of course, in 1:15–20).[43] I infer that Epaphras had not learned enough in his seminary training with Paul in Ephesus, so he traveled from the Lycus Valley down the plain to Ephesus for help dealing with the problems at Colossae. Paul's letter is his response to the conversations with his coworker and friend Epaphras.

Epaphras learns that ministry, perhaps most especially in one's hometown, requires a deep prayer life: "He is always wrestling in his prayers on your behalf, so that you may stand mature and fully assured in everything that God wills" (4:12). He does not mess around in his prayer life, because he knows the problems at Colossae are challenging: he prays that they might stand firm in all that God wills, and he uses terms such as *mature* and *fully assured*, which were connected to the christological confusion at work in the opponents at Colossae.

Paul's theory of friendship is on full display with Epaphras even if the evidence is meager. We learn that Paul was ruggedly committed to him as a person, that he had been noticeably present with Epaphras and was more than willing to share more time with him when a need arose. Further, the meager evidence shows that Paul was the man's biggest advocate in public affirmation. Here are the terms Paul uses for Epaphras in this publicly read letter: "beloved fellow servant" (1:7), "faithful minister" (1:7), and "servant of Christ Jesus" (4:12). The Greek words are of note: *agapētou syndoulou, pistos . . . diakonos*, and *doulos*, all terms that show Paul discerned a growth in the direction of Christoformity in Epaphras. These are major rhetorical moves by Paul to get the Colossians and Laodiceans to trust the man whom Paul himself trusted. This is perhaps one of the major insights we learn in observing the relationship of these two men: Paul trusted this young buck to plant three separate churches. He was not looking over his shoulder; he sent him and awaited in prayer the news of the gospel work in the Lycus Valley.

Paul and Timothy: A Friendship of Equals

At the center of Paul's collegial network of friends was Timothy, a man far too often turned into the trope of a young minister seemingly incapable of being little more than a shadow. Paul's special relationship with Timothy all comes to the surface in one verse in 1 Corinthians 4:17: "For this reason I sent you Timothy, who is *my beloved and faithful child in the Lord*, to remind you of my ways in Christ Jesus, as I teach them everywhere in every church." Paul calls him "child" or "son," a word that reflects Paul's mother-like giving birth and father-like mentoring. It is not the common word for son, *huios*, but the more familial term for the child, *teknon*. Paul expresses his *love* for Timothy, he affirms Timothy, he knows Timothy can accurately tell about Paul's life, and he trusts him. Paul has spent plenty of time *with* his friend Timothy as an expression of their love for each other. Here are the salient facts about his life:[44]

- Timothy's father was a gentile, but his mother a Jew.
- He was probably converted to following Christ during Paul's first missionary journey to Lystra, where Timothy surely saw Paul being stoned.
- Timothy's mother was a believer.
- Paul chose Timothy to be "with" him on his second missionary journey, and Timothy received a special endowment of the Spirit through the laying-on of hands.

- To regulate his "status" Paul had Timothy circumcised.
- When Paul traveled to Athens, Timothy stayed with Silas in Berea and then joined Paul in Athens.
- Timothy encouraged the Christians in Thessalonica and reported good news about the Thessalonians to Paul later, part of that good news expressed by a gift of money for the poor saints in Jerusalem.
- Timothy helped Paul write both 1 and 2 Thessalonians, helped evangelize Corinth, and helped write 2 Corinthians and probably also Romans.[45]
- He traveled with Paul to Jerusalem as Lystra's delegate to the Jerusalem church.
- He helped Paul write Colossians, Philemon, and Philippians.
- Later Paul may have sent him to Philippi; Timothy was encouraged to stay in Ephesus and eventually to meet Paul in Rome (?) during a winter.
- Timothy was imprisoned for the gospel and eventually released.

Timothy was Paul's most common companion from very early in the mission of Paul until, evidently, the very end. If anything displays Paul's theory of friendship, it is his relationship with Timothy: they were ruggedly and affectionately committed to each other; they gave the gift of presence to each other; they were advocates for each other; and they clearly were on the journey of Christoformity with each other.

There is more to be said. Timothy was Paul's best or closest friend. Paul needed him, as Acts 17:15 implies in telling us that Paul wanted Silas and Timothy to "join him as soon as possible." In 2 Timothy 4:9 Paul tells Timothy, "Do your best to come to me soon," and later in the chapter he says, "Do your best to come before winter" (v. 21). This is a man Paul describes as "beloved" or "dear" (1 Cor. 4:17; Philem. 1), "faithful" (1 Cor. 4:17), a man of "worth" (Phil. 2:22), and "son" or "child" (Phil. 2:22; 1 Tim. 1:2, 18).

At times friends in ministry know one another so well they can represent one another, and here we touch on a classical theory of friendship again, for it was Aristotle who said a friend is a "second self" (*Nicomachean Ethics* 9.9.10). Presence and direction in friendship can lead to such a transformation that the two become one in some ways.

Paul often sent Timothy out to represent him, or to put it more theologically: as God sent Jesus and as Jesus sent Paul, so Paul sends the God-and-Jesus-sent Timothy to represent God's act in Christ. The evidence for this abounds: Timothy remained at Berea (Acts 17:14–15), he was sent to communicate for Paul to the Thessalonians (1 Thess. 3:2, 6), and he was trusted as a reliable witness about Paul (1 Cor. 4:17).

Most importantly, Timothy was a cotheologian, coauthor, copastor, and coworker with Paul. Their mutual Christoformity had led to nothing less than the classical ideal of accord. This friend of Paul may not get the credit, but I suspect that on almost every page of every one of Paul's letters Timothy's voice and theology can be heard. If it is right to think Paul wrote his letters in dialogue with his friends (coworkers), then the entire Aristotelian theory of friendship as virtue comes alive in this relationship. These two thought together, prayed together, served God together, and grew in Christ together. Timothy helped write Philemon (1), 1 Thessalonians (1:1), 2 Thessalonians (1:1), Colossians (1:1), 2 Corinthians (1:1), Philippians (1:1), and most importantly Romans: "Timothy, my co-worker, greets you" (16:21). When Paul says in 1 Timothy (1:18), "I am giving you these instructions, Timothy, my child, in accordance with the prophecies made earlier about you, so that by following them you may fight the good fight," and when he shows that he knows Timothy's grandmother's and mother's names and knows from whom the young man learned the faith (2 Tim. 1:5; 3:15), a window opens not only on Timothy's development but also on the closeness of this relationship. Paul knows the man's life.

It is no wonder that Paul's closest friend, Timothy, receives two letters about pastoring and leading churches in the very heart of Paul's missionary work: Ephesus. Timothy was no shadow of Paul; he was no young hanger-on; he was Paul's close associate who took over for Paul when Paul left Ephesus on yet more mission trips.

Conclusion

A first and constant step into the church is friendship, and it is the pastor's calling to nurture friendships that nurture Christoformity. The apostle Paul reworked the classical theory of friendship, with its focus on terms such as *males, elites, equality, virtue, goodwill, consensus, affection*, *trust*, *loyalty*, and *frankness* or *honesty*. How did he rework it? He reframed it first in terms of covenant love, which itself is marked by rugged, affectional commitment, presence, advocacy, and direction. These are the strong foundations of Christian fellowship in a church, and a wise pastor will nurture friendships marked by these themes. Yet the most puzzling element of Paul's obvious network of friends is that there is not one shred of evidence that Paul called his coworkers "friends." Why he did not and what terms he used instead are the subject of the next chapter. We will see that a culture of friendship has such a Christoform direction that it becomes a culture of siblings.

3

A Culture of Siblings

In her wonderful and inevitably intricate novel *Death in Holy Orders*, P. D. James gets the detective Dalgleish into a conversation with one Mrs. Pilbeam about participating in a funeral service by reading from Scripture. Learning of the text chosen for her, Mrs. Pilbeam lets loose on what she'd said to Father Sebastian about the apostle Paul, and it might be a good time for us to bring to the surface in her words what many today sense about Paul:

> Father Sebastian thought I might like to read a passage from St. Paul, but I said I'd rather just say a prayer instead. Somehow I can't take St. Paul. Seems to me he was a bit of a troublemaker. There were those little groups of Christians all minding their own business and getting along all right, by and large. No one's perfect. And then St. Paul arrives unexpectedly and starts bossing and criticizing. Or he'd send them one of his fierce letters. Not the kind of letter I'd care to receive, and so I told Father Sebastian.[1]

It saddens me to think of how many conversations I have had with those like Mrs. Pilbeam, those who think Paul was more problem than solution—though I forgive Mrs. Pilbeam and some of her modern-day followers for not knowing that it was, after all, Paul and his coworker

friends who started those churches. No one as bossy as he sometimes
is made out to be would have had as many friends as Paul did.

Paul's relations with his friends would have appeared in most ways
as friendships did in the Roman Empire, and so also his churches could
look like typical "associations."[2] The so-called associations, however,
were framed by Paul with the word translated as "church" (Greek
ekklēsia, our word "church" and not the Latin *collegia*, "association"),
and so also friendship was framed in Paul's own register of vocabulary
with "loved ones"—*agapētoi*—and not with *philoi*, or "friends," or
with its close equivalent in Greek, *hetairos*.[3] As indicated in the previous chapter, there is something special about the Christian understanding of love, expressed in Paul's writings constantly with the term
agapē, but it is not so much the term itself as it is the revolution of
love through the revelation of God's love in the cross and resurrection
that turns Christian love into something not captured in the Roman
Empire's typical terms. Thus, the Greek and Roman sense of friendship caused Paul to scratch his head more than one time over the best
word to frame his relations with others in Christ. His different framing context is the church. Paul's relation with his coworkers was an
ecclesial, not a social, relation. Here we begin to see the next element
in the culture-nurturing calling of the pastor. The front porch to the
church may be experienced at first as friendship, but it soon gives way
to another category altogether, and it is here that the genius of Paul,
not his bossiness, comes to the fore.

To get this relation-beyond-friendship right we have to step back
and investigate Jesus, the kingdom, contemporary groups at the time
of Jesus, and how Jesus related to those contemporary groups.

The Pharisees and Jesus on the Way toward Paul

When Jesus came on the scene in Galilee, there were more than a few
Pharisees following their special brand of interpreting and observing
the Torah. A later but useful term for the members of these Pharisee
circles is the Hebrew term *haber*, or *haberim* in the plural.[4] To be a
Pharisee was not to belong to a specific synagogue—First Pharisees of
Capernaum—nor were the Pharisees an official denomination approved
by the Sanhedrin of Jerusalem. Rather, to be a Pharisee was to associate

with other Pharisees and to follow a specific set of interpretations, and food laws were smack-dab in the middle of all things Pharisaic.[5]

The word *haber*, as Jacob Neusner has taught us, transcended the idea of "friend" and meant far more: a "fellow-worshipper."[6] This term *haber* may not have been official in the first century, but it does describe something important about the fellowship of Pharisees. This fellowship included both a strict interpretation and observance of how the Torah was to be practiced in rules (*halakoth*). They were creating an underground holiness movement—and this matters most—but they did so in the midst of ordinary Jewish life and while dwelling alongside non-Pharisees. Thus, unlike the Essenes of Qumran, the *haberim* did not withdraw but became what H. Richard Niebuhr called "transformationalists."[7] Hillel is reported to have said, "Do not walk out on the community" (m. Avot 2:4). Pharisees, then, didn't form separate synagogues but instead lived ordinary life in a state of observance of a variety of special commitments. Their presence in Jewish society, however, was awkward because Pharisees were all-out in their observance, and their praxis created differences with those who weren't Pharisees, whom the later rabbis often called, with a harrumph or two, *am ha-arets*, "the people of the land," or ordinary folks.

By all accounts Jesus's followers were mirror images of what I have described above as the Pharisee *haberim*. While it is true that Jesus at times refers to his followers as "friends,"[8] they are more often called "disciples," and Jesus is their rabbi, teacher, and Lord. As such, he ushers them into a new movement called kingdom with a new king. Like the *haberim* of the Pharisees, Jesus and his followers did not withdraw; they did not form their own synagogues; they followed the teaching of their teacher (or rabbi), Jesus; they did not follow the Pharisees' *halakoth* on food or tithing or fasting; they were not so much, then, a purity or holiness movement but a love-God-and-love-others movement; and they were as much fellow worshipers as they were friends. In other words, Jesus's circles of followers were Jesus-following *haberim*, and this sketch of how Jesus's followers operated helps us understand the Pauline churches more than some think.

The Pharisees formed themselves into *haberim*, Jesus framed his vision for Israel with the term *kingdom*, and Paul framed his vision with the term *church*. One could say Jesus formed a kingdom *haber*, whereas Paul formed a church *haber*, but we then are forced to ask why they didn't use *haberim* but instead chose *kingdom* or *church*. Jesus chose *kingdom* to express his vision and *disciple* (Hebrew *talmid*) to express the relation of his followers to himself. Jesus, then, decided *haber* would not work for him. Paul, clearly enough, did not think *haber* or *disciple* or *kingdom* would work for him, so he thought with the term *church*. But the word *church* is not nearly so common in Paul's writings as some may think. He used, in fact, many terms for the people he converted to Christ, and the most common term is the one that will reveal to us why Paul wanted to go beyond friendship. I will argue below that though the Pharisees used *haberim* to describe their members, and Jesus used *disciple*, Paul's favorite term was not *church* but something else.

My concern in this book is how Paul understood pastoral theology and ministry, so there is no reason for us to enter into all the terms or even most of the terms for church at work in Paul's letters.[9] We are now ready to answer why it is that Paul does not call his coworkers "friends" even if they were perceived that way in his world. Paul does not call his coworkers *philoi* because he understands them as brothers and sisters.[10] This stands in contrast to the Old Testament, where, in the summary statement of Saul Olyan, "friends are rarely if ever referred to using familial terminology (e.g., 'brother'), another way in which friends are distinguished from relatives."[11]

Nurturing a local church in which each person is a brother or a sister is the heart of pastoral ministry for the apostle Paul, and such a family of people transcends the sorts of friends seen walking under porticoes along the forum in Athens, Corinth, or Ephesus.[12] For the theme of this book, this now is ready to be said: the pastor is called to nurture friendships into siblingships in the journey toward Christoformity.

Paul's Theology of Siblings

The term *adelphos*, or "brother," occurs 127 times in Paul's letters and 317 times in the New Testament. The term *adelphē*, or "sister," occurs 26 times in the New Testament and a mere 6 times in Paul's letters. If the second term always refers to a female, the first term, *adelphos*, especially in Paul's letters, means "brothers and sisters." That is, the term is used for the whole congregation of Jesus followers. Trebilco says the term occurs 271 times in the New Testament as a nongendered metaphor, which is our concern, and that's enough to show that the idea of siblingship is the dominant self-understanding and self-designation of the church.[13] A metaphor leads a person to think of one thing (the people in Paul's churches) in terms of another (sibling relations). The dense concentration of the term *sibling* means these church folks were to think of themselves more as siblings than as "body of Christ" or "saints" or "fellowship" or even "church."[14] Therefore (as John Barclay and Stephen Barton long ago pointed out) the New Testament both affirms the new family and expresses some ambivalence about one's natural ties in the family when siblings becomes the metaphor for the fictive family, the church of siblings.[15] Paul was nurturing sibling relationships when he formed his mission churches,[16] and we need to bring "siblingship" closer to the heart of our vision of the church and of what pastors are called to do as leaders and pastors.

Metaphors matter because they are words we think with and embody.[17] A student of mine at Northern Seminary, Greg Mamula, has done extensive practical pastoral work on helping Christians in local churches discover and develop sibling relations. He calls it "Welcome to the Family Table," and here is his explanation of the project and the major elements involved in forming a sibling culture: "*Welcome to the Family Table* is a process for learning and experiencing habits of discipleship that connect people to Christ, the church, and one another in powerful ways. The habits of eating together, dwelling in the Word, storytelling, and communion provide participants with space to embody kingdom teachings in their homes and strengthen their Christian brother and sister relationships with one another."[18] His research shows that progress can be made in local churches that truly desire to become more sibling-focused. We need to dig a bit deeper into the metaphor of sibling.

Sibling as Metaphor

As a reality and therefore as a metaphor, siblingship is impossible to extricate from "family" or from "household," which itself was tied into emotional and economic support as well as into educational and cultural formation. Metaphors do not always bring into play the fullness of the term being used (*family*, *sibling*), so Paul's focus on siblings and on the lack of developing ecclesial mothers and fathers—not to ignore the extended family and tenants in one's household—does not mean he plays siblings off against family or the wider household.[19] Paul also does not create a complete map of the church as family. For instance, the father of the siblings is far more God the Father than Paul, though he can speak of himself as both father (1 Cor. 4:15; Phil. 2:22; 1 Thess. 2:11–12; Philem. 10) and mother (1 Cor. 3:1–2; Gal. 4:19; 1 Thess. 2:7) to the siblings.[20] Most importantly, Paul chooses the family and household term *sibling* because it is the relation of brothers and sisters that matters most to him.[21]

It matters how pastors "frame" their congregations. Words matter. Images shape. Metaphors live. Some preacher types think of their churches as audiences; some counselor types think of their congregations as souls; some teacher types think of them as students; sacramental types might think of their congregations as sinners in need of mediation or as needy people. The apostle Paul constantly called his churches siblings, and the constant thinking of them as siblings and calling them siblings built a culture of siblingship rather than a culture of an audience, souls, students, or those in need of mediation. To nurture siblingship in churches, then, will require that the pastor frame his congregants as siblings.

Why Sibling?

Why choose "brothers and sisters" or siblings? We think in metaphors that humans embody reality,[22] so to self-designate the church as a brother- or sisterhood frames the church and our relations with one another in terms of ordinary brothers and sisters. This means we need to understand something about siblings in the world of Paul. The most important text from the time of Paul on this topic comes from Plutarch, *On Brotherly Love*, and Reidar Aasgaard[23] and Paul Trebilco are two who have summarized siblingship in the ancient world.

Family is so central to human relations that one can say all relations are extensions of family relations. Plutarch said all nonfamily relations are "shadows and imitations and images" of family relations. Before there was Israel, before there was a kingdom, and before there was a church, there was family. The foundation of all relations in society is family relations.

Trebilco finds four major themes of family relations:

1. Love
2. Harmony, concord, and cooperation
3. Discord, conflict, leniency, and forgiveness
4. Hierarchy

We are concerned with a theology of siblingship *in Paul* as the portal through which we can enter into an understanding of pastoral ministry as the calling to nurture into a family some formerly nonfamilied people. So I will add one theme to Trebilco's list. I will focus on Plutarch's *On Brotherly Love* as expressing the context for Paul and then show how he adapts each theme. For each, the point is that this is what pastors do in the Pauline mission: they nurture congregants into siblings.

For pastors to nurture friendships into siblingships in the direction of Christoformity, the following five themes are important: sibling relations are marked (1) by love, (2) by love for all siblings, (3) by mutual growth into Christoformity, (4) by recognizing the safety and security of boundaries, and (5) by knowing that sibling relations began with Jesus, our Brother.

Love

First, love is a defining characteristic of family and sibling relations. Homes are where one is loved and where one learns love. Love between siblings finds its way into unity, solidarity, concord, and cooperation. As Plutarch expresses it in *On Brotherly Love*, "And this fact is obvious to everyone: Nature from one seed and one source has created two brothers, or three, or more, not for difference and opposition to each other, but that by being separate they might the more readily co-operate with one another" (2). Brotherly and sisterly love entails prejudice, bias, and favoritism toward one another (20), and any deviance from faithfulness to one's siblings is betrayal. Again, Plutarch: "But the man who quarrels with his brother, and takes as his comrade a stranger from the market-place or the wrestling-floor, appears to be doing nothing but cutting off voluntarily a limb of his own flesh and blood, and taking to himself and joining to his body an extraneous member" (3). What Plutarch means is that brothers and sisters "become united in their emotions and actions" (5).

This is to say, for Paul to frame the church as siblings is to believe Christians are to love one another as brothers and sisters love one another, which means in his world solidarity, unity, prejudicial favor, and emotional attachment. But our development of love as a rugged affectional commitment of presence, advocacy, and direction intensifies ordinary sibling love. With God as the loving Father, the Thessalonians know what it means experientially to be loved by God (1 Thess. 4:9) and how this manifests itself in their sibling relations with siblings throughout Macedonia (4:10–12). And in Romans 12:9–13 we get nothing less than a list of what *sibling love* (*philadelphia*) looks like: zeal in honoring one another, contributing to the needs of the saints, and—to show that sibling love is not entirely exclusive—extending hospitality to strangers. For Paul, love is the central virtue: love knows not to do anything wrong to a neighbor (Rom. 13:10), and, echoing Jesus (Mark 12:28–34), "love is the fulfilling of the law" (Rom. 13:10; Gal. 5:14). Siblings in the church getting along, of course, is the heart of Paul's emphasis on love. He is echoed, with a chill of realism, by Romanian writer Emil Cioran, who is quoted by Joseph Epstein: "Love is an agreement on the part of two people to over-estimate each other."[24] Without some overestimation, love, in the patchwork quilt called a local church, has little chance of success.

What could be more loving than how Paul expresses himself in 2 Corinthians 6:11–13 with 7:2–4? Paul pulls back the veils and reveals his frankness (6:11; 7:4) as well as his restless, vulnerable heart, his desire to have his love for the Corinthians reciprocated, his yearning for full reconciliation: "Our heart is wide open to you," and "There is no restriction in our affections." And in chapter 7 he says, "For I said before that you are in our hearts, to die together and to live together." Their response to Paul was his life or death! So much did he love them.[25]

Love for All

Second, inherent to loving one's siblings is recognizing significant differences. But siblings are siblings, and each sibling is to love his or her siblings in spite of difference, inequalities, and superiorities.[26] Loving each sibling means considering the implications of one's actions and words for the other siblings in the family. It was a reality in the Greek world as it is a reality now: we are not identicals but differents. How does sibling love for each sibling manifest itself when there are differences? Plutarch writes:

> One would therefore advise a brother, in the first place, to make his brothers partners in those respects in which he is considered to be superior, adorning them with a portion of his repute and adopting them into his friendships, and if he is a cleverer speaker than they, to make his eloquence available for their use as though it were no less theirs than his; in the next place, to make manifest to them neither haughtiness nor disdain, but rather, by deferring to them and conforming his character to theirs, to make his superiority secure from envy and to equalize, so far as this is attainable, the disparity of his fortune by his moderation of spirit. (12)

What of the inferior sibling? "Just as Metellus, therefore, thought that Romans should be grateful to the gods because so great a man as Scipio[27] was not born in any other city, so each one of us should pray that, if possible, he himself may succeed beyond all other men, yet if this cannot be, that his brother may have that superiority and influence so coveted by himself" (14).

Hence, unlike a balancing scale, on which, when one goes down, the other goes up in status, the sibling is to rejoice in the rising of the sibling (15). In ways that are like Paul's "body of Christ" metaphors, Plutarch contends siblings are separate fingers and each finger is needed for the hand to do what Nature gave it the ability to do.

Paul, however, takes sibling love to a completely different level. Sibling love is for siblings in Plutarch, but for Paul sibling love is for a much larger family. Paul undoes the elitism-of-friendship approach to relationships in the church not only by admitting that all are sinners but also by imposing the constant obligation to love everyone in the fellowship, regardless of status or virtue. Hence calling church people siblings means expecting that church folks will love *all* their church siblings and not just those of their own gender, age, or status. Three verses jump to the top of anyone's list when this theme comes up for discussion.

> There is no longer Jew or Greek, there is no longer slave or free, there is no longer male and female; for all of you are one in Christ Jesus (Gal. 3:28).
>
> For in the one Spirit we were all baptized into one body—Jews or Greeks, slaves or free—and we were all made to drink of one Spirit (1 Cor. 12:13).
>
> In that renewal there is no longer Greek and Jew, circumcised and uncircumcised, barbarian, Scythian, slave and free; but Christ is all and in all! (Col. 3:11).

The church turns away traditional categories about status and superiorities and inferiorities, because the church turns each person from such categories into one category: sibling. These varied persons are now "one" in Christ, and they are now "one body" and have all been "made to drink of one Spirit," and all this because "Christ is all" and is the sole means of identification and indwells all. And when the apostle turns to this topic of spiritual gifts, what does he call his addressees? "Brothers [and sisters]" (1 Cor. 12:1). The entirety of 1 Corinthians and, in fact, each of Paul's letters can be read through the term *sibling*, and the problems arising are sibling rivalries and tensions, and the solution is to act like loving siblings and family.

It matters what pastors think of when they think of their congregations. Paul's framing thought is that Christians are siblings, and that means they are to love one another. Pastors are to nurture siblings to learn to love all other siblings in the fellowship.

Sibling Growth

Third, siblings are present to one another, they are advocates for one another, and they are committed to mutual development with one another. Toward the end of his essay on sibling relations, Plutarch depicts friends as instruments in moral development: "For friendships shape character and there is no more important indication of a difference in character than the selection of different friends" (20). Because friendships are extensions of families, the next step is logical: If so with friends, how much more so with siblings.

One of Plutarch's great themes is how siblings relate to one another in helping one another along in the life of virtue rather than dominating one another, as elder siblings often did (16). "Nature," he says, "has begotten with the child *at its birth the principle of love*" (italics added). Love is natural and leads in Plutarch to the themes of presence and advocacy, giving way to direction (as I explained in the previous chapter). I will italicize words connected to friendship and love:

> Only after the erring brother has been *defended* in this manner should the other turn to him and *rebuke* him somewhat sharply, pointing out with all *frankness* his errors of commission and of omission. For one should neither give free rein to brothers, nor, again, should one trample on them when they are at fault (for the latter is the act of one who gloats over the sinner, the former that of one who aids and abets him), but should apply his admonition as one who *cares* for his brother and *grieves* with him. Otherwise he who has been the most zealous advocate before his parents becomes before the brother himself the most vehement of accusers. (10)

What is his point? Siblings have a responsibility to foster growth in virtue in one another, and they are thus accountable to one another. Our Western understanding of tolerance has no foothold in either Plutarch or Paul, to whom we now turn for a few major shifts away from Plutarch.

Every letter Paul wrote was an expression of theological ethics. Nuance aside, the point is that over and over Paul tells people how to live. He is calling all Christians into Christoformity. Inherent to such Christoformity is putting sin and the flesh to death and rising to a new life of love and holiness (Col. 2:20–3:17). Inasmuch as Paul was a sibling among siblings and inasmuch as he expected both himself and his friends and churches to follow these teachings about ethics, we can say that the entire mission of Paul was one of moral transformation of sinners into saints, of those who were far from God into those who were becoming Christlike. In this quest for growth in virtue Paul is both like the Roman world of moralists, like Aristotle or Plutarch or Cicero or Seneca, and quite different at the same time: his virtues were

Christoformity and not reducible to the Greek and Roman senses of justice or courage or honor.[28]

Sibling relations with one another turned the churches into homes of Christoformity. Romans 16 reads like a phone book list for the house church movement in Rome. After the opening request to welcome "sister" Phoebe (Rom. 16:1–2), we read of five house churches: that of (1) Prisca and Aquila, then of the family of (2) Aristobulus, then the family of (3) Narcissus, and then (4) a string of names that may well be another house church ("Asyncritus, Phlegon, Hermes, Patrobas, Hermas, and the brothers and sisters who are with them" in 16:14), and perhaps also a house church connected to (5) "Philologus, Julia, Nereus and his sister, and Olympas, and all the saints who are with them" (16:15). It is reasonable to see, then, at least five house churches in Rome, and this has significance for Paul's understanding of church folks as siblings. The natural location for a family and for siblings is the home, and church gatherings centered on a home intensified the siblingship theme in earliest Christianity.[29] Diversity is clear in the names: nineteen Greek names, probably seven Jewish persons, and eight Latin names.[30] House churches, as sibling-shaped space, made transformation into Christoformity pastorally accessible, as anyone who has experience in small-group transformations knows.

I said earlier that the *haberim* of Jesus were not just friends but fellow worshipers. The same is to be said of Paul's *haberim*, who were siblings who fellowshipped and worshiped with one another. The house churches transcended social gatherings, and they were not seminaries or colleges designed for instruction alone. Rather, these were siblings who shared life with one another and who worshiped the same God, made known to them in Jesus the Messiah. The term *siblings* gives a special angle on early Christian house church gatherings: they were intimate because they were in a home; the number of those gathered—no more than thirty and probably often fewer—intensified their siblingship by permitting each to participate; they were focused on a single Lord Messiah, who had redeemed each of them; and they were empowered by a single Lord Spirit, who had given them new life and capacities to transcend their inabilities and to transform their abilities into expressions of sibling fellowship.[31] Again, the sibling character and worship themes of the Christian churches made them homes of Christoformity.

This is perhaps the most notable difference between Paul's theory of sibling relations and Plutarch's theory of sibling relations. For Paul the sibling relation is a spiritually created, "in Christ" relationship that was designed to transcend typical status and honor, and it was designed not simply to shape the fixed boundaries of a family but to expand intentionally in order to create a larger and growing family of new converts to the faith.

It matters not only what pastors *think* of when they think of their congregations but also *what they call their congregations*. Paul's dominant metaphor for the church was not "church" but "siblings." Inherent to the life of siblings is mutual accountability in moral growth. A pastor nurtures siblings into mutual growth toward Christoformity.

Boundaried Community

Fourth, family is foundational to all society and forms a unique set of relationships, as the family forms identity.[32] Maintaining a family's boundaries, honor, and integrity was central to all things Roman, Greek, and Jewish.[33] Siblings form, it should be noticed, a group identity within a group (family, household): siblings are not the whole family or household. *Adelphoi kai adelphai* (brothers and sisters) are not equivalent to *oikos kai oikonomia* (house and household), with the result that family-as-metaphor is not equivalent to siblings-as-metaphor. Both Aristotle and Sirach rank siblings higher on the social scale than friends (*Nicomachean Ethics* 8.12.1–6; Sir. 25:1 [siblings, friends, marriage]). But families and siblings are boundaried by blood relations, and blood relations distinguish families from friends. Plutarch indicates the difference between friendships and siblingship: "So friendships knitted together through long familiarity, even though the friends part company, can be easily resumed again, but when brothers have once broken the bonds of Nature, they cannot readily come together, and even if they do, their reconciliation bears with it a filthy hidden sore of suspicion" (7). The betrayal of siblings, he is arguing, is the deepest wound.

To protect such a special, boundaried relationship, Plutarch urges this: when trivial matters arise, they need to be seen for what they can become and so be dealt with when they arise (16). How so? The one bugged or

bothered is to absorb the problem and grow bigger: "It is therefore of
no slight importance to resist the spirit of contentiousness and jealousy
among brothers when it first creeps in over trivial matters, *practicing the
art of making mutual concessions, of learning to take defeat, and of
taking pleasure in indulging brothers rather than in winning victories
over them*" (17; italics added). When bothered, siblings are to practice
the art of absorption. Genuine alienations are then protected for what
they are. Forgiveness, Plutarch says (18), is an art form learned by practicing forgiving the other. What I find most important about this set of
lines from Plutarch is the special nature of the relation of siblings: it is
a boundaried community of love. Siblings experience a prejudicial love
for one another, unlike the love they will find elsewhere.

To be siblings, then, is to be a boundaried community. What marks
the siblings in the Christian community is baptism, a life of faith under
Christ, and the identity that flows out of those waters. The apostle
Paul breathes this boundary marking on every page of his letters, and
that boundaried community is to learn to know itself as nothing less
than a community of siblings that, like ancient families, is to maintain
its honor by living appropriately as a community of faith. Notice this
from Galatians 6:10: "So then, whenever we have an opportunity, let
us work for the good of all, and especially for those of the family of
faith." It is the word *especially* that reveals the existence of a boundary:
they know who is in the family of faith and who is not.

I will use two examples—the first brief and the second more extensive—of the kind of boundaried community inherent to sibling
relations in a church today. Before we take another step forward, this
must be said: pastors, churches, elders and deacon boards, presbyteries,
and ecclesial groups have used the idea of boundaried communities to
protect, to violate, and to disgrace the name of Christ in our world
today. What is illegal must be reported. Having said that, I want to
sustain the viability of the church-as-siblings being a (legally observant,
voluntary, and uncoerced) boundaried community of the faithful.

BOUNDARIES IN CORINTH

A similar boundary occurs in the odd-but-real passage in 1 Corinthians 6, and this boundary means special work occurs *inside* that is

not to occur *outside*.[34] Inside are siblings (5:11; 6:5–6, 8); outside is the world. (I have altered the NRSV in this instance to bring to the surface the importance of using sibling language.)

> When any of you has a grievance against another, do you dare to take it to court before the unrighteous, instead of taking it before the saints? Do you not know that the saints will judge the world? And if the world is to be judged by you, are you incompetent to try trivial cases? Do you not know that we are to judge angels—to say nothing of ordinary matters? If you have ordinary cases, then, do you appoint as judges those who have no standing in the church? I say this to your shame. Can it be that there is no one among you wise enough to decide between one sibling [Greek *adelphos*] and another, but a sibling [*adelphos*] goes to court against a sibling [*adelphos*]—and before unbelievers at that?
>
> In fact, to have lawsuits at all with one another is already a defeat for you. Why not rather be wronged? Why not rather be defrauded? But you yourselves wrong and defraud—and siblings [*adelphoi*] at that.
>
> Do you not know that wrongdoers will not inherit the kingdom of God? Do not be deceived! Fornicators, idolaters, adulterers, male prostitutes, sodomites, thieves, the greedy, drunkards, revilers, robbers— none of these will inherit the kingdom of God. And this is what some of you used to be. But you were washed, you were sanctified, you were justified in the name of the Lord Jesus Christ and in the Spirit of our God. (1 Cor. 6:1–11)

This, it must be added, has nothing to do with pastoral teams maintaining privacy about criminal activities, such as sexual molestation of children or adults. This has to do with grievances that the church ought to be taking care of inside. Why? Because the siblings of the church know the mind of God, have the Spirit of God, and are destined to judge even angels. This angels bit emphasizes the gravity of the church's capacity to know the truth.

The second paragraph above (vv. 7–8) already shows what ought to be happening inside the boundaried community of siblings. Like blood siblings, they are to take care of matters among themselves, and like good blood siblings, they are to absorb faults for the sake of healing and reconciliation. That boundary then comes splashing out of the water in verses 9–11 when Paul announces the clearest boundary marker of all: moral behaviors. In this passage Paul, no doubt looking out his window onto life in Ephesus or perhaps even pondering what he knows about Corinth itself, describes the notorious sins of notorious sinners and declares such persons will not be in the kingdom.[35] The Corinthian siblings, however, are not like that, because they have been regenerated through the baptismal washing and have been "sanctified" and "justified" in the name of Jesus. Between the washed Corinthians and the worldly Corinthians stands Jesus. He creates the boundary; he is the boundary.

Boundaries in Colossae

Nothing, however, is more forceful about boundaried community life or sibling relations in the church than the letter of Paul to Philemon.[36] The letter concerns Onesimus, the slave, who ran away from Philemon, the slave owner. We do not know why Onesimus ran away, so we are tempted to guess. The evidence is slim enough that we can imagine any number of reasonable scenarios, but imagination is almost all we have. It is likely that, upon departure, Onesimus stole provisions, for that is the most reasonable context for Paul saying in verses 18–19, "If he has wronged you in any way, or owes you anything, charge that to my account. I, Paul, am writing this with my own hand: I will repay it." One of the historical puzzles of this beautiful pastoral letter is why Onesimus ends up in the presence of Paul, for surely Onesimus knew Paul was Philemon's friend ("Philemon our dear friend and co-worker," v. 1). It is less likely that Onesimus was arrested and ended up in the same house arrest as Paul, since the former was a slave. It is more likely that he came to his senses and found out Paul. There is then the possibility that Onesimus was not a runaway (a *fugitivus*) but one who ran to a "friend of the master"—that is, to Paul—to get Paul's advocacy for a grievance against Philemon (hence, an *erro*, a temporary runaway). The evidence of the letter can be explained either way, though I think the theft implication of verses 18–19 tips the scale toward a *fugitivus*.

The drama of the letter now takes on two characteristics. First, this letter will be performed, not simply read, publicly in the (boundaried confines of the) house church of Philemon. Notice verse 2: "and to the church in your house." In the performance of this letter there would be an encounter between the apostle Paul through a letter reader, perhaps Tychicus, and the slave owner Philemon. The letter reader would have been mentored by Paul and Timothy to know to whom to look when reading, to know which emotions to use at which moments, and to pause and speed up when such were needed. Roger Scruton, in a moment of family candor, once said, "It was a peculiar characteristic of our mother that her words never coincided with her facial expressions."[37] This, however, would not work for the reading of this letter: words and face had to coincide to become compelling. In front of everyone in the house church, which most likely included other slaves, the letter became public persuasion. The other slaves are implicated in Onesimus's running away, and now they will hang on every word in the letter, knowing that Philemon's response to him will be his response to them. Furthermore, Philemon's family is present and is surely standing with the slave owner, who has been wounded financially, who can seek justice, and who could—if he chose—inflict serious punishment. I'm thinking of 1 Corinthians 6:1–11 right now, and I hope you are too: Paul wants this stuff to occur inside, among siblings, and not outside, in the world. This is ethics for a boundaried community, and it reveals how to live as a family.

The second characteristic of the drama is the suspense in this letter, which I will now try to re-create. Paul creates this through performance and audience hums and facial expressions and verbal comebacks and questions that cannot be conveyed except in some kind of acting-out of it. (My re-creation is closer to the original than to a summary.) Paul sets up Philemon by taking the side of Onesimus in some important ways. How so? He calls himself at the top of the letter—the second word in Greek—a "prisoner," which means someone of no status, who is suspect and in jeopardy, and this is the only time in all of Paul's letters he opens with such a self-designation. He strokes Philemon's ego in public: Paul calls him "dear friend and co-worker" (v. 1), he blesses him with God's grace in verse 3, he prays for him, and he talks about Philemon's love, faith, and generosity in verses 4–7. The man just got a very thorough public affirmation in front of the whole (boundaried) assembly of siblings.

The suspense continues in a powerful way in verses 8–16. Paul could command Philemon to do something—and what that is has not been stated. Onesimus knows; Tychicus knows; and Philemon and his household know only something's up and the runaway is now in their midst and Paul's got the slave's back. He could command but won't; what he wants done—again, not yet clear—he wants done on the basis of love. Paul backs off and now identifies with Onesimus a little more, though again, Philemon doesn't know what's happening. Paul says he is both "an old man" and a "prisoner." (Feel sorry for me; come to my aid; show me some love.) Now a critical moment in the suspense of this letter comes to the surface: "I am appealing to you *for my child, Onesimus, whose father I have become during my imprisonment*" (v. 10). Onesimus has come to Christ; Paul was his converter. Dramatically, Paul has made him a very special family member: he calls him a "child," the very term he so often uses for Timothy. Onesimus is now inside and no longer outside the boundaried community of siblings, which means he's inside with Paul and Timothy and Philemon and Apphia and Archippus. He's a brother, he's a sibling.

According to Roman law, discovered slaves were to be returned; Paul doesn't want the Romans judging siblings in the church, so he hopes Philemon will drop any charges and forgive the man. Paul, so it seems, wants Onesimus at his side, but he will keep him only with Philemon's permission, and it could be said sibling language is flooding the air in Philemon's presence. Paul even offers a quasi-Calvinist explanation for Onesimus's departure: *perhaps* he was separated by divine providence so Philemon could have him back as an eternal sibling.

But what comes next is the first of two critical turns in this letter. Paul says Philemon is to have Onesimus back "*no longer as a slave but more than a slave, a beloved brother*" (v. 16; see also v. 1). "No longer" expresses the eschatological shift from the world into the *ecclesia*[38] and reminds Bible readers of "no longer two, but one flesh" (Matt. 19:6). The "no longer" of Philemon 16 reverses the prodigal son's confession: "I am no longer worthy to be called your son" (Luke 15:21). As to Paul's own theology, the two most poignant parallels at the theological level are Galatians 4:7 ("So you are no longer a slave, but God's child [*huios*, "son"]"; NIV) and 2 Corinthians 5:16 ("So from now on we regard no one from a worldly point of view. Though we once regarded Christ in this way, we do so no longer" [NIV]; see Gal. 2:20; Eph. 2:19). This musical percolation of "no longers" in the New Testament indicates both a salvation-historical theme of fulfillment and a revolutionary new way of life at the social, ecclesial level.

Kingdom theology means a slave like Onesimus is now a "brother," which is to say, far "better than a slave." Since the "better than" alludes to hierarchy in Roman society, one could translate "higher than a slave." For Paul, Onesimus is a sibling to Philemon, and Philemon is now a sibling to Onesimus, and that has colossal implications: they are to relate to each other and to respond to each other as siblings and not simply—or at all—as master and slave. In the boundaried community they are to be siblings, and the former statuses of master and slave are revolutionized.

The second critical turn occurs in verse 17, and Paul ties his own relationship to Philemon to his relationship to Onesimus to his relationship to Philemon: "So if you consider me a partner [koinōnon], welcome [proslambou] him as you would welcome me." Philemon is cornered and everyone is watching, not least the slaves, who know that if the slave owner welcomes the runaway back, the whole place erupts in joyous celebration. Muted, perhaps, not so visible, but breaking through, and inside the hearts are thumping. The critical turn ends when Paul flat-out changes terms: "Confident of your obedience . . ." (v. 21). And the door flies open when Paul says in verse 22, "Prepare a guest room for me."

Everything in this letter hinges on siblingship and the boundaried relationship of siblings. Because Onesimus is a brother and because Philemon is a brother and because they are now siblings in the boundaried community, different rules apply. If Plutarch said siblings are to be lenient, Paul turns this into the language of grace and reciprocation: now that Philemon is forgiven, he is to forgive. Now that in Christ the siblings are reconciled to God, they are to be reconciled with each other. What distinguishes the Christian community is that *sibling* is the word to think with and to embody. And because sibling is no longer blood sibling but in-Christ sibling, the way of siblings applies to everyone in the family, including runaway slaves.

Pastors are charged to follow Paul right down this road of nurturing cultures of siblings who nurture a culture of reconciliation with one another after fracturing their relationships. *Forgiveness* is the operative word in the ecclesia of siblings. This means pastors have a double task: to recognize a boundary between the church and the world *and* to create and nurture the kind of boundary that is open to and welcomes those on the outside to become part of the church. This is not sectarian or isolationist wall-building but rather a stable family boundary that protects the family, permits growth in the family, and also welcomes the outsider as the family embodies the kingdom of God in the world.

Siblings from Jesus Onward

Plutarch puts in writing a very common relational term in his day: *siblings*. So the Christians weren't the first to use *sibling* for their special, boundaried community relations. Yes, too, the term *brother* refers to fellow Jews in the Old Testament often enough that Paul was equipped with the term from his Roman and Jewish contexts before he became a sibling among siblings in Christ.[39] But this is even more true: Jesus taught that his followers were to be siblings to one another,[40] and Paul's usage of this term in such a concentrated manner distinguishes Paul from others who used sibling language for insider talk. The impetus for Paul's use is Jesus's use. Three passages about Jesus, beginning with my favorite, need to be cited.

> But you are not to be called rabbi, for you have one teacher, and you are all ~~students~~ siblings [Greek, *adelphoi*] (Matt. 23:8; NIV has "brothers").
>
> Then his mother and his brothers came; and standing outside, they sent to him and called him. A crowd was sitting around him; and they said to him, "Your mother and your brothers and sisters are outside, asking for you." And he replied, "Who are *my mother and my brothers?*" And looking at those who sat around him, he said, "Here are *my mother and my brothers!* Whoever does the will of God is *my brother and sister and mother*" (Mark 3:31–35).
>
> Jesus said, "Truly I tell you, there is no one who has left house or brothers or sisters or mother or father or children or fields, for my sake and for the sake of the good news, who will not receive a hundredfold now in this age—houses, *brothers and sisters, mothers and children*, and fields, with persecutions—and in the age to come eternal life (Mark 10:29–30).

These texts illustrate that during Jesus's own lifetime he used the terms for family and siblings to describe his followers and how they were to understand themselves.

The apostle Paul deepens this language when he connects siblingship to one of his favorite terms, *adoption*. Thus, believers have "received a spirit [or "the Spirit"] of adoption," and this means they call God "Father" (Rom. 8:15; Gal. 4:5). Later in Romans 8 Paul says we "groan inwardly while we wait for adoption" (v. 23), and then he connects this to Jesus and says that we are "predestined to be conformed to the image of his Son, in order that he might be the firstborn." I now veer from the NRSV to translate the next phrase "within many siblings" (8:29; NRSV has "within a large family"; Eph. 1:5). The word translated as "adoption" is connected to the Greek term *huiothesia*, which can be rendered "sonship." Christ the Son sends the Spirit to give us new birth, and that becomes for us a metaphorical adoption into the new family; we become children of God. The aim of Christoformity drives the entire process of redemption, which begins in God's foreknowledge, leading to predestination, calling, justification, and glorification (8:29–30). As fellow children, then, we become siblings through the sonship of Jesus.

A Christ-centered understanding of our sibling relations is brought to the fore in the book of Hebrews and needs to be mentioned here to fill in the picture.

> Since, therefore, the *children* [*paidia*] share flesh and blood, he himself likewise shared the same things, so that through death he might destroy the one who has the power of death, that is, the devil, and free those who all their lives were held in slavery by the fear of death. For it is clear that he did not come to help angels, but the descendants of Abraham. Therefore he had to become like *his brothers and sisters* [*adelphoi*] *in every respect*, so that he might be a merciful and faithful high priest in the service of God, to make a sacrifice of atonement for the sins of the people. Because he himself was tested by what he suffered, he is able to help those who are being tested. (2:14–18)

Though Paul was not the author of Hebrews, what is said here is compatible with Paul's writings: the incarnation is Christ's assumption of our flesh and our nature so that he could redeem us. The author calls his fellow Christians Christ's own brothers and sisters. This means Christ is the Brother of brothers. His assumption of our nature establishes our siblingship so that he might become the kind of high priest who knows us, who dies for and as us and with us, and who represents us and therefore can help us as we are tested.

Conclusion

Putting this section together, we must first say that for Paul we are more than friends; friendship is not the goal. Rather, friendship morphs into siblingship. We are siblings because of our Elder Sibling; we become siblings through the work of Christ and the power of the Spirit; we are related as siblings *only because of Christ and his redemption*. This means our Elder Brother Jesus reveals the path of cruciformity and Christoformity, and to be siblings to this Elder Brother means we are to become like him in every way possible. He made us siblings by an act of profound humiliation (Phil. 2:6–11) and therefore set the example of Christoformity. But Christoformity is not so much a moral achievement as it is a divine presence of Christ in us through the Spirit that transforms us into his likeness. Our relation to one another then is not natural but fictive and spiritual; it is not our own achievement but his. We are siblings only through and in Christ, our Elder Brother.[41]

The pastor is called to nurture a culture of Christoformity and the last two chapters have spelled out a double theme: the portal is friendship, but friendship is transcended in the church because the deeper relationship is siblingship. In Christ, we are all brothers and sisters. The pastor nurtures Christoformity by nurturing friendships that become over time siblingships of love.

4

A Culture of Generosity

My six decades of experience with pastors have proven that some pastors have a natural giftedness when it comes to pastoral presence. It's almost style, seen as much in eye contact, facial expressions, capacity to listen, maturity of character, and willingness to lend a hand as it is in actual substance of pastoring. John Ames, that very real fictional pastor in Marilynne Robinson's *Gilead*, describes his own natural giftedness to pastor in these words:

> I've always been taller than most, larger than most. It runs in my family. When I was a boy, people took me to be older than I was and often expected more of me—more common sense, usually—than I could come up with at the time. I got pretty good at pretending I understood more than I did, a skill which has served me through life. I say this because I want you to realize that I am not by any means a saint. My life does not compare with my grandfather's. I get much more respect than I deserve. This seems harmless enough in most cases. People want to respect the pastor and I'm not going to interfere with that. But I've developed a great reputation for wisdom by ordering more books than I ever had time to read, and reading more books, by far, than I learned anything useful from, except, of course, that some very tedious gentlemen have written books. This is not a new insight, but the truth of it is something you have to experience to fully grasp.[1]

Ames's candor is welcome. Some pastors get more respect than they deserve, and there's not much we can do about it, and it's best that we not try. One way to earn that kind of respect is by acquiring wisdom when it comes to money and how to speak to churches about money.

Cajoling and guilting are not the ways of wisdom, but neither is it wise to avoid speaking of discipleship and stewardship in the same breath. The pastor who leads with a front foot shaped by respect for others and their economic decisions will gain the confidence of her congregation. One can always lampoon congregants as easily as pastors when it comes to how money is allocated, and exposing opulence among the clerics was the way of Anthony Trollope,[2] but the aim of the pastor is Christoformity. Pastors who take cues from Paul are called to nurture economic Christoformity. If Christ is Lord over all of life, if money and resources and possessions form one of the most important dimensions of life, and if pastors are called to nurture Christoformity in all ways, then the pastor is called to nurture economic Christoformity.

But Paul . . .

A long tradition claims that the apostle Paul abandoned the economic justice consciousness of Jesus. Mary's Magnificat extolled the poor and castigated the rich (Luke 1:46–55), Zechariah's Benedictus at least sounds notes of the restoring the fortunes of peace (1:67–79), and John the Baptist's prophetic demand was nothing less than breathtaking economic justice (3:10–14). So, when Jesus stood up to read the lection from Isaiah 61 and then sat down to utter that that Scripture's justice was fulfilled on that very day (4:16–30), when he opened the sermon on the gentle slope on the northern edge of the Sea of Galilee by blessing the poor and cursing the rich (6:20–26), and when his common practice of fellowship was among the poor of Galilee, he set the tone for economic justice in his kingdom mission. Those in tune with Jesus cannot, then, be one bit taken by surprise when the first fellowship in Jerusalem after Pentecost becomes economically just (Acts 2:42–47; 4:32–36).

Some then ask, What happened to Paul? Why, scholars have accusingly asked for a century or more, so little concern for economic justice and the poor? Earle Ellis, a highly regarded New Testament professor of yesteryear, once observed that, "like Jesus and the New Testament writers generally, he displayed no interest in using his ministry for broader humanitarian concerns. Unlike a Cynic preacher (or John the Baptist), he did not reproach the licentiousness of Berenice and generally saw no obligation as Christ's minister to judge or to reform the society of Caesar." Ellis continues, "This attitude . . . was, rather, rooted in the Apostle's total theological outlook, which, like early Christianity generally, had more affinities with Epicurean withdrawal from society than with Stoic engagement with it."[3] Ellis isn't a Scrooge, for he does think Christians are to love their neighbors and to do good, but he makes little space for Paul having a social justice vision. In this Ellis enters a circle of scholarship that—the circle, not Ellis—thinks Paul abandoned the liberating social vision of Jesus and went sectarian.

Bruce Longenecker, from the generation after Ellis, points a long, accusing finger at Ellis. Longenecker is right in this: Ellis does not think Paul's vision is for the empire. Longenecker is wrong in this: Ellis does think the church has a "social" vision, but he thinks it is for the church and that, what is more, that vision will influence the larger society.[4] Let us say that Ellis is an influentialist, while Longenecker is a liberationist or progressivist.[5] Longenecker finds a *social* consciousness in Paul, whereas Ellis finds an *ecclesial* consciousness. Briefly, a third set of voices: Verlyn Verbrugge and Keith Krell, in their recent book *Paul and Money*, relegate nearly all of Paul's vision about money to how individual Christians use their money—generously, wisely—and very little to no attention to whether Paul had a social or ecclesial economic vision.[6]

Who gets Paul right? Let us grant that Jesus did have more of an economic vision for a wider circle than his followers: Does Paul abandon that vision? The answer to this question matters—let's be honest—in the weekly offerings of churches. Are pastors called to nurture economic Christoformity for the church, for the world, or for the church and the world? Many pastors dread anything like a Stewardship Sunday. Would Paul have dreaded it? Ellis, Longenecker, and Verbrugge with Krell each have at least a different nuance to their answers to these questions.

Pastors as Economic Stewards in Recent Discussion

Two recent studies make the case that Paul himself had far more of a socioeconomic vision, and I shall summarize briefly both of these academic studies and then launch into a study of Paul's own mission as nurturing economic generosity in his mission churches.

The Original Bishops

I begin with Alistair Stewart's lengthy study *The Original Bishops*.[7] Stewart moves seamlessly at times between the New Testament's letters and patristic evidence to form a set of theses that generate eye-popping conclusions, including his agreement with this statement by R. Alastair Campbell on the nonspecificity of the term *elder*: "The main contention of this thesis is that in the ancient world the elders are those who bear a title of honor, not of office, a title that is imprecise, collective and representative, and rooted in the ancient family or household. To put it another way, we do not know who is referred to by the term 'the elders' unless we know the context and even then we do not know whom the term includes or excludes."[8]

More importantly for our study, the bishop was also the one in charge of almsgiving and financial matters, and especially of providing for common meals and fellowship. A distinctive point of Stewart is that from the outset bishops were financial overseers and stewards in the community of faith on behalf of the church folks and others in the community as the funds were available. In other words, bishops were charged with being economic stewards for the sake of generosity in the community. Stewart's conclusions draw scholars back to the old study of Edwin Hatch called *The Organization of the Early Christian Churches*, which articulates this same theme with largely the same conclusion, a conclusion that has largely been ignored but deserves far more attention today.[9] It would take pages to describe and evaluate Stewart's work, but that is not necessary here.[10] All to say this: if Hatch and Stewart are even close to accurate, Paul did in fact have a deep concern with economic justice, and the primary leader of each church was charged with nurturing a culture of generosity.

Remember the Poor

Bruce Longenecker, in *Remember the Poor*, contends that Paul's mission strategy was shaped by the famous fasting-as-economic-justice passage in Isaiah 58. Though often ignored, some passages in Paul's letters, if strung out into a list, demonstrate that Paul urged all of his churches to "remember the poor." Longenecker emphasizes that these "poor" include not only the ecclesial poor but all who are poor. He focuses on Acts 20:35; Romans 12:13, 16; Galatians 2:10; 6:9–10; Ephesians 4:28; 1 Thessalonians 5:14; 2 Thessalonians 3:6–12; 1 Timothy 5:3–16; 6:18; and Titus 3:14, and he contends that each of these Pauline texts more or less speaks to a social consciousness for economic justice.

We cannot pause here to sketch this important study by Longenecker—which includes a fascinating discussion of socioeconomic levels in the Roman Empire[11]—except to make two observations: first, Paul in fact did care for the poor from the front to the back porch of his life and ministry, and this care for the poor demonstrated solidarity with the Jewish world;[12] second, the issue is how broad Paul's concern for the poor was and how integrated it was into a kind of socioeconomic vision for the empire. Was he concerned for the empire's poor, or for the ecclesia's poor? And if the latter, did his concern also entail an influentialist direction and a spillover into the local community? I will not be able to answer these questions until the end of this chapter, but I will suggest that Longenecker's final landing place is, ironically, closer to Ellis than he seems to think.

The Collection for the Saints

Where to begin to examine Paul's belief that pastors were called to nurture economic Christoformity? I suggest we dig into the collection for the saints.[13]

Galatians 2 and Acts 11 and 12

Here is a traditional sketch of the evidence: Paul's second visit to Jerusalem came to a peace accord with "the pillars" (Gal. 2:9) that included the pillars' request for Paul to remember the poor (Acts 11:27–30; 12:25; Gal. 2:1–10).[14] This request generated a two-decades-long passionate ministry within the apostolate of Paul of collecting funds for the saints in Jerusalem. Alternatively, some believe there were two collections: one indicated in Galatians 2:1–10 and based in Syrian Antioch, and another occurring during Paul's third mission trip.[15]

1 and 2 Corinthians, Romans

The second major trace of the collection is in the Corinthian correspondence, and any sorting-out of dates and orders of sections, especially of 2 Corinthians, requires more space than can be given here.[16] First Corinthians 16:1–4 reads, "Now concerning the collection for the saints: you should follow the directions I gave to the churches of Galatia. On the first day of every week, each of you is to put aside and save whatever extra you earn, so that collections need not be taken when I come. And when I arrive, I will send any whom you approve with letters to take your gift to Jerusalem. If it seems advisable that I should go also, they will accompany me."

It seems wise to me to understand 2 Corinthians 8–9 as one or perhaps a combination of two letters concerning the collection, and it provides abundant evidence for Paul's thought about the collection. Finally, in Romans 15:14–32 we hear the final words from Paul about the collection. In verse 16 Paul describes the collection as "the priestly service of the gospel of God" and "offering of [i.e., to or by] the Gentiles," in 15:25 he calls it a "ministry to the saints," and in 15:27 a "service to them in material things." Clearly anticipating a negative response to his collection, Paul then speaks of it as "my ministry to Jerusalem" and prays it will be "acceptable to the saints" (v. 31).

Participants in the Collection

From whom did Paul collect funds? A maximal view uses both explicit mentions of the collection and references to representatives on Paul's trip to Jerusalem, because that view assumes Paul worked each congregation for support. Thus, we could say he collected funds from the Galatian region (1 Cor. 16:1); Derbe, Lystra, Berea, and Thessalonica (Acts 16:1; 20:4); Macedonia (2 Cor. 8:1–5; 9:2, 4); and Philippi (Acts 16:12, 16; 20:6). We can also add Corinth (Rom. 15:26; 1 Cor. 16:1–4) and perhaps Mysia and Ephesus (Acts 20:4), and Troas (vv. 5–6). One can also wonder whether Paul drew support from Tyre (21:3–4), Ptolemais (v. 7), Cyprus and Caesarea (v. 16), and even Rome (compare Rom. 12:13; 15:26 with 2 Cor. 8:4; 9:13; and Rom. 1:13 with 2 Cor. 9:6–10 in their uses of "reap" and "harvests").

A Noticeable Silence

What is perhaps most noteworthy is the absence of a report in Jerusalem of Paul handing over the collection and the absence of a response from the "saints" in Jerusalem. Paul does say in Acts 24:17, in his trial before Felix, "Now after some years I came to bring alms [a more acceptable term for Felix than a direct mention of his collection for poor Christians in Jerusalem?] to my nation and to offer sacrifices." But in Acts 21:17–26, when Paul arrives we get only this sparse information:

> When we arrived in Jerusalem, the brothers welcomed us warmly. The next day Paul went with us to visit James; and all the elders were present. After greeting them, he related one by one the things that God had done among the Gentiles through his ministry. When they heard it, they praised God. Then they said to him, "You see, brother, how many thousands of believers there are among the Jews, and they are all zealous for the law. They have been told about you that you teach all the Jews living among the Gentiles to forsake Moses, and that you tell them not to circumcise their children or observe the customs. What then is to be done? They will certainly hear that you have come. So do what we tell you. We have four men who are under a vow. Join these men, go through the rite of purification with them, and pay for the shaving of their heads. Thus all will know that there is nothing in what they have been told about you, but that you yourself observe and guard the law. But as for the Gentiles who have become believers, we have sent a letter with our judgment that they should abstain from what has been sacrificed to idols and from blood and from what is strangled and from fornication." Then Paul took the men, and the next day, having purified himself, he entered the temple with them, making public the completion of the days of purification when the sacrifice would be made for each of them.

Not a word, and the absence of that information indicates for many today that the collection was rejected and was therefore diverted to more pragmatic uses: namely, the funds were used for the rite of purification for four Jewish males and Paul. My less-than-confident judgment is both that Acts 24:17 refers to the collection, now reframed into almsgiving for a Jewish audience, and that the warm welcome reported in 21:17 is a slight indicator that the collection was accepted. The evidence is not clear enough to be confident.

Accepted or not, the collection makes clear that Paul believed each of his mission churches was to be generous to Jerusalem's poor saints, and to accomplish these acts of generosity Paul nurtured economic Christoformity.

A Theology of Economic Christoformity

In the history of discussion there have been a number of proposals for why Paul was collecting money for the poor (saints), including the genuinely important reason of simply helping the poor,[17] but most want a more theological and symbolic understanding of the collection than simple relief (no matter how important relief is).[18] Hence, some have suggested vigorously that the collection demonstrated to the leaders in Jerusalem both that Paul had a connection to Jerusalem's church as the mother church and that Paul was not doing his own thing. In other words, the collection was ecumenical in that it was simultaneously an expression of unity and an appeal by Paul to Jerusalem to embrace his mission of the one true God and the one true gospel.[19] Others have argued this was an act to provoke the eschatological reality of the end-time gathering of the people of God from the whole world to Jerusalem.[20] Yet others consider the collection from the angle of patronage and reciprocal benevolence and mutual obligation.[21] A South African scholar of the collection, Stephan Joubert, in fact, says the Pauline churches' "basic motivation . . . was not in the first instance the economic plight of believers in Jerusalem, but rather *the repayment of their own debts* to the mother church."[22] Inasmuch as almsgiving was seen by Jews of that time as a virtual substitute for sacrifices, it has been argued that Paul's collection was a gentile sacrifice and support for Jerusalem as the home of the church. More recently, David Downs has argued that the collection was an "act of cultic worship" that elicited praise of God (see Phil. 4:18). Rather than narrowing the meaning of the collection to one view, in what follows I will offer a broader perspective on the collection as part of Paul's overall theology of economic Christoformity.[23]

One reason it is unwise to narrow the collection to one theme is the terms Paul uses for the collection, which themselves provide a wider panorama of vision to his theology of the collection. It is a collection (1 Cor. 16:1–2),

a grace/gift (16:3; 2 Cor. 8:6),

a blessing (2 Cor. 9:5 [*eulogian*; NRSV, "bountiful gift"]),

a liturgy (9:12 [*leitourgias*; NRSV, "ministry"]),

a service/ministry (Rom. 15:31; 1 Cor. 16:15; 2 Cor. 8:4), and

a fellowship (Rom. 15:26 [*koinōnia*; NRSV, "resources"]).

Each of the purposes of the collection mentioned above and each of the terms Paul uses for the collection frames the collection slightly differently, and each then yields a slightly different approach to how to understand it, meaning that their combination yields a multifaceted approach to the purpose of the collection. At least five themes surface. If pastors nurture Christoformity, economic Christoformity means (1) care for the poor, (2) wise uses of money and resources, (3) unity, (4) worship, and (5) equality.

Care for the Poor

Sometimes kingdom theology so overtakes discussions of Jesus that one misses the obvious: Jesus loved people and wanted to make them whole, and he relieved their needs with miracles. The same applies to the collection: some theologies of the collection are so absorbed by its theological nature that we forget the obvious. The poor saints were suffering, and Paul wanted to offer them economic relief. When Paul tells the Galatians, "Let us not grow weary in doing what is right," and, "Let us work for the good of all, and especially for those of the family of faith" (6:9–10), he is dealing in the language of alms and economic relief. These two verses echo Galatians 2:10's exhortation to remember the poor. Longenecker calls these expressions not vague generalities but "cruciform morality."[24] He's right, and he summons support from Bruce Winter's exceptional study, *Seek the Welfare of the City*, in which Winter contends that "doing good" means caring for the poor.[25] A second text is Ephesians 4:28, where the apostle urges followers of Jesus to cease a life of theft and instead work for a living. Why? "So as to have something to share with the needy." The Greek word behind "the needy," *chreia*, often refers to financial needs, so we are on safe ground contending that

Paul thought it was the duty of each Christian to become an agent of charity.

Care for the poor runs deep in the Bible, especially from Deuteronomy on, in contrast to the predominant attitude of the Greco-Roman world. That world nearly uniformly despised the poor and did not see almsgiving as a virtuous activity—not to say that care for the poor was unheard of. Strabo, speaking of the Rhodians, said this in *Geography* (14.2.5): "The Rhodians are concerned for the people in general, although their rule is not democratic; still they wish to take care of their multitude of poor people. Accordingly, the people are supplied with provisions and the needy are supported by the well-to-do; and there are certain liturgies [orders] that supply provisions, so that at the same time the poor man receives his sustenance and the city does not run short of useful men." In reference to Greeks and Romans generally, we can state bluntly that they lacked compassion, but then we must nuance that statement given what we know of folks like those on the island of Rhodes. Yet the Jewish world offered a resounding alternative to the common Greco-Roman way of dealing with the poor: in that world, to give alms was the height of virtue.[26] When Queen Helena of Adiabene was converted to Judaism, she visited Jerusalem, and in arriving provided abundant supplies for the poor (Josephus, *Antiquities* 20.34–53). Sirach is loaded with a theology of almsgiving and its redemptive value (7:10; 12:3; 29:12; 35:2). Jesus and the apostles, not least James the brother of Jesus, continued this Jewish virtue, and by this they countered the Roman way of life.

The emphasis on economic Christoformity in the Pastoral Epistles, whether it concerns widows or others, reveals both how vital economic discipleship is for Paul's perception of leaders and how his churches functioned. The "rich" in Paul's churches—and his eye here is on Ephesus—are "to do good, to be rich in good works, generous, and ready to share" (1 Tim. 6:18). In accord with the Jewish belief in a treasury of merits for those who trust God and not social reciprocation for their reward,[27] Paul says next that in this way they will be "storing up for themselves the treasure of a good foundation for the future, so that they may take hold of the life that really is life" (6:19; Titus 3:14). In this Paul sees himself as an example of charity: "In all this I have given you an example that by such work we must support the weak, remembering the words of the Lord Jesus, for he himself said, 'It is more blessed to give than to receive'" (Acts 20:35). Pastors who follow the lights of Paul are to be examples as well as nurturers of economic Christoformity, which means caring for the poor.

I pause in this next observation for a pastoral stop at the request of several pastor friends.

Wise Economics

Too many Western-world Christians are unwise with their spending, with their allocation of funds, and with their planning for the future. In a chapter that focuses on generosity, not least in helping those who are poor, it will not hurt us to pause to look into other dimensions of the Christian and economic Christoformity. It is not Christoform to spend more than we have or to generate debts well beyond our income potential, and it is also not wise to spend now without regard for our future.

About 75 percent of American garages have no cars in them because a car won't fit, while 90 percent of American garages are crammed with between 300 and 650 boxes of stuff. American homes are saturated with possessions, and this has all been revealingly detailed in statistics, stories, and high-quality images in *Life at Home in the Twenty-First Century*.[28] Whenever I've talked about the subject of Christians and generosity, I hear a common pastoral observation: "I agree that Paul and the Bible teach economic justice, but what I find as a pastor is the need for so many in my church to learn how to manage their own money. So many are maxed out on their credit cards and loans, and many either have no margin or are below water. What we need most is what Paul says about managing the money we've got with wisdom." Americans, in general, are gluttons for things, and Paul has a few things that might help.

Here are a few thoughts, and there is not space for this to be developed.[29] First, Paul believed in labor, Paul himself labored, and the majority world knows that without labor a person dies (2 Thess. 3:6–12). The connection between labor and survival is strong throughout human history, and only the privileged in history—and, far more commonly, in late modernity—sever the connection. Many today feel entitled to luxuries. But labor and survival remain locked for much of the world today. Second, we work in order to provide for our families (1 Tim. 5:8) but also to bless others (Eph. 4:28). If we have choice in these matters and margin in our budgets, then we need to examine our expenditures—possessions, gluttony, consumerism, lust for things—to determine a Christoform proportionality. Third, we need, especially in the affluent world, to spend below our budgets, and many of us will have to grab ourselves by the scruff of the neck and begin to practice wise spending (1 Cor. 16:1–4). Fourth—which I will develop below— Christoformity means generosity. Or, as David Roseberry explains, it means giving up and giving our all to our God, who is generous, and learning generosity from our God.[30] After years of nurturing a culture of generosity, he offers these wise words: "Building a culture of generosity means that the emphasis in the church month by month is consistent and clear. Focusing on the virtue and value of generosity is not phenomenal; that is, it is not extraordinary, but ordinary. The virtue should not be special; it is routine. It is not highlighted in one season and ignored after that; it is foundational."[31]

But there are other themes pastors have asked me about, including one that Paul himself at times had to address, what he called intentional idleness and irresponsibility. Some need to be taught the basic way of life: developing a sense of responsibility for one's life and family; nurturing a proper kind of ambition to flourish; preparing oneself in life for how life works (educationally and vocationally); developing a healthy sense of accountability for how we conduct our life before God, self, family, and others (including our community, state, and nation); paying our dues and exhibiting a growth in vocation in order to experience promotion; and wisely transmitting the wisdoms of life to our children and the next generation.

These, and surely more, deserve to be taught in our congregations if we want to nurture economic Christoformity.

Unity

Paul recounts a meeting in Jerusalem in which both the ministry of Peter to the Jews and that of Paul to the gentiles is affirmed by the pillars (Gal. 2:1–10). Connected to that affirmation of unity is an obligation on the part of Paul and Barnabas to "remember the poor" (2:10). This connection of the gentile churches to the Jerusalem church's poor explodes from the surface in Romans. After informing the Roman churches that the Macedonians and Achaians volunteered alms for the "poor among the saints in Jerusalem" (15:26), Paul says, "They were pleased to do this, and indeed they owe it to them; for if the Gentiles have come to share in their spiritual blessings, they ought also to be of service to them in material things" (v. 27). Notice those words "they owe it to them" and the rationale for that obligation: spiritual blessings that have come to the Macedonians and Achaians entail reciprocal material blessings toward Jerusalem. This theme of reciprocating unity between Paul's mission churches sends us back to Romans 11:11–24 and forward to Ephesians 2:11–22, two passages emphasizing the unity of Jews and gentiles in the mission churches of Paul. So the words of Paul in Acts 24:17 that Paul came to Jerusalem to "bring alms to my nation" explains rather clearly how Paul understood what he was doing: he was expressing his love for Israel and embodying a commonality and unity in his gift.

This could be developed further, but at this point I will say this: Paul knows not only that a social bond is created by gifts from the mother church to the gentile mission churches but also that reciprocation establishes yet more social bonding between the two parties (giver, receiver). This can be explained simply and even exclusively as a mechanism of social relations.[32] But Paul digs deeper and wider into how he himself understands the collection. To be sure, when the wealthy offer direct relief to the poor, the poor will be grateful, and a social bond of unity can be established. But Paul wants the social bond grounded in something deeper: spiritual unity in Christ. He says it has to do with a spiritual gift (the Jerusalem side of the equation) and material reciprocation (the Corinthian side). This spiritual-material reciprocation builds unity between the Pauline mission church and the mother church in Jerusalem.

Worship

The evidence that Paul understood the collection as an act of worship is compelling and pastorally significant.[33] I begin with 1 Corinthians

16:1–4 and 2 Corinthians 8–9. The collection is front to back the grace of God. Paul calls the gift of the Corinthians just that: a gift, using a Greek word often translated "grace" (1 Cor. 16:3). The same is said of the Macedonians: "We want you to know, brothers and sisters, about *the grace of God that has been granted to the churches of Macedonia*" (2 Cor. 8:1). Here grace is a power of God unleashed in the redemption of the Macedonians, but that grace became an active power that turned them into agents of generosity. There is nothing more Christoform than generosity! Their generosity/grace was embodied in Christ: "For you know the generous act of our Lord Jesus Christ, that though he was rich, yet for your sakes he became poor, so that by his poverty you might become rich" (8:9). But this theme of grace reaches nothing less than a religious crescendo in 9:8, where it is all anchored in God's own grace: "And God is able to provide you with every blessing [grace] in abundance, so that by always having enough of everything, you may share abundantly in every good work." God initiates the reciprocal cycle: God grants grace and empowers others to grant grace to others as an act of (worshipful) response.

Even more, Paul explicitly uses worship language for the collection. First, in 1 Corinthians 16:1–4 Paul urges the Corinthians to set aside money. When? On "the first day of every week." Who does this? "Each of you." As part of their weekly gathering for worship, the Corinthians are to give to the poor saints in Jerusalem. Second, some of the terms Paul uses when describing the collection are distinctively worship terms, and when gathered together, they express an undeniable worship theme. Paul uses *logeia* in 1 Corinthians 16:1, a term that was most frequently used for religious collections.[34] He also anchors the collection in the self-offering of Christ for our redemption (2 Cor. 8:9), using language clearly connected to temple worship. The term *epiteleō*, found in 2 Corinthians 8:11, like *logeia* in 1 Corinthians 16:1, is another term used most commonly for religious obligations. Thus, 2 Corinthians 8:11: "Now *finish* doing it, so that your eagerness may be matched by *completing* it according to your means." Throughout the inscriptions found on objects preserved from the classical world, this term refers to the performance of sacred rites.[35] A worship context is evident also in Paul's seeing the act of the representatives as something that will serve "the glory of Christ" (8:23), and in 9:11–13 it is God's glory that gains our attention. That is, the generosity of the Corinthians will not bring them honor but instead—subverting the Roman honor system—will "produce thanksgiving to God through us" (9:11; see also 9:12, 13, 15).

No surprise, then, that Paul describes the collection as a liturgy, or a *leitourgias* in Greek (2 Cor. 9:12). Thus, "the rendering of this ministry" translates *hē diakonia tēs leitourgias*, which could be translated as "this service that you perform" (NIV) or "your ministry of this service to God's people" (CEB). Again, this term is used in the writings surrounding Paul—including the Septuagint, the Greek translation of the Old Testament—as a priestly kind of work (e.g., Num. 7:5; 8:22, 25; 16:9). We need also to mention Philippians 4:18, where, in speaking of the gifts from the Philippians, Paul describes them as "a fragrant offering, a sacrifice acceptable and pleasing to God."

But the worship orientation of this economic Christoformity comes into full display in Romans 15:14–32.[36] Downs contends vigorously that "the offering of the gentiles" in verse 16 is the financial gifts given to Jerusalem *by* the gentiles (subjective genitive). This is of less significance to us in this context than the worship atmosphere Paul creates around this economic stewardship: what the gentiles are doing in sending donations to Jerusalem is giving an "offering." In addition, other terms in verses 15–16, with echoes in verses 25–32, are connected to worship: "I have written to you rather boldly . . . because of the *grace* given me by God to be a *minister* [*leitourgon*] of Christ Jesus to the Gentiles in the *priestly service* [*hierourgounta*] of the gospel of God, so that the *offering* [*prosphora*] of the Gentiles may be *acceptable*, *sanctified* [*euprosdektos, hēgiasmenē*] by the Holy Spirit." What the gentiles are doing when they send donations to Jerusalem is an act of cultic worship. It has to be stated boldly because space prohibits development of the idea that in turning the entire act of benefaction for the poor saints into an act of the worship of Israel's God, the entire Greco-Roman system of honor and status is either abandoned or intentionally subverted.[37] Instead of understanding the collection as glorifying the giver in the typical social-bonding way of life, Paul understands it as an act of worshiping God.

Economic Christoformity transforms gift giving and reciprocation into worship of God, and the pastor is called to the challenge of both subverting the economic ways of life in the Western world and teaching his congregation to see gift giving as worship.

Equality

It is by now clear that for the apostle Paul pastoring is more than spiritual direction and more than preaching and more than leading. For Paul pastoring meant embodying, teaching, and nurturing a culture of Christoformity. For him (and for us), this also means nurturing economic availability and accountability to fellow siblings in the body of Christ. The most neglected text, when it comes to the collection for the saints, is a text that tells us more about Paul's understanding of economic Christoformity than any other.[38]

The Chiasm of 2 Corinthians 8:13–15

I speak of 2 Corinthians 8:13–15, and I emphasize the words of focus and reformat it to make the chiasm-like structure visible:

[Thesis:] I do not mean that there should be relief for others and pressure on you, but it is a question of a **fair balance** between

A   your present <u>abundance</u>
  B   and their *need*,
A   so that their <u>abundance</u>
  B   may be for your *need*,

[Thesis repeated:] in order that there may be a **fair balance**.

As it is written,
  "The one who had much did not have too much,
    and the one who had little did not have too little." (NRSV)

Isotēs is translated as "fair balance" in the NRSV, though it's translated in the KJV, ASV, CEB, and the NIV (1984, 2011) as "equality." The ESV echoes the NRSV with a slight change to "fairness." The operative term is the Greek term *isotēs*. This is the most significant term Paul uses for his collection, since it expresses the aim of his collection.[39]

What Does *Isotēs* Mean?

We need to examine this term in some depth before we can move into the pastoral implications. The standard lexicon for New Testament studies is referred to as Bauer-Danker-Arndt-Gingrich (BDAG; this refers to the book by the last names of the editors. The title is *Greek-English Lexicon of the New Testament and Other Early Christian Literature*). Here is the word's primary definition: "state of matters being held in proper balance, equality." The lexicon cites Pseudo-Phocylides (137), which reads, "Render to all their due, and impartiality [*isotēs*] is best in every way." The editors of BDAG cite our two verses in 2 Corinthians 8 and move to a second usage: "state of being fair, fairness."[40] Ceslas Spicq, in his extraordinary work on New Testament words, *Theological Lexicon of the New Testament*, understands the term to mean "equality."[41] General definitions don't always speak clearly in specific contexts, so we need to probe deeper than general definitions.

Isotēs has a history and nuance in various contexts. In the Letter of Aristeas it means "equality."[42] When asked to whom one was to show favor, the answer is, first, to one's parents. "Next (and closely connected) he reckons the honor due to friends." How is this understood? It is demonstrated in "calling the friend an equal of one's own self" (228). The text has a theme of friendship: "You do well if you bring all men into friendship with yourself." The Letter of Aristeas does this in the next instance of *isotēs*, for we read, "How can one find welcome abroad among strangers?" The answer is, by treating them as friends. How so? "By equal treatment to everyone" (257). In the Letter of Aristeas the image of God is combined with social equality not too far from that advocated by the apostle Paul. The Letter of Aristeas also plumbs *isotēs* as "justice," a theme found throughout Philo: to treat another as an "equal" is to treat that person justly (*On the Special Laws* 4.231; *Who Is the Heir?*, 141–206). So the term now has two primary nodes of meaning: equality and justice.

In the New Testament we encounter the following senses of this term and its cognates: Jesus was *equal* with God (John 5:18; Phil. 2:6); all Christians have received the *same* gift of the Spirit (Acts 11:17) and have a faith that gives them the *same status* as the apostles (2 Pet. 1:1) even though there is no *equal* to Timothy (Phil. 2:20). Those who worked all day complained about those who worked less because they had been made *equal* (Matt. 20:12). In one of Paul's most radical moves, he says masters are to treat their slaves as *equals* (Col. 4:1). Again entering the world of reciprocation, we read in Luke 6:34 that "even sinners lend to sinners, to receive *as much again*" (= equal reciprocation).

BACK TO 2 CORINTHIANS 8:13–14

All of which leads us to 2 Corinthians 8:13–14. What do such ideas as equality or justice actually look like in reality for Paul? We could ask thirty questions at this point, but let's move on. By way of context, Paul is urging the Corinthians to donate to the poor in Jerusalem; he grounds benevolence in the pattern of Christ, who became poor so others might become rich; he urges the Corinthians to complete what they have already begun; and he is keen to state that he has no intent of making them poor (as Christ himself became), but rather of seeing them give according to their means (1 Cor. 16:2). The appeal is rooted in their "present abundance" and the Jerusalem saints' "need" (2 Cor. 8:14). Noticeably, he quotes from the manna text in Exodus 16:18. That text is both about everyone having what they need and about everyone having no more than they need, but it also has another theme: when gathering the manna some needed more and gathered more, while others needed less and so gathered less. Supply is determined by need in the manna story of Exodus 16.[43] Some need more than others.

The thrust of these verses in 2 Corinthians is material distribution and reciprocation, and therefore it evokes the Greco-Roman world's sense of friendship and reciprocal gift exchange. There is no better image of this than the one used by Seneca in *On Benefits*. Ever since reading it in conjunction with Barclay's *Paul and the Gift*, I have remembered the imagery, so citing it in full may have the same effect on you:

> I would like to use the example of ball playing advanced by the Stoic Chrysippus. There is no doubt that when the ball is dropped it could be the fault of either the thrower or the catcher. The game goes along nicely when the ball is thrown and caught by both in a suitable manner, back and forth between the hands of thrower and catcher. But a good player needs to throw the ball differently to a tall partner and to a short one. It is the same with granting benefits: unless it is adjusted to the social roles of both parties, the giver and the recipient, the benefit will

not actually be given by the one nor be received by the other in the right manner. If we are dealing with an experienced player who is in good condition, we will throw the ball more adventurously, knowing that however it comes at him his quick and nimble hand will knock it back. If we are playing with an untrained novice, however, we will not send it to him in such a firm and percussive manner, but more gently, and we will just barely meet it when it's volleyed back to us, guiding it right into his hand. We should do the same with benefits; some people we should treat like students and we should think it sufficient if they make an effort, if they will take a chance, if they are willing. But generally we make people ungrateful and foster this feeling in them, as though the final proof that we have given an impressive gift is their inability to return the favor. This is how mean-spirited players plan to trick the other player—though of course it ruins the game, which can only carry on as long as both want to play.[44]

This is the way gift exchange worked in the Roman Empire (and it is fundamentally common to humans in general). Gift giving, as Plutarch reuses the image of playing catch, implies obligation of reception and return: "He who refuses to accept the favour [*charis*], like the man who refuses to catch a well-directed ball, disgraces it, allowing it to fall to the ground without achieving its end" (*On the Sign of Socrates*). These contemporaries are not Paul, and neither of them is Jewish, but their vision of reciprocation is not at all unlike what Paul is saying in 2 Corinthians 8:13–14.

The same can be said of the famous passages in Acts (2:42–47; 4:32–37). Here we find mutual responsibility, accountability for one another, and voluntary generosity, and all seemingly for a limited time. While the Essene experiment in communal living was a permanent arrangement with rules (1QS), the actions of Acts are spontaneous, generous, and temporary. Perhaps the most significant lines, echoes of Israel's own experience, are in Acts 2:45's "as any had need" and 4:34's "not a needy person among them" (see also Deut. 15:4). If one posits these Acts descriptions as reliable, we have here an excellent example of what the apostle Paul means by *isotēs* in 2 Corinthians 8:13–14.

Paul, however, creates a theological narrative for the collection: it (1) begins in God's own gift (grace), (2) is embodied in Christ the gift, then (3) is experienced by faith among all the Christians, both in

Jerusalem and in the diaspora, (4) results in thanksgiving to God and God alone (noticeably, rather than listing names of givers on a monument, the glory and honor goes to God[45]), and (5) leads to a culture of generosity among those who have experienced God's grace in Christ. The experience of the gift and its orientation toward God organically obligate the Christians to be gift givers themselves, and (6) their reciprocation creates social bonds between the churches of Paul and the Jerusalem church.

This gift-exchange context (God in Christ to humans and humans back to God and to one another) for *isotēs* suggests that the word refers to the mutual reciprocation of material things in such a way that people's needs are met and God is thanked and glorified. Even more, it refers to reciprocation in such a way that each church has its needs met because of the network of supply created in the Pauline mission.[46]

To ask whether one should translate *isotēs* as "equality" or "fair shares" or "fair balance" is to steer the cart into the ditch. The issue is mutual material availability and accountability to one another, because each church is part of the body of Christ, and each church is composed of a universal brotherhood and sisterhood of equals. Paul thinks all Christians are drawn into a network of supplying for one another. What is even more clear is that those living in abundance are immediately summoned by Paul to become generous to those in need. One who has come to this conclusion is David Horrell: "The aim, for Paul, of economic redistribution is not that Christians with something to give might impoverish themselves, but that a state of equality might be attained. The self-lowering [like Christ] of the relatively wealthy is a means of achieving this equality, which is rooted in the will of God, but is to be realized through responsible human action."[47] We are right to ask what this equality looked like in "responsible human action." Murray Harris clarifies this, first by seeing equality as central to the collection: "One of the purposes of the collection project" is "the achievement of 'equality.'" But he goes further into the meaning of *isotēs*: it "involves (negatively) the equalization of economic burdens and (positively) the equal supply of the necessities of life."[48] Equality and sufficiency, components of justice, then, are nearly synonymous here.

THE CUP OF PYTHAGORAS

Greek philosopher-mathematician Pythagoras (ca. 570 BC–495 BC), from the Greek island Samos, not far from the coast of Ephesus in the Aegean Sea, had a cup, and whether it was a practical joke doesn't matter. Whether Pythagoras himself invented this doesn't matter either since I'm going to tell this story as an illustration of Paul's theology of equality and sufficiency. Pythagoras's cup looks normal until you peer inside and see a central column rising about three-quarters of the way to the top. The column is a warning to the one pouring wine that if one pours more than his (or her) share, the device inside the column will siphon off the entire contents of the cup, and wine will be spilled on the table or on a person's foot. The Pythagorean cup, then, is a visible symbol of *isotēs* and the manna story—namely, take your share and no more, so that each can have what each needs. It appears to me that Paul thinks pastors ought to keep the Pythagorean cup in mind more often.

Conclusion

Will Willimon, in his magnificent book on pastoring, tells a story about the relationship of a pastor to givers in a congregation and about the tie of giving to discipleship.

> Early in my ministry, our church sought to raise a large amount of money to build a service center for the poor in our city.
>
> We engaged a church fund-raiser to help us manage the campaign. At his first meeting he asked me to make a list of the top twenty givers in the congregation, along with a list of those who were not giving up to their potential. I told him proudly that I knew nothing of the specific giving patterns of my congregation. He replied, "That is irresponsible. If I were to ask you to name the ten model marriages in your congregation, or the ten marriages in the most trouble, could you tell me?"
>
> I could.
>
> The church fund-raiser said, "Jesus repeatedly stressed the dangers of money. You ought to hold up before your congregation the opportunity to respond to Jesus's teachings on wealth."[49]

You may well have the same response as I did. I wanted to hear what Willimon told the fund-raiser and what he said to his congregation. He doesn't tell us, so I'll move to one who did.

Not long ago I was teaching a doctor of ministry course at Northern Seminary, and we were discussing Alistair Stewart's theory, mentioned early in this chapter, that the original bishops were economic stewards. A conversation about whether pastors ought to know who gives what in churches enlivened the entire class. Some were strenuously opposed, while others were at least open to knowing. Before any kind of consensus emerged, if such were to emerge, Bill Shiell, a former pastor and now president of Northern Seminary, walked in, and so we asked him. His answer surprised the class and its professor. "Of course the pastor ought to know." Why? we asked. "Because money is a serious element of life and discipleship, and how can the pastor disciple a congregation if that important element of life is off the table?" In this the apostle Paul would at least partly agree: money is important; the pastor nurtures economic Christoformity; and the pastor's responsibility is to embody and create a culture of generosity toward other churches and Christians.

Bruce Longenecker makes caring for the poor central to the gospel itself when he writes these words near the beginning of *Remember the Poor*: "Instead, falling within the essentials of the good news, care for the poor [and he means all poor, not just the Christian poor] was thought by Paul to be a necessary hallmark of the corporate life of Jesus-followers who lived in conformity with the good news of the early Jesus-movement."[50] While I think it is over the top to think of caring for the poor as part of the "essentials of the good news," which is defined by 1 Corinthians 15:1–9, Longenecker is surely correct in seeing care for the poor as indicative of Christoformity. Back, then, to Earle Ellis and Longenecker's long, accusing finger. How broad were Paul's concerns for the poor? Did he care for the poor of Rome, or did he care for the poor in (to use Longenecker's term) the Jesus-movement? There is a way to untie this knot, and Longenecker, so it seems to me, has done so.

I read Bruce Longenecker as saying care for the poor in general led Paul to work to provide for the poor among the Christians.[51] I believe the direction needs to be reversed. Paul learned in Judaism a care for the (Jewish) poor, and he followed his tradition by focusing it on the household-of-faith (Christian) poor (Gal. 6:10). Paul's practice of alms was learned in Judaism and practiced as it was in Judaism: first to those in the "family" and then also to others. Longenecker suggests this very orientation when he says, "It is most likely that care for the poor was primarily practiced intra-communally within Jesus-groups." In fact, he knows how poor the churches were, so he says, "It would be foolhardy to imagine much other than an intra-communal practice of extending support in limited supply to a few within a community. Anything beyond that was probably unlikely to transpire."[52] In conceding this orientation of the giving by early Christians, Longenecker now stands much closer to Ellis than one might have suspected. David Downs is right: "There is no indication in Paul's letters . . . that the collection was intended for any group other than the Jewish-Christian community in Jerusalem." In fact, he says those who see the collection as something designed for the poor in general miss "the ecclesiocentric focus of the relief fund in Paul's mission and theology."[53] Downs is right, and so is Ellis.

I stand with Paul: first to the household of faith. As a pastor of mission churches for at least three decades, Paul spent some of his time nurturing generosity in gentile believers. His collection for the saints put his entire theology—gospel, church, mission—on full display because he saw in the acts of benevolence an embrace of the fullness of God's people.

5

A Culture of Storytellers

We are born storytellers, and, consciously or not, we all indwell a story. We make sense of life with a story we tell ourselves, and when something doesn't fit—a tragedy, a death, a failed marriage, a broken career—we find a story that turns what doesn't fit into something that does fit. We also love to read stories, and some enter the world of fiction to escape the dominant ideological narratives of our day—that is, to find a better world to indwell. Many of us find in J. R. R. Tolkien, C. S. Lewis, Ernest Hemingway, Ralph Ellison, Kent Haruf, Annie Dillard, Anne Rice, Marilynne Robinson, or J. M. Coetzee something that makes even better sense of life. These storytellers generate hope and stimulate the imagination to be a better person or work for a better world with a better story. Both Jesus and the rabbis told parables to stimulate listeners to imagine a different kind of world. Paul, too, was a storyteller and sought to capture his mission churches into his narrative web called the gospel.

I wrote the first draft of this chapter in the Old Town of Rhodes on the island of Rhodes in Greece, at least one location claimed by locals for Paul's visit (Acts 21:1). While there, I pondered how Paul read the Old Testament, read major studies of Paul's use of the Old Testament, and reformulated ideas about Paul that I'd been developing. Kris and I warmly thank Chrysoula, Despina, Themis, and Demetrios Brokou of the Avalon Boutique for warm hospitality. I am also grateful to Matthew Bates for a careful reading that led to some corrections and adjustments.

Paul's gospel story exploded from his reading of the Old Testament. If one pays close attention to the cross-references in footnotes in a Bible, one quickly sees how often Paul's letters are laced up in citation, in echo, in image, and in narrative with the Scriptures of Israel. In his career-defining book on how Paul used the Old Testament, Richard Longenecker tallied a list of eighty-three quotations of Scripture.[1] If one were to add to explicit quotations what many today call echoes or allusions, the number of cross-references would triple, if not grow even more. "But it is not that he quotes" the Bible, Eugene Peterson once observed in his essay on Paul as pastor. No, he

> *inhabits* the story, he gives the impression of being on familiar terms with everything written by his prophet ancestors, totally at ease in this richly expansive narrative of God's Word. The scriptures have become for him "all autobiographical" (Alexander Whyte's phrase). . . . There is a sense in which nothing in Scripture is ever "out of context" for Paul. He is so at home in the entire country of Scripture that he has an intuitive sense of what fits and where. He has not used his intellect to rearrange or correct or improve upon what he has been given; he enters it as a guest and receives with gratitude everything set before him, trusting the Host to see to his needs.[2]

But where are we today? What is our story? Which story do we inhabit? America is having nothing less than a story crisis today.

Statism, the New American Story

I agree with Peggy Noonan that Americans are afraid and are in search of a story or something to take away the fear. Here's how she puts our American condition: "Something's up. And deep down, where the body meets the soul, we are fearful. We fear, down so deep it hasn't even risen to the point of articulation, that with all our comforts and amusements, with all our toys and bells and whistles . . . we wonder if what we really have is . . . a first-class stateroom on the Titanic. Everything's wonderful, but a world is ending and we sense it."[3]

Many are searching to conquer their fears—this constant turmoil of the amygdala and worry that we are on a Titanic about to sink—in activism and have ramped it all up to apocalyptic proportions. The solution to the fear, it is believed, is the state. America's dominant narrative today is statism, the theory that the state ought to rule and the state can solve our problems. (One could of course approach the ruling American story through a number of narratives, such as racism or capitalism or elitism, but I will focus here on statism.[4])

Statism as Americans know it goes back to the time of Constantine, and since that time the church's relationship with the state has been complicated on more than, but at least, two fronts: how much Christianizing the state can accomplish and how much politicking the church ought to be doing. From the days of the Holy Roman Empire until now, especially during the founding of the United States,[5] the churches of Europe and North America have told a nation's story, though since the rise of modernity the church has gradually lost that power.

Skip to the famous study of the US by H. Richard Niebuhr, *Christ and Culture*, and a typology of the relationship of the church and state/culture found its language: Christ of culture, Christ with culture, Christ above culture, Christ against culture, Christ and culture in paradox, and Christ transforming culture. When every Wheaton student was reading Niebuhr, a Reformed theologian named Abraham Kuyper began to make a different influence felt among American evangelicals. The Kuyperians turned "transforming culture" into a political agenda. This transformationalist approach gained strength in the heady days of Ronald Reagan and was spearheaded by Francis Schaeffer, James Kennedy, Jerry Falwell, James Dobson, and Billy Graham; Graham's influence was nonpareil.[6] American evangelical conservatives, as the so-called moral majority, became glued in new ways to the Republican Party, while the more progressive moral "minority" became attached in similar ways to the Democratic Party. The church was politicized.[7] Whether they were Kuyperian, Niebuhrian, or some bricolage of them and others isn't the issue.

At no time in my life have I seen the church more engaged in politics and more absorbed by a political story than now. I'm not referring here simply to Republican versus Democrat or conservative versus progressive. Rather, I mean the belief that what matters most is what happens in DC and that if we get the right candidate elected, America can be saved. Blogs, Facebook updates, Twitter posts, and websites are tied together and double-knotted with this political narrative. It is so pervasive many don't even know it's running and ruining our public and private lives. Ask them about a candidate, and their blood pressure pops or their mouth spews or their mind runs into the wall of exasperation. The political narrative of today makes for a mesmerizing story: there are problems, we are strung along for two years or more with potential winning or losing, and then voting day comes and the story's next chapter starts. We may even give the story's centrality a break for a year or so, and then we start up all over again. But make no mistake, the American story is increasingly statism.

More significantly, statism entails an inherent belief, either explicit or implicit, in the state. It is a belief that solutions to our biggest problems are found in the state and that the Christian's responsibility from the Left or the Right is to get involved and acquire political power. It is a belief that legislation is morality, that more laws will make for better people. *Statism* as I am using it here refers to the idol of making a human, an office, a seat of power, a constitution the world's true ruler. Statism exalts humans and human plans and voting and laws and government. Statism centers its faith in the future on who rules in DC. Statism makes government a god. Statism is a secular eschatology and soteriology; for those who have left their childhood religion, it has become their new religion.[8]

No one, of course, says or even admits it, but our lives betray our words. Except Marilynne Robinson, my favorite contrarian. Her net of concern is broader and wider, but she's getting to the same point when she says, "I know that before we devoted ourselves to Darwinism and Marxism and Freudianism and capitalism it was theology that was meant to inhibit thought, and that these successor monisms modeled their claims on the old claims of religious orthodoxy. We human beings never can make a truly fresh start."[9] Theology, she claims, is the original claim on all of life, and the deterministic ideologies that replace it will assume the original claim. *Idolatry* is another term for the replacements. Contrarian indeed!

Statism is the story many tell; it's the story even more indwell; it's the only narrative some 24/7 TV news shows tell, and 24/7 TV and news and social media make statism omnipresent. Statism has become America's narrative. Don't make the mistake of accusing others of the statism narrative: it's as much the story of conservatives and

Republicans as of progressives and Democrats, or Social Democrats, as well as of the holdout independents. The Tea Party, which loved to pat itself on the back for advocating small government, was just as deeply committed to statism. Put more bluntly, the vitriol that is spewed today about President Trump is the vitriol of those who want control, who would then generate vitriol from the other side if control switched. Public vitriol demonstrates statism. Here's how one can see the statism at work in the so-called prophetic criticisms of our day: if someone offers a criticism of the current administration, it inevitably comes off as support for the other side of the political spectrum. When it is a one-or-the-other zero-sum game, it is statism. Is there an alternative?

Some of our fellow Americans on either side use the Bible in their statist narratives. But to use the Bible's narrative this way is nothing more than baptizing statism. Our political narrative is not the Bible's narrative, but human beings are inescapably storytellers, and it is their stories that make sense of life for them. Is there an alternative? Yes, but it is dying, and only pastors can resurrect the alternative.

The Bible as the Great Story

The Old Story Is Dying

The story of Christians today is shifting quickly. I read a book recently on how the founding fathers used the Bible.[10] The more Daniel Dreisbach studied the topic, the more obvious the problem became: the Bible was so pervasive in the speeches and writings and journals of the founding fathers that the boundary between its words and theirs was nearly undetectable. When, we are led to ask of the founders, was it the Bible and when was it the way the founders expressed themselves? For instance, does exclaiming "May it never be!" constitute a quotation of the apostle Paul? The essential story of the colonies was the story of Israel as the story of the Puritans (and others who were within earshot of sermons or pamphlets). For some leaders such as John Winthrop the colonies, like Israel, were to be a "light to the nations," and from Jesus they decided to be a "light on a hill." The Bible's story was their story, and their story was the Bible's. That story, I want to emphasize, is the Bible's narrative re-actualized—the German word is *vergegenwärtigung*—in the American consciousness.

But our founders' allusions to and echoes of the Bible today lie, like a precious item from early American centuries, one foot under our feet on an open plain, undetected because we don't know the narrative. I recently also read another book about the Old Testament among American Christians, a book called *The Old Testament Is Dying*, by Brent Strawn.[11] Among other things, and with a profusion of support, Strawn wonders what will happen to the narrative of Christians, their essential story, when the Old Testament narratives are eclipsed from their stories. The conclusion is that, without the Old Testament narratives to draw on, the church and we as individuals will be impoverished. He's right. Leading me to ask, as I read Strawn: What is our story when the Bible's story is no longer our story? Will it be statism's versions of progressivism, liberalism, socialism, conservatism, materialism, or hedonism? Or, perhaps, is Henri Nouwen right when he says we won't have a single story, but instead we will hold in our hands little more than "ideological fragments"?[12] Fragments do not a story make.

We need a better (than statism) story. We need to recapture the Bible's own story.

Israel's Faith: A Story

Israel's faith was not formed as a systematic theology, nor was it formed into a creed. Israel's faith was a story, and it was lived. A good portal into the storied core of Israel's faith can be found in many biblical and extrabiblical sources, which summarize the Bible's story.[13]

As the Bible's own story develops, each new summary builds on earlier summaries. The additional summary recaptures the narratives that have been told up to that point and gives them new shape. These summaries are, to use the words of David Steinmetz, "second narratives" that give shape to the "ramshackle" stories and events and characters in the narrative.[14] Here, then, is where we begin: Israel's many authors were storytellers, Jesus was a storyteller, Paul was a storyteller, and I believe the pastor, too, can follow Paul in storytelling. There were many stories to tell, but no one, I emphasize, turned that story into a creed or set of beliefs.[15] Their theology was their story, and their story was their theology. That's Paul's world, and it is one that pastors today can recapture if they wish to nurture Christoformity.

New Testament scholars are on the prowl to find the secret key that will unlock the mysteries to Paul's own way of reading the Bible.[16] What matters most is the explicit framing of the story by the apostle Paul himself. So, here's our first clue for nurturing a culture of Christoformity when it comes to forming a storytelling culture: we need to *begin* with Paul's explicit framing narrative.[17] What is that? Paul's explicit framing narrative, his "second" narrative, is the gospel. In the contexts of America today, if the gospel is the story, then statism collapses into idolatry if it is claimed as Christian storytelling. It gives to Caesar what is God's alone.

The Story Told by Paul Is the Gospel

Jesus and the apostles were gospel centered, and the New Testament provides two crisp definitions of the gospel, both in the writings of Paul. One is a tradition passed on in the early churches that Paul is quoting, and the other one comes from what many would say is the last of Paul's writings.[18] They are found in 1 Corinthians 15:3–8 (or 15:3–28 along with Rom. 1:3–4) and 2 Timothy 2:8 (or 2:8–13).[19]

First, in 2 Timothy we learn the gospel is to make claims about Jesus: that he is the Messiah, that he was raised from the dead, and that he descended from David. "That," Paul then utters, "is my gospel." We perhaps need to stare these words in the face. The gospel is to make claims about Jesus: that he was the Messiah, that he was raised, and that he is a descendant of David. Paul has summarized his gospel, and it's all about Jesus. Paul spells out the implications of his Jesus-centered gospel in verses 9–14: cruciformity, redemption, and the faithfulness of Christ.

Second, from 1 Corinthians 15 we learn that the gospel itself narrates major elements in the life of Jesus. Paul is not here making something up: he is repeating or passing on the tradition of the apostles about the gospel (vv. 1–2). That traditional gospel Paul was passing on told of the life of Jesus, the death, the burial, the resurrection, and appearances of Jesus (vv. 3–8). Then, with an aside on the importance of the resurrection (vv. 12–19), Paul resumes his gospel narrative in verses

20–28. And these verses press us to say that the gospel is the narrative of Jesus's entire life: from birth to his handing over his kingdom to the Father so that "God may be all in all."

Third, in 1 Corinthians 15 the apostle Paul extends the narrative about Jesus in two ways: he says "in accordance with the Scriptures" twice (15:3, 4), which means the story of Jesus emerges from the story of Israel. Paul's second extension appears immediately: Jesus died "for our sins." That is, the death of Jesus is redemptive.

The order that emerges from these three brief points is important: the gospel (1) narrates the story of Jesus and his death / his person and (2) is redemptive. For many today the gospel is about (1) redemption and (2) Jesus bringing the redemption. That is, the subject for some is redemption, while for the apostle Paul the subject, the number-one item, is Jesus, and the implication of the gospel is redemption.[20] For modern gospel presentations the subject is salvation or redemption, and Jesus becomes the means of our redemption. I repeat myself: for the apostle Paul and the gospel tradition prior to him that he passes on, we first learn Christology/Jesus, and then, second, redemption. That is the apostolic order. I have written a brief book about this topic called *The King Jesus Gospel* and can only briefly summarize it here, but more can be found by reading that treatment.

Let this now be said clearly: the story of Paul is the gospel, and the gospel of Paul is the story about Jesus, and that means the story to be nurtured in churches is the story about Jesus. Pastors nurture Christoformity when they tell the story of Jesus.

The Gospel's Shortest Statement

The shortest summary of the gospel in the New Testament is to be found in Romans 10:9–10, where we read these words: "because if you confess with your lips that Jesus is Lord and believe in your heart that God raised him from the dead, you will be saved. For one believes with the heart and so is justified, and one confesses with the mouth and so is saved."

The gospel is to announce that Jesus—the Galilean, the son of Mary and Joseph, the miracle worker, the parable teller, the controversialist, the one who was dragged before Pilate, the one who was crucified, the one who cracked the tomb open on Easter morning, the one who ascended—this Jesus is the world's only true Lord.

To call Jesus *kyrios*, or "Lord," which in Hebrew would most likely have been *adonai*, a term used for God, was at least to cast a suspicious or skeptical eye on what was happening all over the Roman Empire. It is unwise to assign Jewish or Christian understandings of God to what the emperors made of themselves, but this, at least, is clear: upon their deaths, starting with Julius Caesar, some of the emperors—Caesar Augustus (Octavian) and Claudius—were "deified" in a way not unlike how popes in the Roman Catholic tradition have announced that some people are made saints. Deification, however, is more than being made a saint. The Roman senators announced that the emperors were now part of the pantheon of the gods.

Well before his death, for example, Nero was being more or less deified both in Western Asia Minor and in Greece, though he played his cards more cleverly in Rome itself. Most noticeably, immediately after the famous fire of Rome, Nero planned a massive complex in the heart of Rome, and at the entrance to the famous Domus Aurea, his own palace, he had a one-hundred-foot tower reconstructed, a Colossus Neronis, on which stood Nero-Helios (or perhaps it was Nero-Apollo). The message being sent was that the sun god and Nero were more or less indistinguishable. At the time, coins of Nero were occasionally imprinted with sunrays emanating from his head. For Romans themselves this quasi-deification-before-death was sacrilegious, while for Jews it was nothing more than arrogance and idolatry. While these actions come later, in the mid-60s and later, already in Jesus's time the themes of deification were in place, and the arrogance was more than set for what did happen, so to call Jesus "Lord" was asking for trouble with Nero on the throne and Christianity known in Rome.[21]

That Romans expose the folly of deification, at least when they were out of earshot or protected by superior powers, is well known. The title of Seneca's famous book *Apocolocyntosis divi Claudii*, written to "honor" Claudius after his death, has usually been translated "the pumpkinification" of the deified Claudius. It is, if anything, a lampooning of Claudius in order to elevate the place of Nero, whom it was Seneca's job to mentor and teach.[22]

What armed Jews like the apostle was a long history of prescriptions and descriptions of the just, peace-making, and Torah-observant king:

> Some take pride in chariots, and some in horses,
>   but our pride is in the name of the LORD our God. (Ps. 20:7)

> Give the king your justice, O God,
>   and your righteousness to a king's son.
> May he judge your people with righteousness,
>   and your poor with justice.
> May the mountains yield prosperity for the people,
>   and the hills, in righteousness.
> May he defend the cause of the poor of the people,
>   give deliverance to the needy,
>   and crush the oppressor. (72:1–4)

> I will sing of loyalty and of justice;
>   to you, O LORD, I will sing.
> I will study the way that is blameless.
>   When shall I attain it?
> I will walk with integrity of heart
>   within my house;
> I will not set before my eyes
>   anything that is base. (101:1–3)

One Jewish author after another called out the pagan kings and nations for their idolatries. Thus, today, statism, as it did in ancient times, easily becomes idolatry. How so? By elevating humans on the towers of honors and adoration, modern statism questions the lordship of Jesus every time one or another version of it becomes our ruling narrative. The alternative to statism, then, is the gospel, the courageous announcement that Jesus is our Lord.

Lord over Israel's Story[23]

The gospel taught Paul to read the Bible afresh; the gospel gave Paul a second narrative by which he learned to read the first narrative. Once he embraced Jesus as the Messiah, he could never read the Bible the same way again. Paul's rearrangements of Israel's story in Galatians

3–4 derive exclusively from his gospel, his hermeneutic. Because he is
convinced Jesus is the Lord, because he is convinced Jesus was raised
from the dead and appeared, because he is convinced Jesus's death is
redemptive, and because he is convinced all of history will be wrapped
up by Jesus and handed over to the Father, Paul reads the Old Testament with fresh eyes. Our passage reveals nothing less than a gospel
hermeneutic. What happens?

First, redemption in Christ, for all, by faith alone—provokes Paul
to reanchor Israel's story in *Abraham*, not Moses. In doing so, Paul
refocuses the story on *promise* and not as much on covenant and law.
Any reading of the summaries of Israel's story I mentioned earlier
(Deut. 6:20–24; 26:5–9; 30; 32; Josh. 24:2–13; Neh. 9:6–37; Pss. 78; 105;
135:8–12; 136) will not find Abraham as he is found in Paul's story,
and neither does one find Moses located in them as one finds him here
in Paul. Abraham is elevated, Moses is diminished. Why? Because the
gospel pointed to Jesus as the redemptive agent by faith alone. The
original promise was given to Abraham, so anything added later does
not annul the promise. Abraham has precedence for Paul. Here are
Paul's words in Galatians 3:17: "My point is this: the law, which came
four hundred thirty years later, does not annul a covenant previously
ratified by God, so as to nullify the promise." Paul's Lord-centered
hermeneutic puts Moses in his place, as it also puts Abraham in his
place. The big point for Paul is the "inheritance," and that was given
by "promise," not by "law" (3:18).

Second, this forces Paul's hand. He must now clarify, especially because he's being dogged by the agitators of Galatia, why the law was
even given if it was not given to supersede the arrangement made with
Abraham. Paul's words in Galatians 3:19–26 stunningly reveal his Lord-
centered hermeneutic. The big idea is that the law was given to Israel for
a limited time and for a limited purpose. The Mosaic covenant (notice
the term) is not the Abraham promise (notice the term), and it is the
Abrahamic promise that is the eternal arrangement for the relationship
of the people of God with God. The limited reason for the law was
that it was added only because of "transgressions" (3:19a; see also 3:22,
23), and it was added for that purpose only "until the offspring would
come" (3:19b)—that is, until the Lord Jesus. The diminishment here of
Moses is palpable: the law, which was the burden in the gospel of the

agitators of Galatia, had done its work and had its time. There is now a new day, what Paul calls in another context "new creation" (2 Cor. 5:17). Furthermore, the law was mediated—that is, "through angels by a mediator" (Moses; cf. the LXX's use of "angels" in Deut. 33:2). The promise, however, came directly from God (as Gen. 15 clearly shows). Hence, the law is inferior to the promise and therefore cannot supersede the promise, and this has huge implications for the agitators' message. The agitators in Galatia are getting things backward, Paul says, because he's learned to read the Bible backward in light of the gospel about Jesus. What is perhaps most breathtaking for Paul is that now that Christ has come, the time of the law is complete: "But now that faith has come, we are no longer subject to a disciplinarian" (3:25).

Third, Paul's gospel hermeneutic is Christocentric. In our passage Paul spins a daring hermeneutical move. In Genesis 17:8 (or 13:15; 24:7) the term translated as "seed" (Hebrew: *zera*; Greek: *sperma*), which is singular in grammatical form, referred corporately to Abraham's descendants through Isaac, but Paul says this singular is used to refer to one person in particular—namely, Christ (3:16). Paul is referring to Christ here as the representative of all the faithful descendants of Abraham, or, as an alternative, to a less comprehensive and more singularly focused Jesus alone in a messianic interpretation. Either way, one gets the same result: the gospel-centered Bible reader Paul sees in that promise to Abraham a prediction or a fulfillment in Jesus the Messiah.

I want to back out of this discussion for a breath of air. What we see here is Paul as storyteller, and the story he is telling is the story about Jesus as Messiah. Jesus is the fulfillment of Israel's story; he is the seed of Abraham; he is the Righteous One who has faithfulness; he is the promise, and he puts Moses's covenant in its place in history as a temporary affair with a limited purpose. Jesus brings the inheritance, he makes us all sons of Abraham, and he brings us into a new community called the church. This is the story pastors tell: how the whole of Israel's history comes to its focal point in Jesus and how the whole of the church derives from Jesus.[24] Any narrative that we indwell—whether it is statism in general or one of its attractive temptations—whose fundamental point is not that Jesus is Lord, the Lord over history and our narrative, is idolatrous.

Lord over the Cosmos

There is a fierceness in Paul's theology of the lordship of Christ. If one has the courage to look it squarely in the eye, it is awe-inspiring and breathtaking. This is what I mean by breathtaking: the Christian story tells the story of all humanity from the beginning of human history to the end of human history. It tells not just the story of Israel but the stories of Egypt, Assyria, Asia Minor, Rome, Africa, Asia, and Europe. Unless we have the courage to grab it all, we will never comprehend this story as it is meant to be understood. Paul begins at (what he knew to be) the beginning, with Adam and Eve in the garden of Eden (Acts 17:26–28; Rom. 5:12–21; 1 Cor. 15:21–22, 45–49). We turn for confirmation of such expansiveness to two of Paul's gospel-centered hymns, which Paul is probably quoting from liturgies used in the early churches: Philippians 2:6–11 and Colossians 1:15–20.[25] Once again, the lordship of Jesus ushers him into breathtaking visions of time and redemption, but in these two hymns the story becomes cosmic. The words Paul uses here for Jesus—and the gospel is about Jesus—stun the first-century reader into sudden awakenings.

First, both of these hymns affirm the preexistence of Jesus and an unusually high Christology.[26] Philippians 2:6 states that Jesus, "though he was in the form of God, did not regard equality with God as something to be exploited."[27] No matter where you cut the cards, to be in the *morphē theou* (form of God) and to be *isa theō* (equal to God) are high claims for someone who two decades earlier was wearing sandals and eating fish from the Sea of Galilee. Paul's choice of *ekenōsen* (emptied) in verse 7 shows that by becoming incarnate, the Son took on a new *morphē* (form), the "form of a slave"—that is, he became human. Jesus freely chose to die on a cross; then God "highly exalted him" (v. 9), giving him the highest of names. Like 1 Corinthians 15:1–28, this passage tells the life story of Jesus Christ the Lord: he was incarnated as a human, he lived, he died on the cross, he was raised, he was exalted, and all this "to the glory of God the Father" (Phil. 2:11).

The Colossians hymn takes us one more step backward in time, for here Paul calls Jesus the "image of the invisible God" (Col. 1:15) and says, "In him all the fullness of God was pleased to dwell" (v. 19).

But something other than what we saw in Philippians 2 happens here: noticeably, this Image of God Jesus is creator of all (vv. 16–17). And as in the Philippians hymn, his self-degrading work on earth leads to his exaltation: "so that he might come to have first place in everything" (v. 18). Even more, all of creation is from him, all of creation is sustained by him, and all of creation's telos is him (v. 16).[28] These are breathtaking claims about our story: that our Lord Jesus is creator of all and the point of it all. That's what a Christoform storyteller has to tell, and it is a story to be nurtured by pastors.

Second, when we consider side by side these two hymns' claims about the very life of Jesus, the implication of the gospel comes to the fore in redemption. Redemption is less prominent in Philippians than in Colossians, though it seems at least begging for a bit of attention in Philippians 2:11, where we are told that "every tongue should confess." However, in Colossians the redemptive theme is powerful: "Through him God was pleased to reconcile to himself all things, whether on earth or in heaven, by making peace through the blood of his cross" (1:20). Cosmic confession and cosmic reconciliation—that's how vast Paul's vision of Jesus as Lord has become.

The pastor as storyteller has a model here: not only does Paul tell of the life of Jesus in his gospel-definition passages (1 Cor. 15:1–28; 2 Tim. 2:8–13), and not only does he use that gospel-centered hermeneutic to put Jesus in a story about Abraham's promise and Moses's covenant and law, but in this passage Paul the storyteller also sees the very human Jesus of the gospel definitions as nothing less than divine. To tell the story of Jesus is to tell the story of God. The point is that Paul depicts Jesus as the preexistent equal to God, as the preexistent one prior to creation, as the Creator, as creation's sustainer, and as the goal of all creation: "All things have been created through him and for him" (Col. 1:16). Jesus, then, is not only the Second Adam; he is also the creator of Adam (and Eve).

Again, statism exalts a human, a president, someone who can be elected; it exalts a government, a collective of human powers. The gospel exalts God in the face of his Son, Jesus Christ, as the world's one true ruler and Lord. If our Lord Jesus Christ is the Lord of the cosmos, we have a story to tell the world that can strip statism of its fake trappings in rulership and imperial ideologies.

Lord over Evil

Pastors are summoned to tell a story about life, about new creation, and about life over death. In a world of evil, they are to tell a story where evil is not the last word. Whether at the graveside of a saint or in the oncology unit in a hospital, or perhaps, more generally, in considering the potential for some new convert's life to become something brand new, or perhaps at someone's baptism, or in a sermon at Easter, or, if you are lectionary driven, every Sunday—the narrative of Jesus the Lord is a narrative that announces that Jesus is the Lord of life over evil. Whether in the face of unspeakable human tragedies, unexplainable events that take innocent human lives, or unimaginable horrors that rip innocence or an anticipated life from people—even children—the pastor is to pastor people into the victory of God over evil.

The themes of evil in Paul are sin, death, and the principalities and powers. This unholy trinity of evil in our world needs to be pictured together for us to see the lordship of Jesus over these lordless lords. This unholy trinity of evil has recently been tied together in an academic study called *The Emergence of Sin*, by Matthew Croasmun.[29] Wondering how one is to understand sin in Romans, whether uppercase *Sin* or lowercase *sin*, whether some kind of power or tyrant or mythology as well as the acts of an individual human who sins, Croasmun dives deep into emergence theory to explain the complexity of evil. To make a complicated story short, he contends individual sins are the "supervenience" or causal basis of something that emerges out of those sins. What emerges from nothing other than the global or local accumulation of those sins is what may be named a self or a person—that is, something altogether real and distinguishable from individual sins that can be called Sin, a cosmic tyrant. Uppercase Sin takes on agency and the power to act on individuals to keep them in line. Now the crucial factor: if sins are the supervenience base, then the collectivity of sins by humans emerges into Sin and takes on the power and agency of "downward causation," that is, the ability to affect the individual sinners. How so? Sin constrains sinners to keep on sinning, and this, as it were, feeds the beast of Sin. Sin then becomes both what we do and, through emergence into Sin, a systemic self that protects itself by pressing us into more sins. Sins and Sin have one goal:

death. This systemic understanding of sins and Sin, then, is a cycle or a feedback loop. This unholy trinity of evil—sin, death, and Sin (and we will add another dimension to Sin when we look at principalities and powers)—has been entered, defeated, and conquered by Jesus. I will begin with the aim of Sin and sins: death.

Death

But this story of Jesus's lordship over evil will only work if we acknowledge two gospel truths: that *sin is real* and that *sin leads to death*. Death is the consequence of sin. We anchor our faith in this connection in Genesis 3, but here we are focusing on Paul, so we go to both Romans 5:12–21 and 1 Corinthians 15 yet again. A few observations about Paul's theology of death. First, sin is the action of a human being, and it brings death and condemnation: "Therefore, just as sin came into the world through one man, and death came through sin, and so death spread to all because all have sinned . . ." (Rom. 5:12). Even more, Paul says the consequence of one man's sin is humans sinning so much that he can say "death exercised dominion" (NRSV) or "death reigned" (NIV; see also vv. 17, 21). He says death is nothing less than God's "condemnation" (v. 16).

Second, Jesus entered into our death in order to slay death and put death to death once and for all. Enter here, of course, all the discussions of atonement theory.[30] I believe the best summary is to see Jesus identifying with humans and humanity in their sinfulness and Sinfulness in order to take our blame, our guilt, and our punishment on himself—all to rescue us from our condition and liberate us to become the people of God. I call this "identification for incorporation," and it shares much with both Christus Victor and substitutionary atonement. Hence, the "death of [God's] Son" (Rom. 5:10) is an entry into our death so that Jesus can become Lord over death by resurrection—that is, by ushering in justification and new creation life (vv. 15, 16, 17, 18, 19, 21). Now life rules or exercises dominion (v. 17).

Third, Jesus's dealing death to death itself creates new life beyond death, which is nothing more than a dominion of life (Rom. 5:17). This happened "so that, just as sin exercised dominion in death, so grace might also exercise dominion through justification leading to eternal life through Jesus Christ our Lord." As Romans 6:9 puts it, "We know that Christ, being raised from the dead, will never die again; death no longer has dominion over him."

Finally, Jesus thus becomes the Lord of life over death, and death has lost its place in history:

> The last enemy to be destroyed is death. . . .
> . . . When this perishable body puts on imperishability, and this mortal body puts on immortality, then the saying that is written will be fulfilled:

> "Death has been swallowed up in victory."
> "Where, O death, is your victory?
> Where, O death, is your sting?" (1 Cor. 15:26, 54–55)

Statism's narrative is the story of death—seemingly about half of our citizens feel a death each time their candidate loses. It is death, too, because nations wax and wane and are not eternal: not Alexandria, not Rome, and not Washington, DC. Every generation renews its own idols to worship in the heads of state. I'm old enough to have weathered many elections and withered under the hopes of America's most common idolatry. It is not that I don't think who gets elected matters. The elections matter, but they don't matter like the lordship of Jesus. The "last president" standing will be Jesus.

Jesus asked the right question: Whose image is on this coin? (Mark 12:13–17). That's the question the Lord Jesus asks of us as we consider the gospel of life over death. "Give to the emperor," he said to his interrogators, "the things that are the emperor's, and to God the things that are God's."[31] Statism gives to the party or president the things that are God's.

I began at the end, or the aim of sins and Sin, with death, so now we turn to the means of death in the systemic feedback loop called evil, with sin.

Sin

In discussing Jesus as Lord of life over death, we saw sin come into the picture, but this discussion has been focused on individual sins, and I will turn to the impact of the collectivity of sin when I turn to Sin, or The Powers. Sin (uppercase) in the Jewish tradition can be sorted into a number of metaphors and terms, such as staining or violating or rebelling or transgression against law or idolatry or failing to love or acting unjustly or turning against the way of peace. All these and more are at work when we speak here of sins. When it comes to Paul's understanding of Jesus as Lord over evil and over sin as a manifestation of evil, I turn to Romans 6 and Paul's argument that Jesus has conquered sinning in the life of the believer.

The issue of sin or transgression is provoked by a question: "Should we continue in sin in order that grace may abound?" (Rom. 6:1). Someone thinks sin magnifies God's grace, so let's get on with it in spades! Paul gives them what the Germans call an *Ohrfeige*, a boxing of the ears, with his "By no means!" (6:2). His solution to the presence and even attractiveness of sinning in the life of the believer is baptism. Baptism is burial: "Do you not know that all of us who have been baptized into Christ Jesus were baptized into his death?" (6:3). This clarifies what he just said in 6:2: "we who died." In 6:6 he says in baptism we know "that our old self was crucified" with Christ, so that "we might no longer be enslaved to sin." In baptism the Christian dies to sin, because in that baptism the believer is plunged into the death of Christ, whose death slew death. Baptism is the sacrament of death that brings new life.

This is to say, baptism is also life, new life after the sin-death-life. Thus, Romans 6:4: "Therefore we have been buried with him by baptism into death, so that, just as Christ was raised from the dead by the glory of the Father, so we too might walk in newness of life." Or, as he puts it at the end of this paragraph, "So you also must consider yourselves dead to sin and alive to God in Christ Jesus" (6:11). In Paul's programmatic or thematic statement of how the believers in Rome were to live in Romans 12:1–2, he frames the Christian life in both a death way and a life way, only here that life is framed by two other terms: "Do not be conformed to this world, but be transformed by the renewing of your minds, so that you may discern what is the will of God—what is good and acceptable and perfect" (12:2). The baptism into death emerges here as "do not be conformed to this world," while the "raised to new life" comes out as "be transformed by the renewing of your minds."

Jesus entered death on our behalf and died our death. But he did not remain in the grave, because Easter is the Christian's true story. The Easter story is that Jesus defeated death and replaced it with new

life, both now and into eternity. Our baptisms are embodied partici-
pations in that death and resurrection of Jesus, and that means that
our baptisms are fundamentally Christoformity. Our baptisms are our
story, the one and only story we have to tell: we tell the story that Jesus
has entered death, snapped its shackles to us, and set us free for new
life. But *our* story is not really ours. Our story is Jesus's story, and
that means his story is ours: he died and he was raised; we are in him;
therefore, we have died and we are raised. We have the capacity to live
a life of love, of world-denying nonconformity and grace-affirming
"renewing," because our Lord has paved the way for us and we are
merely sucked into his wake of victory. David deSilva, a professor of
New Testament, has captured Jesus's lordship over sin and over our
participation in his lordship in these terms: "God offers you the means
to become reconciled with him and to become a new person who will
want and love and do what is pleasing to him because the Spirit of his
Son will live in you and *change* you. The result of God's kindness and
activity is that you will live a new kind of life now and, after death,
live forever with him."[32]

Jesus, then, is the Lord over sin at work in the feedback loop of
evil/Sin. That means we have the power in our Lord and in the Spirit
to overcome sin, to live a life of love, justice, the fruit of the Spirit,
and obedience. Statism merely offers the possibility of changing the
structures by creating and enforcing laws, regulations, and ordinances.
Statism cannot tell a story of personal transformation by the indwelling
Spirit and God's personal presence. Statism regulates people; Jesus the
Lord re-creates them and renews them.

The Powers

Evil has a third component in Pauline theology: not just sins and
death, but Sin ramped up into The Powers. At the heart of statism is
something far too often unrecognized: behind statism are the "principalities and powers," often simplified into The Powers (the term I will
use now). The context of The Powers can be presented by quoting two
verses in Colossians:

> For in him all things in heaven and on earth were created, things
> visible and *invisible, whether thrones or dominions or rulers or*

> *powers*—all things have been created through him and for him
> (1:16).

He disarmed the rulers and authorities and made a public example
of them, triumphing over them in it (2:15).

In the first verse, The Powers are created by God and therefore good; in
the second, The Powers are corrupted, rebellious, and evil but conquered
by Jesus in his death and resurrection. What then are The Powers?[33] Andrew Lincoln sketches three options: (1) they were supernatural forces
and are to be so yet today, a view held by many evangelicals; (2) they
were supernatural forces but are appropriated today as ideologies and
social structures; and (3) they were supernatural *and* social structures
then and can be so today.[34] I want to make a brief case for the third
view, and in this the system of evil is unmasked: sins-leading-to-Sin is
joined by the spirits to create a larger sense of Sin called The Powers,
who then through "downward causation" affect both the structures of
this world and humans in their sin. If the aim of sin is death, the aim
of Jesus is to bring new creation life through defeating sin and death
and conquering The Powers.

I begin by gathering a few shards of evidence from the Bible to
sort out this third view. Daniel 7 mentions The Powers in the terms
"sovereignty, power and greatness of all the kingdoms" (7:27 NIV; see
"princes" and "prince" in 10:13, 20). Paul speaks in 1 Corinthians of
the "rulers of this age" (2:8), and in his consummate summary of the
end of endings he says Christ will hand "over the kingdom to God
the Father, after he has destroyed every ruler and every authority and
power. For he must reign until he has put all his enemies under his feet"
(15:24–25). The last enemy, it may be remembered, is death (v. 26). That
Jesus has erased death out of history and will usher in eternal life means
all enemies of life will be defeated, and here are Paul's terms: "For I am
convinced that neither death, nor life, nor angels, nor rulers, nor things
present, nor things to come, nor powers, nor height, nor depth, nor
anything else in all creation, will be able to separate us from the love
of God in Christ Jesus our Lord" (Rom. 8:38–39). The various terms
in these and similar passages describe human rulers at times (13:1) but
seem to be transhuman realities as well. The Powers, then, in Colossians (1:16; 2:15) are connected with the near parallel in Ephesians

1:21; 3:10; 6:12, with the terms "rule and authority and power and dominion" and "rulers and authorities *in the heavenly places*," and then with language describing the cosmic conflict in which Christians engage in the power of the Spirit and in the victory achieved by Christ, a conflict "against the rulers, against the authorities, against the cosmic powers *of this present darkness, against the spiritual forces of evil in the heavenly places.*" This language undeniably describes spiritual and cosmic forces at work in this world, forces that Paul in Ephesians attributes to "the ruler of the power of the air, the spirit that is now at work among those who are disobedient" (2:2). Yet some of this language is routinely used for, say, Roman structures and institutions. In other words, "The Powers" refers to dark cosmic forces that are at work in the structures of God's world.

In The Powers, then, we are drawn into a story: God's created structures pollute themselves and are polluted by humans sinning because they choose to align with Satan. The battle of bringing the enemy under the footstool (Ps. 110:1; cf. a similar idea in Ps. 8:6) is on,[35] and no one has captured the meaning of this battle better than Tremper Longman and Daniel Reid:

> The contours of the story are of one sent from heaven to subject the cosmos to its Creator and Lord. Born of a woman (Gal 4:4) and taking human form (Php 2:7), he engaged the enemy, was victorious in an epochal battle (Col 2:15; cf. 1:12–14), and was exalted to God's right hand, where he now reigns as cosmic Lord (1 Co 15:24–26; Eph 1:20–22; Php 2:9 Col 3:1; 1 Ti 3:16), building his new temple (1 Co 3:16–17; 2 Co 6:16; Eph 2:19–22), and receiving praise and obeisance (Php 2:10–11). He will come again at the end of the age and conclude his defeat of the enemy, who will have waged a final revolt (2Th 2:8). In the end, death, the final enemy, will stand defeated along with every other hostile power, and Christ will hand over the kingdom to God (1 Co 15:24–28). But in the meantime, the people of the Messiah stand between two episodes—climax and resolution—in the eschatological warfare, enjoying the benefits and advantage of Christ's defeat of the enemy at the cross (Ro 8:37). Yet, as they await their Lord to descend from heaven on the final day (1 Th 4:16–17), they are till beset by a hostile foe (Eph 6:10–17).

This story of conflict and triumph presumes enemies. And Paul selected and fashioned a rich vocabulary to describe them in their various aspects. These enemies consisted not of Romans or Greeks but of "prin-cipalities and powers," sin, flesh, death, law, and a final enemy he called the "man of lawlessness."[36]

My conclusion is that The Powers are malevolent created beings/ spirits at work in divinely created but now corrupted structures in our world. Human sins become Sin, and Sin becomes The Powers, and The Powers do their dirty work on humans by promoting sins. In the Bible, a noticeable emphasis within the theme of The Powers is on kings and princes (cf. Dan. 7:2–8; 10:13, 20–21; Rom. 13:1; 1 Cor. 2:6–8;[37] 15:24–26) or death (1 Cor. 15:26), but empowering or influencing or shaping them are evil spirits (Rom. 8:38–39; Eph. 6:12). We are to see in The Powers more than injustices in this world,[38] more than Sin, and The Powers are more than an "inner reality." Rather, in Paul's mind there are real demonic beings out to destroy God's work. I find something of this in Joseph Conrad's *Heart of Darkness*. In a famous descrip-tion of Kurtz, Marlowe wonders whether the man is not connected to darker forces: "Everything belonged to him—but that was a trifle. The thing was to know what he belonged to, how many powers of darkness claimed him for their own."[39]

The statism story is now unmasked for what it can be, for what it is at times, or for what it has been over and over in history. One need not mention many examples, but I am thinking of Nero and the Roman Empire in the time of Paul, the atrocities of Hitler and Stalin, and the duplicitous evil of modern apartheids, not to ignore the systemic racist and sexist structures very much alive in the United States today. While God created The Powers (structures and spirits) to be good,[40] they are corrupted and out from under the lordship of Christ. They are in fact at war with the Lord. While Christian citizens can strive with all their might to do good and to influence the state in the direction of God's will, there ought to be a holy reserve about the reality of The Powers at work in the structures and a renewed commitment to the lordship of Christ over his people, the church, which is our next theme.

God knows and sees our sins, Sin, and The Powers at work, and so God sent his Son to reverse the feedback loop: by absorbing our sins (2 Cor. 5:21), the Son is able to break the powers of death and Sin and The Powers and to conquer evil. The evil of our world is not the last word; a word beyond that word is the lordship of Christ, who has brought life into the world and turned the feedback loop into the message of life, righteousness, and a system of righteousness and justice and peace that then through downward causation guides those in Christ in the ways of Christoformity.

Lord over Church

No place can embody, or ought to embody, the gospel story of Jesus as Lord like the church, and by this I mean especially a local church. I'm no idealist about the church, and I stand with Dietrich Bonhoeffer's famous line about entering the church only to become disappointed, disaffected, and actually destructive to the church if we expect it to live up to our wish dreams.[41] But Jesus is the "head"[42] of his body, the church, and I cite three texts from Ephesians.

> And he [God] has put all things under his [Christ's] feet and has made him the head over all things for the church (1:22).
> But speaking the truth in love, we must grow up in every way into him who is the head, into Christ (4:15).
> For the husband is the head of the wife just as Christ is the head of the church, the body of which he is the Savior (5:23).

But the most important lines in this word study of *head* are found in Colossians 1:18, which reads, "He is the head of the body, the church; he is the beginning, the firstborn from the dead, so that he might come to have first place in everything" (see also 2:10, 19).

It is The Powers at work even in the church that turn The Head, Jesus the Lord, into a subordinate and that turn a human pastor, who ought to be subordinate, into the head. The temptations to power and celebrity come to life in churches, too. My point is that these things ought not to be, because the Lord of the church and of every local church is Jesus and Jesus alone. Clamoring for governmental influence or seeking publicity and fame or attention are not the ways of Christoformity. The one true way of Christoformity in a local church is to make it clear to one and all that Jesus is Lord in the house of God. That's the story we have, and that's the story we are to tell.

Conclusion

We have one simple gospel story, whose theme is Jesus is Lord.

We nurture Christoformity in a local church when we tell the story of Jesus as Lord over and over and let it soak into our bones and muscles and sinews. Our Lord is the one who was crucified and raised, and so the Christoform story is the story of death and resurrection, not just the story of conquest and triumph. The path of our Lord was to empty himself in order to redeem others, and through his sacrifice and self-negation he was exalted. His mission was redemption, not attention and not celebrity. His mission was to hand over to God the defeated Powers and the redeemed people of God.

To let any other story gain ascendance or centrality in a church, statism included, is idolatry.

6

A Culture of Witness

I once informed a professor that my favorite definition of a sermon was "truth on fire." The professor shot back that he thought sermons ought to be absent of emotion, and then he said they also ought to be absent of personal stories. I was now officially stuck on both sides, because I believed both were ingredients of the best sermons I had heard. Not sermons that are all stories but sermons with the right story at the right time struck magic for me. Some preachers, such as Fred Craddock and Barbara Brown Taylor, are the preachers they are because of their genius in combining Bible and personal story and turning the whole sermon into a story itself. Or some create a living relationship between the Bible's theology and the congregation, such as Fleming Rutledge. Others, such as Ellen Davis and Eugene Peterson, are much less inclined to tell stories and more known for entering into the text itself in their acts of imagination. Yet others, such as John R. W. Stott, seek to expound a text with an eye on the believer and the congregation.[1] Different preachers find their way with a variety of giftedness and approaches, but the preacher is obliged, at times (and not too often), to tell her own story.[2] (Yes, all Christians are obliged to tell their own stories.)

The pastor is first and foremost a *witness*.[3] In his spectacular sketch of the meaning of *witness* (Greek *martys*), Ceslas Spicq breaks the term into five components: a New Testament witness to the gospel is someone who

1. was present when something was said or done,
2. is active to announce, proclaim, or describe what the witness observed or heard,
3. identifies with what was seen or heard and believes (the gospel that Jesus is Lord),
4. embodies that witness even to the point of death (as does a martyr), and
5. has hearers or observers render decisions on the basis of the witness's witness.[4]

If this is the case for first-generation witnesses during the New Testament period, then for the pastor to witness in our day means the pastor has experienced redemption in Christ and can witness to the truth of the gospel verbally and behaviorally. This is what I mean then when I say a pastor is a witness, or that the pastor has a (personal) story to tell. Like Barbara Brown Taylor, who is a witness to her own odd kind of conversion story, which she told when some college classmates hit her up for some quick-fix evangelism. The one most surprised is Taylor and perhaps her fans, like me, today:

> The whole thing took less than twenty minutes. It was quick, simple, direct. They did not have any questions about who Jesus was. You are here, God is there, Jesus is the bridge. Say these words and you are a Christian. Abracadabra. Amen. It is still hard for me to describe my frame of mind at the time. I was half-serious, half-amused. I cooperated as much out of curiosity as anything, and because I thought that going along with them would get them out of my room faster than arguing with them. . . . Most of it was just embarrassing, the kind of simplistic faith I liked the least, but something happened to me that afternoon. After they left I went out for a walk and the world looked funny to me, different. Peoples' faces looked different to me; I had never noticed so many details before. I stared at them like portraits in a gallery, and my own face burned for over an hour. Meanwhile, it was hard to walk. The ground was spongy under my feet. I felt weightless, and it was all I could do to keep myself from floating up and getting stuck in the trees.[5]

She had no other story to tell, for that was her story, even if it didn't live up to her or her Episcopalian expectations.

There are three stories, not just one, every pastor is to nurture in a church in order to foster Christoformity. The three stories are the Bible's gospel story, the pastor's personal story, and the story of the congregation as part of the story of the church. By telling the first, the pastor nurtures the environment where the second and third belong. One is not exaggerating to say the pastor's calling is to embody the gospel as a witness, not in the sense that the pastor is idolized or idealized or the central hero in the story, but in the sense that the pastor's life directly leads to and speaks of Christ. That is, the pastor's life is a witness to the gospel, not to the pastor him- or herself. The pastor nurtures a storytelling culture when the pastor's story becomes Christoform. When the pastor's story itself becomes Christoform, the church learns to tell the gospel story well.

So then, we are not talking about preachers who are armed with one story after another. Such preachers have so many stories that one wants to ask whether the Bible might make a cameo appearance. It is not inaccurate to say such pastors tend to do what is said of the man in Kent Haruf's novel *Eventide* who "would sit and visit with other old men in town and tell stories that were not exaggerated so much as they were simply enlarged a little."[6] And neither are we talking about dramatics or theatrics when it comes to the pastor's story. I know a pastor who announced that he *only* became a Christian because as a young boy his sister walked forward and he was afraid to remain in his pew—so he walked forward, too, and accepted Jesus into his heart, and it stuck and he was a pastor for some four decades. One of America's finest evangelical writers is Alan Jacobs, and his conversion story combines a Spirit-shaped, naive experience with a desire to impress a girl (who became his wife) that altered his life.[7] Jacobs, it should be observed, can neither date nor doubt his conversion. I know others who tell dramatic stories of conversion from drugs, sex, crime, and other things that Christians love to hear about. However, there is—and this could be underlined—a fine line of difference between a storyteller who ends up being the hero and the storyteller who exalts Christ. Dietrich Bonhoeffer offers what we constantly need to be reminded of: "The call to be extraordinary is the great, inevitable danger of discipleship."[8]

Speaking of Bonhoeffer, scholars do not know when Bonhoeffer was converted, though time has allowed us to fill in much of his story because he left behind so many letters and papers, and, far more importantly, his best friend, Eberhard Bethge, told Bonhoeffer's story.[9] If you read Bonhoeffer's sermons or major works, you quickly discover that the story is not about him but about God, about Christ, about the German church's survival through the Confessing Church, and about God's powerful grace in the midst of suffering. Only by reading his letters do we learn about Bonhoeffer's personal life and story. Those letters were only preserved because his assassination drew us to his writings and then to what we could learn about him. Again, we have hero-ized him not because he told us about himself but because his story takes us to a higher plane in the Christian life. Or to use other terms, because his story takes us to the gospel story itself. Pastor Bonhoeffer was a witness.

What about Paul? Did he tell his story? Was Paul a witness? I'll answer this question with a resounding yes, and I'll direct us to Eugene Peterson, who said it this way: "[Paul] is a scarred veteran in the political and spiritual conflicts of the first century. Paul is far too honest to have been bribed to write something he didn't believe in. He is far too experienced to have any untested illusions about life. He is far too authentic a man to pass on to us anything he had not already incorporated into his own life."[10] Yes, Paul was a witness, and every word he wrote was a witness born in experience.

Paul and the Term *Egō*

In a number of locations in Paul's letters, he turns from "we" language to "I" language (to witness). Romans 7 alone contains sixteen "we" and "I" references, and within that chapter no transition is more dramatic than that from Romans 7:4–7 to 7:8–11.[11] Here's the "we" language:

> In the same way, my friends, you have died to the law through the body of Christ, so that you may belong to another, to him who has been raised from the dead in order that **we** may bear fruit for God. While **we** were living in the flesh, **our** sinful passions, aroused by the law, were at work in **our** members to bear fruit for death. But now **we** are

discharged from the law, dead to that which held **us** captive, so that **we** are slaves not under the old written code but in the new life of the Spirit. (vv. 4–6)

Then it turns to "I" language:

> But sin, seizing an opportunity in the commandment, produced in **me** all kinds of covetousness. Apart from the law sin lies dead. I [*egō*]was once alive apart from the law, but when the commandment came, sin revived and I [*egō*] died, and the very commandment that promised life proved to be death to **me**. For sin, seizing an opportunity in the commandment, deceived **me** and through it killed **me**. (vv. 8–11)

You may know that more than a few debates are raging about how to read Romans 7 and the word *egō*, including whether the "we" is actually an "I" and whether the "I" is actually a "we." For the moment, I will ask only that we see Paul's own witness behind these words in some way.

We can find another example in Galatians 2. After confronting Peter publicly over Peter's shifting viewpoints, Paul turns to a "we"-and-"I"-language witness to the gospel (vv. 15–21). Again, let's look at the "we" language first:

> **We** ourselves are Jews by birth and not Gentile sinners; yet **we** know that a person is justified not by the works of the law but through faith in Jesus Christ. And **we** have come to believe in Christ Jesus, so that **we** might be justified by faith in Christ, and not by doing the works of the law, because no one will be justified by the works of the law. But if, in **our** effort to be justified in Christ, we **ourselves** have been found to be sinners, is Christ then a servant of sin? Certainly not! (vv. 15–17)

In verse 18 Paul turns to "I" language:

> But if I build up again the very things that I once tore down, then I demonstrate that I am a transgressor. For through the law I [*egō*] died to the law, so that I might live to God. I have been crucified with Christ; and it is no longer I [*egō*] who live, but it is Christ who lives in **me**. And the life I now live in the flesh I live by faith in the Son of God, who loved **me**

and gave himself for **me**. I do not nullify the grace of God; for if justification comes through the law, then Christ died for nothing. (vv. 18–21)

We find the same problem here as in Romans 7: Is the "we" an "I" or
the "I" a "we"? Even if one sees much "we" in the "I," the personal
witness of Paul's own life in the "I" is not diminished.

This is enough to begin to see that Paul can become a witness and
use his personal story to tell the story of Christ and the gospel. Four
more texts in Galatians reveal Pastor Paul as a witness:

Am I now seeking human approval, or God's approval? Or am I trying to please people? If I were still pleasing people, I would not
be a servant of Christ (1:10).

Friends, I beg you, become as I am, for I also have become as you
are (4:12).

I am confident about you in the Lord that you will not think other-
wise. But whoever it is that is confusing you will pay the penalty.
But my friends, why am I still being persecuted if I am still preaching circumcision? In that case the offense of the cross has been
removed (5:10–11).

May I never boast of anything except the cross of our Lord Jesus
Christ, by which the world has been crucified to me, and I to the
world (6:14).

We can understand Paul's "I" as a witness because he tells his own
story in Galatians 1–2, summarizes it in 1:10, and then encourages
his audience, "Become as I am," in 4:12. He then appeals to his own
practice as a model in 5:10–11 and, in effect, sums up the Christian life
by pointing to his own cruciform life in 6:14.

A pastor in the Pauline mode is a personal, embodied witness to the
gospel about Jesus. To deny the personal is to deny embodiment of
the gospel and is to deny the pastor as witness, but a genuine witness
in personal storytelling is one who tells the "I" story as both a "we"
story and, more importantly, the "Christ" story. In this chapter I want
to examine "Paul as convert" as a paradigm for understanding the
"pastor as convert,"[12] and in doing so I aim to move beyond "Paul as
convert" to "Paul as embodied witness."

Was Paul a Convert? Considering Our Options

It may be a surprise that some Pauline scholars think Paul was not a convert. Rather, they think he was *called* rather than *converted*.[13] Which was it? The answer to this question will open the door to understanding Paul as embodied witness and will provide a paradigm for the pastor as one who can nurture a witness culture of Christoformity.

A Conscience Pricked

Perhaps the most popular reading of Paul's story is that he was converted in (what is often said to be) an Augustinian and Lutheran sort of way.[14] Many read Paul's story through the lens of Romans 7 as the cry of an anguished soul, even if that reading of Paul is not embraced by the guild of Pauline scholars today, or for that matter by Augustine or Luther. That is, Paul struggled with a troubled and "pricked" (Acts 26:14) conscience over his sin and guilt and also struggled to be accepted by God until he simply gave up, admitting he was a sinner who was striving to please God on his own merits. In so admitting his sinful striving, Paul simultaneously embraced the righteousness that alone is found in Christ and that Christ provides for us.

A pile of important theological words end up in this sort of explanation of Paul's conversion—*satisfaction* and *double imputation* and *alien righteousness* and *merit-seeking* and *total depravity* and *legalism* and *works righteousness*—but our concern here is not with those. Most Pauline scholars have not only called into question this reading of Romans 7 but, even more, abandoned this way of reading Paul's life.[15] For those scholars who are in what is now called the new perspective on Paul,[16] the struggle of the "I" in Romans 7:7–25 does not fit well with the lack of struggle in Paul's clear autobiographical reflections. That is, we don't see a titanic ego struggle either in Galatians 1:13–14, where Paul looks back with some pride at his zeal and his success in Torah (or tradition) observance, or in Philippians 3:6, where Paul says "as to righteousness under the law" he was "blameless" (*amemptos*). In the words of Stendahl, who thought Paul did not have that classic Lutheran "introspective conscience,"[17] Paul "experiences no troubles, no problems, no qualms of conscience, no feelings of shortcomings. He is a star pupil . . . a very happy Jew." Beverly Gaventa agrees: "His own statements do not indicate that Paul was tormented by guilt or unhappiness in his early life. . . . If Paul was aware of a prolonged period of searching and questioning, he gives the reader no indication of this struggle."[18] So the "conscience pricked" theory has lost ground in contemporary scholarship.

Switching Religions

Another theory has been older and bolder: Paul changed religions in moving from Judaism to Christianity. This view lingers despite the gallant efforts and brilliant studies of numerous scholars who have each in their own way impressed on generations of students how embedded messianic Judaism was in the diverse Judaism of its day. Jesus the Jew was followed up by Paul the Jew (Acts 22:3; Rom. 11:1). No matter how much ground has been gained in this direction of appreciating the continued Jewishness of Paul's gospel, many simply have not heard the message. For such persons, Judaism is something that existed until Jesus, and then, with one big bang of a resurrection, it all changed, and from Pentecost on, Judaism was done with and everything was now Christian. But what if Paul is right when he says, "I *am* [not *was*] a Pharisee" (Acts 23:6)? So, though a follower of Jesus he remains a Pharisee somehow? What fascinates, then, is the question, What happens to Paul's conversion if he never changed religions, if he remained within Judaism with a kind of messianic Judaism? Is that still conversion? For some, once one admits that neither Jesus nor Paul started a new religion, the word *conversion* morphs into the word *call* or *commission*.

But I've left the switching-religions theory with a lingering problem. For some, once we settle on whether Paul remained a Jew and "within Judaism," we can then conclude "yes" or "no." If he remained inside the walls of Judaism in his faith in Jesus as Messiah, then he didn't convert. If he didn't remain in those walls, then he was a convert. In some ways, this is the point of Stendahl's famous essay, which notes,[19] "The emphasis in the accounts is always on this assignment [of Paul to the gentiles], not on the conversion. Rather than being 'converted,' Paul was called to the specific task—made clear to him by his experience of the risen Lord—of apostleship to the Gentiles, one hand-picked through Jesus Christ on behalf of the one God of Jews and Gentiles. The mission is the point. It is a call to mission rather than a conversion." Stendahl's framing of the issues masks the lingering problem; namely, we need to ask, What is *conversion*? If conversion, as Stendahl says, means switching religions, then sure, Paul's not a convert. But what if *conversion* has a more nuanced meaning? In other words, Stendahl answered his question—Was Paul a convert or not?—by assuming a meaning of conversion not accepted by some others who have addressed the question.[20]

Was Paul a Convert? Examining the Telltale Sign

Conversion has been examined by biblical scholars but also by sociologists and psychologists.[21] Since many biblical scholars are now at a stalemate—conversion or calling?—I propose that sociologist Lewis Rambo has provided for us a paradigm for resolving the biblical scholars' dilemma, and it is this sociologist's resolution that will clarify the role of the pastor as called to nurture Christoformity by being a witness.

First, what is conversion? Rambo answers with this direct and then abstract, nonreligious language: "Conversion is what a group or person *says* it is. The process of conversion is a product of interactions among the convert's aspirations, needs, and orientations, the nature of the group into which she or he is being converted, and the particular social matrix in which these processes are taking place."[22] Conversion involves three elements: the group into which one is converting, the individual, and the interaction of the two. First the group.

Group

If we convert this into Christian theological language, conversion implies an *ecclesiology*. Now let's make this real: it is not just an ecclesiology, as if converts were moving into some theological box or into some ideological shelf of books. Conversion is ecclesiological at the most particular, concrete, and local of levels. Conversion is what a specific church says it is. Since one is moving into a church, and since a church is, in most cases, a stable organization, conversion

will mean taking on the ethics, ideas, practices, beliefs, and relationships of a concrete, local church. This happens at such a pervasive
level that it is invisible. Conversion, indeed, is what a group says it
is. An illustration of a person converting by belonging can be seen in
Nancy Mairs's lovely line: "Instead of being denied communion unless I converted, I was given communion until I felt strong enough to
convert."[23]

This is why there is an interactive phase in conversion: the individual
and the group size each other up, and the group renders judgment of
acceptance. Alan Segal has said this well. He notes that a convert's
story "is always mediated through the values of the convert's new
community, which defines what a conversion is and actually teaches
the convert how to think of it. . . . Thus [moving into Paul himself], the
accounts of Paul's and other ancient conversions, even the first-person
accounts, are *retrospective retellings of events, greatly enhanced by
group norms learned and appropriated in the years prior to the writing.*"[24] That last observation is salient: it is not uncommon to watch
a convert's story express and also adapt to the group's expectations.
The aim, of course, is to gain approval by the group. Alan Jacobs, in
his study of conversion stories, notes that "one of the purposes of
'giving one's testimony' is to ratify one's place in the community, to
prove oneself a valid member of it."[25]

Ego and Identity

If group is one important element of a conversion, so is the individual or, more penetratingly, one's ego. James Fowler, in his classic
Stages of Faith, defines conversion as "a significant recentering of one's
previous conscious or unconscious images of value and power, and
the conscious adoption of a new set of master stories in the commitment to reshape one's life in a new community of interpretation and
action."[26] In another of Fowler's books this definition had a morning
shave and gained a cleaner appearance. He says, "By conversion I mean
an ongoing process . . . *through which people (or a group) gradually
bring the lived story of their lives into congruence with the core story
of the Christian faith.*"[27] Even with a morning shave, that definition
lives up to Peggy Noonan's barb: "There are few things you can rely

on in this turbulent world, but one is the tendency of academics to use language poorly."[28] Here's my summary: conversion happens when a person acquires a new autobiography. When a person says, "Once I was *that*, but now I am *this*," they are a convert.

Above, I mentioned that theologians and biblical experts came to a stalemate about conversion, and I have now shown that sociologists of conversion offer a way to end the stalemate. One might object that using modern sociology imposes modern categories on ancient texts. That this is not merely modern theory is confirmed by the examination of conversion among ancient Romans and Greeks by classical scholar Abraham Malherbe.[29] If conversion to various philosophers and philosophies was normally a "gradual process," those precipitated by speeches tended to be sudden.[30] The advocates for these conversions to philosophies expected intellectual and practical transformation, but they were fully aware that conversions could often also lead to confusion and displacement.[31] Importantly, and once again confirming the recent study of sociologists, Malherbe contends philosophers encapsulated the recent convert; that is, they surrounded converts with other philosophers and a new community shaped with fictive relationships. Why? So conversion would deepen and stick.[32] What Malherbe points out in his brief study is that conversion involved "the redefinition of personal identity."[33] What he also shows is that conversion was an interaction between a group and an individual. Rambo's and Fowler's theories, then, are confirmed in important ways by Malherbe's study of conversion among the philosophers.

Summary

Conversion, then, was and is a complex affair involving transformation at the level of personal identity. What mattered most was what happened at the level of one's own self-perception and identity formation. It is inaccurate, then, to say that since Paul stayed within Judaism, he was not a convert. We have to ask two other questions behind the switching-of-religions question: Did Paul change groups? Did his personal identity shift? How, then, do you detect a conversion? The answer can be found if one examines whether the person was involved in (1) switching groups and (2) revising their autobiography.

Paul, Finally

Now we can ask our question again, Was Paul a convert? The answer can be found by asking whether Paul changed primary groups and whether he revised his autobiography. Paul clearly began to associate with "messianic" Jewish groups, and in fact he began to form them! So we can answer yes to the first half of that question. Our focus can now turn to the second half.

The key is to ask how Paul told his story. However we understand texts such as Galatians 2:15–21 and Romans 7:7–25, those texts will continue to indicate that Paul revised his own story and learned to tell it as a movement from a life centered on Torah to a life centered on Christ, grace, and the gospel.[34] If one believes that the stories of Paul's "conversion" in the book of Acts (9; 22; 26) are reliable, we have a profound example of witness in which Paul both revises his own story and testifies to a movement from his life of zealous persecution to a life of gospel preaching. His master story, in other words, is a messianic story that moves away from his old story, and such a move is a sign of conversion. Conversion, then, is all about how a person tells her story as an identity-shaping narrative.

Are there other passages that indicate a revision of his autobiography? The answer is yes, and we'll see this in looking at two passages: Galatians 1:13–16 and Philippians 3:4–16. I'll concentrate on Galatians and set in bold the first-person singulars and underline the two chapters of his life:

> You have heard, no doubt, of **my earlier life in Judaism**. **I** was violently persecuting the church of God and was trying to destroy it. **I** advanced in Judaism beyond many among **my** people of the same age, for **I** was far more zealous for the traditions of **my** ancestors. But when God, who had set **me** apart before **I** was born and called **me** through his grace, was pleased to reveal his Son to **me**, so that **I** might proclaim him among the Gentiles, **I** did not confer with any human being.

Paul has divided his life into chapters. One might be called "Earlier Life in Judaism," when he was a persecutor and destroyer of the church; it was also a time of advancement in Torah observance. But in a new chapter, perhaps called "But When God," that former life all somehow came to a screeching halt when Paul encountered Christ in a revelation by God that Jesus was indeed God's Son. The new chapter of Paul's life is characterized by "gospeling" Christ among the gentiles.

Whether or not the exegetes and theologians want to call Paul a convert, sociologists and psychologists who detect conversions on the basis of how one tells one's own story have this to say: Paul is an obvious convert. That doesn't quite sound right, so I'll say it this way: the pervasive presence in Paul's writing of a self-reflected revision of his own story, a story cut up into pre- and post-Jesus days, is a telltale sign of conversion. Paul, I conclude, was a convert. He had a personal story to tell, and he told it. Paul was a witness.

How did he frame his story of conversion?

Paul's Conversion: From What to What?

To answer this question, we turn to Philippians 3:2–16. This passage is tailored for conversion theorists. First, Paul cuts his life in half. The first half is marked by his Jewish ethnicity ("flesh" and "Israel" and "tribe of Benjamin," vv. 4–5), Torah-observant credentials ("circumcised" and "Pharisee" and "righteousness under the law, blameless," vv. 5–6), and strenuous opposition to Jesus and the church ("zeal" and "persecutor of the church," v. 6). Second, the transition from one world to another world is framed in typical words of converts—namely, in words of contempt for one's past: "loss" and "rubbish" (vv. 7–8; *skybala* could be translated in a variety of ways, not all of them church language). It is common for converts to insult their former group, and the language is sometimes labeled "antirhetoric." Third, the second half of his life is framed in terms of glory: "surpassing value of knowing Christ Jesus my Lord" (v. 8) and "righteousness from God based on faith" (v. 9), which contrasts with "a righteousness of my own [or, my righteousness] that comes from the law" (v. 9). In addition, his terms of glory include "the power of his resurrection" (v. 10) as well as "sharing of his sufferings by becoming like him in his death" (v. 10). Finally, Paul has not ultimately arrived, so he tells the Philippians that he is pressing on in the faith. Here Paul makes it clear that for him saving faith is allegiance to Jesus as Messiah, Lord, and Redeemer.[35]

Paul's Witness Is to Christ's Story

The life Paul sketches of himself in Philippians 3:2–16 has sufficient parallels with the life he sketches of Christ in 2:6–11 for this conclusion: Paul shaped his own self-identity and story as an expression of Christoformity. As Christ had credentials but surrendered them for the sake of others, so Paul sacrificed his credentials for the sake of Christ and others. Noticeably, then, Paul in chapter 3 focuses on "loss" (3:7–8) as Christ "emptied himself" (2:7). As Christ suffered but was raised (2:8–9), so Paul suffers in the hope of resurrection (3:10–11). One can put it this way: the Christoform story of Christ led Paul to tell his own story in Christoform. Paul's story is a witness to Christ's story, not to himself.

A Christian convert, then, is someone who shifts from self-lordship to the lordship of Christ. The singular feature that rises to the surface in this account is the place of Jesus Christ in Paul's story. It all—every bit of it—hinges on who Christ is and what Christ has accomplished, and only then on what benefits shift to Paul because of his association with and allegiance to Christ. His radical change in his view of Jesus created a radical change in Paul's life. Thus, there are three elements to the personal story of Paul:

1. Jesus, who formed the church and whose story becomes the source of its story (with Israel as the backstory)
2. Paul's entrance and participation in the church's story of Jesus
3. The redemptive benefit that Paul discovers in the church's story about Jesus

We are not done, but we now need to pause for a moment to consider the pastor as witness and as one who nurtures Christoformity by telling her story. Remember, Paul told his story in such a way that it told the story of Christ. That story is of the Lord who suffered and was raised. Paul's own story parallels that story in such a way that we call it "Christoform." A pastor is a witness to Jesus, a witness to Jesus in the context of Jesus's people called the church, and an embodied witness to the redemption that comes to those who are "in Christ" and who enter into the body of Christ. Pastors who diminish the centrality of Jesus as Messiah and Lord and Redeemer are failing their pastoral calling because that is the gospel story to be told. Pastors who diminish the centrality of the body of Christ as the embodied witness about Jesus are failing their calling because the Jesus of the story is the Jesus who formed the body of Christ.

But this is not all. There is at least one more element to Paul's story of conversion that connects directly to the pastor who is called to nurture Christoformity as a witness, and that is that he told his story in a Christoform pattern. Paul does this even more than is sometimes observed.

Paul as Embodied Witness

I'll jump right to the conclusion before discussion. Paul believed that he—Mr. Saul Paul from Tarsus—embodied what God was doing in the world. That is, Paul saw himself embodying the gospel, and his personal embodiment made his gospel credible to his audiences.[36] So much did Paul frame his own story as a service to the gospel that we can say Paul's own stories of himself—his *egō* narratives—are nothing less than a diminishment of himself and a display of God's grace and the gospel itself. In other words, he is not making his story important; he uses his story to make the story of Christ, the gospel, important. In so doing, he uses "I" in his letters in diverse ways, sometimes emphasizing himself over against some false teachers but at other times spinning an "I" into a paradigm of the gospel itself.[37] Barbara Brown Taylor captures this in a sermon in breathtaking prose:

> By choosing Christ to flesh out the word, God made a lasting decision in favor of incarnation. Those of us who are his body in the world need not shy away from the fact that our own flesh and blood continue to be where the word of God is made known. We are living libraries of God's word. Our stories are God's stories. Sometimes they are comedies and sometimes they are tragedies; sometimes faith shines through them and other times they end in darkness, but every one of them bears witness to the truth of God's word. Preachers cannot "stay out of" their sermons any more than singers can stay out of their songs. Our words are embodied, which means we bring all that we are to their expression.[38]

I'm sure you caught that lovely "living libraries of God's word," as I did, but that's only one line in this treasure trove. She's got it exactly right: "Our stories are God's stories." We find our story only when we lose it in God's story in Christ.

The most important story Paul tells of himself in his letters is found in Galatians 1–2, a section often marked off in outlines as the "auto-biographical" argument for his gospel. The story he tells is the story of a man who persecuted the church with zeal (1:13, 23) and who was on the highest of levels of respect among fellow Pharisees and Jews (v. 14). But that honorable man was dethroned by the revelation of God in Christ, and he surrendered his ego to Christ and became a gospeler of Jesus (vv. 15–24). Are people heroizing Paul? No, they are praising God (v. 24).

Paul then paradoxically submitted his gospel message to the Jerusalem leaders, knowing full well he had God's approval (Gal. 2:1–10). His confrontation with Peter in 2:11–14 is yet another example of the story he has told so far: it does not glorify him but instead turns full attention to the gospel of grace for all who turn to Jesus. One has to wonder whether Paul is embarrassed by his own behavior while at the same time he glories in the opportunity to exalt the wideness of God's grace. My reading of this incident is not that I like what Paul did, for I don't. Instead, I see here a man who uses bad behavior in order to keep grace uppermost in a difficult moment. If we but circle back, we are astounded by what has happened: the Torah-observant, church-persecuting budding rabbi has become an out-and-out gospeler about God's grace. What happens to Paul is nothing short of a miracle, and we come away thinking about nothing but the power of God's grace to take his worst enemy and make him a friend.

Turn again to Galatians 2:15–21:

We ourselves are Jews by birth and not Gentile sinners; yet we know that a person is justified not by the works of the law but through faith in Jesus Christ. And we have come to believe in Christ Jesus, so that we might be justified by faith in Christ, and not by doing the works of the law, because no one will be justified by the works of the law. But if, in our effort to be justified in Christ, we ourselves have been found to be sinners, is Christ then a servant of sin? Certainly not!

To repeat, in verse 18 Paul turns to "I" language:

> But if **I** build up again the very things that **I** once tore down, then **I** demonstrate that I am a transgressor. For through the law I died to the law, so that I might live to God. I have been crucified with Christ; and it is no longer I who live, but it is Christ who lives in **me**. And the life I now live in the flesh I live by faith in the Son of God, who loved **me** and gave himself for **me**. I do not nullify the grace of God; for if justification comes through the law, then Christ died for nothing.

Paul slides from "we" language into "I" language not because he wants us to focus on him but because he wants us to know that his experience is the common experience. I use an analogy to what is called the personal essay, found in writers as diverse as Plutarch, Michel de Montaigne, Samuel Johnson, William Hazlitt, George Orwell, Hubert Butler, H. L. Mencken, E. B. White, Mary McCarthy, Joan Didion, and Joseph Epstein. What distinguishes personal essayists is the ability to talk about themselves and their own experiences in a way that opens up their stories and experiences.[39] The analogy is this: the ability to tell one's own story as common to others/all is what Paul himself is doing in Galatians. So, when Paul says "I," he is saying not only "we" but also "This is what all of us experience in Christ." This explains why Paul can say in Galatians 4:12, "Become as I am, for I also have become as you are." That is, he and his readers have the same experience of God's gracious claim on their life. His "I" is their "we."

Let's tie this together now: Paul's autobiography in Galatians 1:13–2:10 is then representative of the "we" of 2:11–17 and the "I" of 2:18–21. His autobiography is, to use the words of Beverly Gaventa, "paradigmatic."[40] As John Barclay puts it, "Precisely *in* his individuality and uniqueness is played out a common story of grace."[41] This leads to the following observation: Paul does not make himself a hero or the subject of a special story but instead depicts his story as the story of Christ taking up space in his life as it does in the life of other followers of Jesus.

Christoform witness, then, is an act of gospeling: Paul thinks he embodies the gospel, and therefore his life is a display of the gospel. I like how Eugene Peterson ties the incarnation to our own embodiments: "When God chose to reveal himself to us completely, he didn't do it in words or ideas. He became flesh and lived in the neighborhood with us. Which means that our bodies are capable of receiving God and participating in God, not just with our minds or our emotions or our 'hearts' as we sometimes say, but with these actual flesh-and-blood, skin-and-muscle *bodies*."[42]

Paul is then not a special case or a super-Christian; he is nothing more than what happens to a person when Christ indwells them and takes control of a body. Paul embodies Christoformity, and it makes his embodied life a witness to Christ. We turn to Galatians 6: "May I never boast of anything except the cross of our Lord Jesus Christ, by which the world has been crucified to me, and I to the world. For neither circumcision nor uncircumcision is anything; but a new creation is everything! As for those who will follow this rule [*kanoni*]—peace be upon them, and mercy, and upon the Israel of God" (vv. 14–16). The "I" of these verses is a crucified "I," and that crucified ego—cruciformity, Christoformity—is the rule or *canon* of what it means to be a Christian.

Paul's embodied witness—his life in the body—is not, then, what is so often heard on Christian stages: see how bad I was—enter sex, drugs, alcohol, crime—and see how much I *have changed*! No, his story is "I was Saul but now I am a living embodiment of Christ!" Barclay, again, gets it just right: "Thus any first-person narrative can only be secondarily about Paul himself: it will be primarily about the gospel of which he is the instrument and witness."[43]

The Embodied Witness as Christoformity

Paul's courageous gospeling from Jerusalem to Rome is an embodied witness to what God had planned all along. In this section I will explain how Paul saw his own mission as an embodiment of Christoformity. A bold claim on Paul's part, to be sure.

Bold, indeed, and nothing is bolder on this theme than Colossians 1:24: "I am now rejoicing in my sufferings for your sake, and in my flesh I am completing what is lacking in Christ's afflictions for the sake of his body, that is, the church." In Paul's mind, because he is gospel saturated, the sufferings of Christ not only are the core of the life and death of Jesus but also were announced in advance in the Scriptures (1 Cor. 15:3–5). Hence, sufferings are gospel themes. Paul's Scripture-shaped

imagination about the sufferings of Christ led him to see his own sufferings as an embodiment of the sufferings of Christ in such a way
that they were "completing what [was] lacking in Christ's afflictions
for the sake of his body." That's bold!

The big picture is that Paul is explaining or interpreting his sufferings
in order to locate those sufferings in a meaning-creating story.[44] The inter-
pretive history here is intense, and so I want to restrict the options to the
genuinely possible. Some see here a moral-exemplary theory of a Christ-
kind-of-suffering (he suffered like Christ), while a second view contends
for a mystical or union theory or a corporate-Christ, even cosmic-Christ,
concept and think the verb refers to a "union-with-Christ kind of suffering" (in suffering Paul is at one with Christ). The apocalyptic or eschatological view has become the most attractive theory today: as there was
an appointed number of sufferings in the "messianic woes," or the exilic
conditions of Israel,[45] so Christ absorbed many or most of them, but
some suffering yet remains (his sufferings are the end-time sufferings).

Each of these approaches makes important contributions, but it appears to me that a more eclectic approach is required, one that might
clumsily be called the missional-Christoformity theory. Paul understands his gospel-mission sufferings as an intentional and pastoral entrance into sufferings of Christ, and, like Christ, the more Christoform
he becomes, the more he suffers for the benefit of the church. Furthermore, he understands his suffering as experiencing the fire instead of
and for the benefit of the Colossians.[46] In this view, Paul sees his sufferings as completing the sufferings of Christ because he is engaging
in the same kind of intentionally shaped pastoral work and suffering
after the death of Jesus that Jesus performed at the cross.[47] Here's the
big point, then: Paul's story is the story of Christ, not his own story.
So lost is Paul in the story of Christ that his story is only meaningful
if it is the story of Christ.

But what does this suffering look like? Are words like these only for the
apostle Paul? Dietrich Bonhoeffer's theology of discipleship illustrates
this last view of how to read the sufferings of Paul in Colossians 1:24:

> Even though Jesus Christ has already accomplished all the vicarious
> suffering necessary for our redemption, his sufferings in this world are
> not finished yet. In his grace, he has left something unfinished . . . in his

suffering, which his church-community is to complete in this last period before his second coming. This suffering will benefit the body of Christ, the church. . . . What is clear, however, is that those suffering in the power of the body of Christ suffer in a vicariously representative [*stellvertretend*, probably the most significant term in German theological discussion about atonement] action "for" the church-community, "for" the body of Christ. They are permitted to bear what others are spared.[48]

We thus see in this paragraph from Bonhoeffer a missional-ecclesial focus, along with a Christoformity for the sake of others. That, so it appears to me, is what Paul was talking about for his own ministry.

One more time: Paul is an embodied witness of Christ.

Conclusion

I return to Spicq's fivefold breakdown of the New Testament idea of a witness, summarized at the beginning of this chapter: a New Testament witness to the gospel is someone who

1. was present when something was said or done,
2. is active in to announce, proclaim, or describe what the witness observed or heard,
3. identifies with what was seen or heard and believes (the gospel that Jesus is Lord),
4. embodies that witness even to the point of death (as does a martyr), and
5. has hearers or observers render decisions on the basis of the witness's witness.

Paul was such a witness, and the pastor today is to be such a witness. The pastor's experience of Christ in conversion—from "what I was to what I now am"—becomes an opportunity for the pastor to announce the story about Christ. The pastor embodies that story in how she lives, how she talks, and how she conducts herself throughout the day. On the basis of this embodied witness the pastor can then call others to turn to Christ and find redemption in Christ. The pastor's story is not the story but a witness to the story, and that story is Christ.

7

A Culture of World Subversion

Pastors do not always tell the whole truth. Some carry on ministry with a subtle fear of losing their jobs, so they mute their subversions. One pastor recently explained that he and the leadership wanted to guide their church away from such strong political affiliation and into a kingdom-centered life. He admitted mistakes along the way that had almost derailed the process. He said now he has to be extra vigilant about any language that sounds like he's guiding them away from their political and statist orientations. What this pastor knows is that sometimes the pastor has to subvert if nurturing Christoformity is the task. Eugene Peterson once explained his subversive pastoral task in these words:

> Most of the individuals in this amalgam [in his congregation] suppose that the goals they have for themselves and the goals God has for them are the same. It is the oldest religious mistake: refusing to countenance any real difference between God and us, imagining God to be a vague extrapolation of our own desires, and then hiring a priest to manage the affairs between self and the extrapolation. And I, one of the priests they hired, am having none of it.
>
> But if I'm not willing to help them become what they want to be, what am I doing taking their pay? I am being subversive. I am undermining the kingdom of self and establishing the kingdom of God. I am helping them to become what God wants them to be, using the methods of subversion.

Surely this is deceptive, I mutter to myself. But I read on, and he offers this response to my mutterings about deception: "Not exactly, for I'm not misrepresenting myself. I'm simply taking my words and acts at a level of seriousness that would throw them into a state of catatonic disbelief if they ever knew."[1] My experience with many pastors is that this is exactly how they understand their vocation, and it is the intent of their craft: to subvert worldliness in the congregation. As James Thompson gently pressed this point, "Ministry becomes not the clarification of the congregation's own values but the transforming of its values through the Christian message."[2]

The apostle Peter, facing churches of Asia Minor that are facing persecution as he is facing it himself, looks to Christ and the cross for his paradigm, and he subverts worldliness in doing so. His words ring the bell to start this chapter: "For to this you have been called, because Christ also suffered for you, leaving you an example, so that you should follow in his steps. 'He committed no sin, and no deceit was found in his mouth.' When he was abused, he did not return abuse; when he suffered, he did not threaten; but he entrusted himself to the one who judges justly" (1 Pet. 2:21–23). What Peter, who played a cowardly role in the front seat at The Event itself, remembered was how Jesus responded to his assailants. He seemed not aloof but above and beyond their accusations. The Gospel stories themselves confirm Peter's words. In Gethsemane one of the disciples swung a sword with piercing accuracy and cut off the ear of a Roman soldier. The Synoptic Evangelists conspire together to hide his identity, but John lets us in on the secret—it was Peter (compare Luke 22:50 with John 18:10). Jesus's words at that very moment illustrate what Peter meant when he wrote, "When he was abused, he did not return abuse." Here's what Jesus says in John: "Put your sword back into its sheath. Am I not to drink the cup that the Father has given me?" (18:11). Over and over in the Gospels Jesus responds to threats by turning the other cheek. It was Jesus who said his mission was to give himself for others, and it was therefore the same mission for his followers (Mark 10:35–45).

From Jesus the apostles all learned that the way of Jesus was the cross, and that meant nonretaliation as well as redemptive suffering. What they learned, to quote Craig Hill, was "everything exactly backwards."[3] I will avoid at this point a disquisition on pacifism in the

Christian tradition and instead shift to the topic of how the apostle Paul responded to accusations in a world-subverting way.[4] Where to begin? In nearly every letter Paul writes there are either direct accusations against him or at least hints of probable-to-possible accusations that we can tease out. Some must have told the Galatians that Paul was still preaching circumcision, and Paul wishes they'd just castrate themselves (Gal. 5:11–12). At Thessalonica he must have been accused of trickery (1 Thess. 2:3), but it's in his volatile relationship with the Corinthians that the accusations come to the surface most completely and clearly.[5]

Pastor Paul and Verbal Crucifixion

If high-status Corinthians were Paul's critics in Corinth—and they were—then 2 Corinthians 10–13[6] is the text that reveals the substance of their criticisms, or at least Paul's caricature of those criticisms.[7] One may summarize Paul's problems with Corinth in this way: after his first visit, there was a rather sudden incursion or development of local opposition to Paul's message and manner of ministry, spearheaded by some visiting teachers who formed a front of competition for the Corinthian congregants.[8] What was the big issue? Bruce Winter sums up the alliance against Paul as *Romanitas*—that is, the way of the Romans was infecting the Corinthians, and this Romanization was at odds with Paul's way of the cross.[9] I agree and will begin with that general picture.[10] For Paul the pastor, his challenge was to subvert *Romanitas* by nurturing Christoformity.

The alliance against him saw things differently, and we find a record of their specific problems with Paul in 2 Corinthians 10–13. If you read those chapters as a mirror of what his opponents were saying, you will be ushered into a Corinthian house church to hear the common complaints about Paul. Here are some of the major criticisms, all in Paul's own terms:

10:1: "I who am humble when face to face with you, but bold toward you when I am away!" (see also 13:10a).

10:2: ". . . those who think we are acting according to human standards."

10:7: "Do you decide on the basis of appearance?" (my translation).

10:9–10: "I do not want to seem as though I am trying to frighten you with my letters. For they say, 'His letters are weighty and strong, but his bodily presence is weak, and his speech contemptible.'"

10:14: "Boasting," which is about publicly claiming one's honor and status[11] (see more below).

10:15: "We do not boast beyond limits, that is, in the labors of others" (cf. 12:1).

11:5–6: "Think that I am not in the least inferior to these super-apostles. I may be untrained in speech, but not in knowledge; certainly in every way and in all things we have made this evident to you."

11:7–8: "Did I commit a sin by humbling myself so that you might be exalted, because I proclaimed God's good news to you free of charge? I robbed other churches by accepting support from them in order to serve you."

11:11: "Because I do not love you? God knows I do!"

11:12–13: "And what I do I will also continue to do, in order to deny an opportunity to those who want an opportunity to be recognized as our equals in what they boast about. For such boasters are false apostles, deceitful workers, disguising themselves as apostles of Christ."

11:20–21a: "For you put up with it when someone makes slaves of you, or preys upon you, or takes advantage of you, or puts on airs, or gives you a slap in the face. To my shame, I must say, we were too weak for that!"

11:21b–23a: "But whatever anyone dares to boast of—I am speaking as a fool—I also dare to boast of that. Are they Hebrews? So am I. Are they Israelites? So am I. Are they descendants of Abraham? So am I. Are they ministers of Christ?"

12:11: "For I am not at all inferior to these super-apostles, even though I am nothing." (They accuse him of being "nothing.")

12:12: "The signs of a true apostle were performed among you with utmost patience, signs and wonders and mighty works."

12:13–14: "How have you been worse off than the other churches, except that I myself did not burden you? Forgive me this wrong!

... And I will not be a burden, because I do not want what is yours but you; for children ought not to lay up for their parents, but parents for their children."

12:15b–18: "If I love you more, am I to be loved less? Let it be assumed that I did not burden you. Nevertheless (you say) since I was crafty, I took you in by deceit. Did I take advantage of you through any of those whom I sent to you? I urged Titus to go, and sent the brother with him. Titus did not take advantage of you, did he? Did we not conduct ourselves with the same spirit? Did we not take the same steps?"

13:3: ". . . since you desire proof that Christ is speaking in me."

Is Paul exaggerating or embellishing? To ape his words, "Much in every way." The accumulation of accusations, some on the mark and some embellished, creates the opportunity for the Corinthians to experience Paul's emotional state and how he wants them to respond. Very few pastors have weathered such an attack, no one wants this kind of attack, most of us would run from this attack, and all but a slim minority would at least call into question their calling to ministry if they suffered such attacks. What we have here is nothing less than verbal crucifixion. They targeted the core of his being as an apostle and as a minister, his gifts, his physical appearance, and his integrity in dealing with money.

One of course wonders how pastors make it, how they weather the criticisms, how they respond with any kind of grace and mercy to their critics. One can't help but wonder how, when faced with such evaluations, a minister can go on without getting burned out or calling it quits to do something else. Ellen Davis once preached an ordination service in which she said:

Being a priest is not a matter of winning victories for God. Countless stories, movies, television, and now video games have burned into our imaginations a certain heroic plot: the brave adventurer sent forth on a Mission Impossible, and eventually winning against all odds. Yet this is not, and never can be, the pattern of Christian ministry, for the simple reason that it is not the pattern of the gospel—which, as you know, is all about human defeat, the shattering of human hope, the excruciatingly painful disappointment of human desires . . . and after all that, in spite of all that, even through all that, God's victory becomes perceptible. That is why being a priest is such a lousy job for an incurable optimist, because disappointment is so fundamentally built into the job.[12]

She's right: failure and disappointment and criticism are written into the job description of pastor. You, pastor friend, have a friend in Paul.

How did Paul respond to this verbal crucifixion? Again, "Much in every way!" But before going there I want to dig a bit more into the world of his opponents. Their world, I will show, was Paul's worldliness.

The World: Roman Ambition and Status in Corinth

Everywhere Rome went, its culture went, and a singular mark of Roman culture was the insatiable quest by upper-class males (especially) to climb the social ladder to be honored, often with a monument or statue, for their accomplishments.[13] Historians of the ancient world as well as scholars of contemporary cultures often describe such societies as honor-shame cultures.[14] Honor is both one's perception of one's own status and simultaneously (and more importantly) affirmation by one's peers or important others. Honor thus becomes public verdict. It also becomes intoxicating. In another context, the famous novelist Gore Vidal said, "Glory is a drug more addictive than any others."[15] That drug was abundantly available in the Roman Empire.

Rome remains the ultimate version of a status-conscious society, and, while colonies of Rome were not the same as cities in the empire, the organization of many of the cities in which Paul ministered is strikingly similar. Furthermore, the Roman and Greek models of leadership had structural impacts on more local organizations and associations and synagogues. What the upper class did, the others imitated. Hence, those Corinthians who were noble of birth, generous with wealth, courageous in battle, capacious in persuasive powers in public speaking, or virtuous—and therefore enhanced the reputation and safety of the colony—could pursue an ascent up the *cursus honorum*, the path to public honor and glory, and were often rewarded for their efforts and benefactions. This path was competitive to the core, and once there, one marked one's status in what one wore, in one's occupation, in where one sat at public events and banquets, and how one got along in the legal system.[16] The actual *cursus honorum* was available to very few, but it became systemic to all of society, for each of the various associations and clubs and subcultures, including the slaves in a household, adopted a system of honor and shame.

Quest for Honor in the Church of Corinth

This path of competition for honor both shaped Corinthian public life and infected the Christian church, and it is not an overstatement to say the *cursus honorum* shaped at least some, if not most, of the accusations against Paul. Paul seemed intent on undermining the *cursus honorum*—the path to honor—with what Joseph Hellerman has called *cursus pudorum*, the path to shame or degradation![17] David Starling, New Testament lecturer at Morling College in Sydney, calls the quest for honor in the house churches of Corinth the "Corinthianization" of leadership.[18] Here is his definition, which summarizes what this section is about: "The 'Corinthianization' of leadership is the uncritical absorption and imitation of the mindset and power-structures of the surrounding culture—particularly the kind of mindset and power-structures that were prominent and influential in first-century Roman Corinth."[19] For the Corinthians status mattered, which is why Paul had to say—with his eyes on the ignoble and the noble at the same time— "Consider your own call, brothers and sisters: not many of you were wise by human standards, not many were powerful, not many were of noble birth" (1 Cor. 1:26).[20] He says it this way because some in the church were people of status (Erastus, Gaius, Crispus, Stephanus), and they had a lopsided influence on the church culture, but the majority in the churches of Corinth were not people of status. With his eyes on both, Paul reminds the lowly that they matter and the high-status folks that he's got his eye on them! But the culture being formed in the churches of Corinth was closer to Rome than to Paul.

Boasting and Status

If the quest for honor marked the Roman way, boasting about it was the inevitable implication. Not only was it acceptable to boast; it was required to boast of oneself to establish credentials. I want to labor this point through three rather complete examples because boasting has to be seen for what it was, and Paul's response, therefore, for what it was.

The Boasts of Augustus

Caesar Augustus, a military commander of some three hundred thousand troops with thousands more in his navy and praetorian guard, near the end of his life wrote up, in effect, his own narrative of accomplishments, called *Res Gestae Divi Augusti* (the achievements of the deified Augustus).[21] His record of his own accomplishments focuses on military conquests, charity for Romans, and the buildings he has constructed.[22]

> Twice I have celebrated triumphal ovations and three times I have driven triumphal chariots and I have been hailed twenty-one times as victorious general, although the senate voted me more triumphs, from all of which I abstained. I deposited the laurel from my *fasces* in the Capitoline temple, in fulfillment of the vows which I had taken in each war. On account of affairs successfully accomplished by land and sea by me or through my deputies under my auspices the senate fifty-five times decreed that thanksgiving should be offered to the immortal gods. Moreover the days during which thanksgiving has been offered by decree of the senate have amounted to 890. In my triumphs nine kings or kings' children have been led in front of my chariot. I had been consul thirteen times at the time of writing, and I was the holder of tribunician power thirty-seven times [as of AD 14]. (4.1–4)

You get the impression, but what must be seen here is that this form of self-promotion is expected. Augustus nurtured a status and boasting culture, the Corinthians were for it, and Paul was against it.

The Boasts of Josephus

Not just emperors boasted. Jewish priest, scholar, and historian Josephus begins his own autobiography with boasting: "My family is no ignoble one, tracing its descent pedigree far back to priestly ancestors. Different races base their claim to nobility on various grounds; with us a connexion with the priesthood is the hallmark of an illustrious line. Not only, however, were my ancestors priests, but they belonged to the first of the twenty-four courses—a peculiar distinction—and to the most eminent of its constituent clans. Moreover, on my mother's side I am of royal blood" (*The Life* 1–2). He continues: "Brought up with Matthias, my own brother by both parents, I made great progress in my education, gaining a reputation for an excellent memory and understanding. While still a mere boy, about fourteen years old, I won universal applause for my love of letters; insomuch that the chief priests and the leading men of the city used constantly to come to me for precise information on some particular in our ordinances" (*The Life* 89).

Paul and Boasting

The apostle Paul provides us with one way of telling his own story in Philippians 3:4–6: "If anyone else has reason to be confident in the flesh, I have more: circumcised on the eighth day, a member of the people of Israel, of the tribe of Benjamin, a Hebrew born of Hebrews; as to the law, a Pharisee; as to zeal, a persecutor of the church; as to righteousness under the law, blameless." That he subverts this story in the verses that follow is not the point, because we catch a glimpse of Paul's former boasting in these verses. The influential, wealthy, and powerful in the house churches of Corinth developed a patronage or party system of allegiance and zeal shored up by boasting, seen most noticeably in 1 Corinthians 1:12: "What I mean is that each of you says, 'I belong to Paul,' or 'I belong to Apollos,' or 'I belong to Cephas,' or 'I belong to Christ.'" What we see here is an example of personality cults.[23] To make one's way up the *cursus honorum* in the Roman world, one became an adherent of someone with status. So, what mattered most to those secular leaders in the Corinthian church was a person's status, not a person's holiness, love, wisdom, or faithfulness to the gospel. Paul's accusation is worldliness or fleshliness: "For as long as there is jealousy and quarreling among you, are you not of the flesh, and behaving according to human inclinations? For when one says, 'I belong to Paul,' and another, 'I belong to Apollos,' are you not merely human?" (1 Cor. 3:3–4). What mattered to them was their worldly *wisdom*, their strength of status, their honor, and their ability to boast about each (4:10). What mattered to Paul was that their wisdom was *worldly*.

The problem for the Corinthians was that Paul did not fit into their model of boasting about status, achievement, and honor. How did Paul respond to their desire for Paul to fit in? The apostle's strategy was to surrender to them, to turn leadership upside down, and to form a theology of leadership rooted in the life of Jesus, the cross, and the resurrection-ascension.[24] That is, his theology of how to lead in the church was *bio*-form, *cruci*-form, and *anastasi*-form. In other words, Paul denounced Roman power systems and offered Christoform leadership. Paul's response was nothing less than subversion of their world.[25]

The Cruciform Pastor Responds to Corinthian Worldliness

Many leaders fear that if they give in, if they humble themselves before a criticism, and if they don't live up to expectations, their authority, their influence, and their ministry will be diminished. Paul did not agree with that theory of leadership. Paul took the leadership marks of the Corinthians—wealth, status, eloquence, power, birth lineage, patronage—and subverted them.[26] But he subverted in a Christoform manner. As Andrew Clarke concluded, "Much of Paul's response to the Corinthians, therefore, effectively yields ground to those Corinthians who considered that Paul did not cut a fine figure of leadership according to the much lauded, standard measures of Corinthian society."[27] I completely agree.

Take the matter of personality cults (1 Cor. 1:26–31; 3:18–23; 4:6–7). Paul will have none of this patronage and personality-cult system so redolent of the Corinthian expectations for how Paul ought to be acting as an apostle and leader. Or take the matter of message: the Jews want "signs" to prove someone's status, the Greeks want "wisdom" (1:22). What about Paul? The cross! "We proclaim Christ crucified" (v. 23).

1 Corinthians 4: A Subversive Reading

Before we turn to five elements in Paul's subversion of Corinthian worldliness, I offer a subversive reading of 1 Corinthians 4:8–13:

> Already you have all you want! Already you have become rich! Quite apart from us you have become kings! Indeed, I wish that you had become kings, so that we might be kings with you! For I think that God has exhibited us apostles as last of all, as though sentenced to death,

because we have become a spectacle to the world, to angels and to mortals. We are fools for the sake of Christ, but you are wise in Christ. We are weak, but you are strong. You are held in honor, but we in disrepute. To the present hour we are hungry and thirsty, we are poorly clothed and beaten and homeless, and we grow weary from the work of our own hands. When reviled, we bless; when persecuted, we endure; when slandered, we speak kindly. We have become like the rubbish of the world, the dregs of all things, to this very day.

Paul takes their terms and their definitions—namely, status and honor—and with potent irony unmasks them. That is, he says to them, you have "all you want" and you are "rich" and "kings" (v. 8). Then he shows that their terms and definitions make him a loser—which is his glory. The second sentence of verse 8 says, "I wish that you had been kings"—indicating they really had not—"so that we might become kings with you!" Surely he doesn't want the world's honor like that, but he plays right into their language game because he wants to subvert the world's system of honor. Going beyond the biting sarcasm at the end of verse 8, in verse 9 Paul shows the Corinthians what the world's system makes of Paul: "last of all" and "sentenced to death" and a "spectacle to the world, to angels and to mortals." In verse 10 he says that he is assigned to be with the "fools" and be "weak" and "in disrepute" but that the Corinthians, in their worldly system of honor, are "wise" and "strong" and "held in honor." In fact, he doesn't have the necessities of life (v. 11) and so has to work with his hands (v. 12). His gospel work leads to his being "reviled" and "persecuted" and "slandered" (vv. 12–13), but his response is one of blessings and endurance and kind speech (vv. 12–13).

As Gordon Fee says, "How they perceive themselves, masterfully overstated twice (vv. 8 and 10), is undoubtedly the way they think *he* ought to be. But the way he actually is, set forth in the concluding rhetoric (vv. 11–13), is the way *they* all ought to be."[28] The effect of taking their system and playing it to its logical extreme is to subvert their worldly honor system and replace it with Christoformity. The stinger in this passage can be found in the verse before the passage quoted: "What do you have that you did not receive? And if you received it, why do you boast as if it were not a gift?" (4:7). It's all a gift anyway, so their boasting and clamoring for status deny the gift. When gift or grace becomes the reigning idea in the Pauline paradigm of church relations, including leadership, a subversive power is unleashed.[29]

In what follows, then, I will outline five elements of how Paul subverted the worldliness of the Corinthian approach to leadership.

Christ the Paradigm

Paul's image for the Christian and the pastor is Christ, and this can't be emphasized enough. This means Christoformity is to be the culture of the Pauline mission churches, which can't be exaggerated. The image of Christ at work in Paul's communications with Corinth can be found in 1 Corinthians 1:18–25, but I want to focus more narrowly on the famous hymn in Philippians 2:5–11 as the theological paradigm behind Paul's subversion of Corinthian worldliness. Because that hymn is often ripped from its context like a set of Bible verses in a memory packet, I want to cite these verses beginning at verse 1:

> If then there is any encouragement in Christ, any consolation from love, any sharing in the Spirit, any compassion and sympathy, make my joy complete: be of the same mind, having the same love, being in full accord and of one mind. Do nothing from selfish ambition or conceit, but in humility regard others as better than yourselves. Let each of you look not to your own interests, but to the interests of others. Let the same mind be in you that was in Christ Jesus,
>
>> who, though he was in the form of God,
>> did not regard equality with God
>> as something to be exploited,
>> but emptied himself,
>> taking the form of a slave,
>> being born in human likeness.
>> And being found in human form,
>> he humbled himself
>> and became obedient to the point of death—
>> even death on a cross.
>>
>> Therefore God also highly exalted him
>> and gave him the name
>> that is above every name,

> so that at the name of Jesus
> every knee should bend,
> in heaven and on earth and under the earth,
> and every tongue should confess
> that Jesus Christ is Lord,
> to the glory of God the Father.

Paul's response to their verbal crucifixion of him boggled their minds. Why? Because he did not defend himself, he did not assert his honor, and he did not boast. Rather, he degraded himself in order to subvert their worldly system of patronage, eloquence, and honor. Why? Because, as the above lines from Paul reveal, God revealed his power in Christ, and that power was the power of the cross, the power of sacrifice for the sake of others, the power of a path toward a death that led to a resurrection. In the words of Mark Finney, "The cultural lust for upward mobility, greater influence, or higher status in the eyes of the world by changes in circumstances is now to be abandoned for it is ultimately irrelevant."[30] Status was for Paul irrelevant.

Michael Gorman sees cruciformity as the crystallization not only of Christoformity but also of theosis (transformation into Godlikeness).[31] This, Gorman shows, is Paul's "master story,"[32] so much so that when Paul takes the side of the loser in the Corinthian narrative, he is participating in Christ's own narrative. I quote Gorman again: "Paul's apostolic status is most truly and fully exercised, not in throwing his weight around—coercively making use of his power to compel or order others to act in certain ways—or making use of his right to financial support, but in practicing self-giving, Christlike, parental love (1 Thess. 2) or enslaving himself by working with his hands in self-support so as not to be a burden to others (1 Cor. 9)."[33] Amen! Paul's pastoral response to the verbal crucifixion of the Corinthians is to subvert their theory of honor and status by appealing to the ultimate degradation, the crucifixion of Christ, as the model for the Christian life. I move now from Christ as the paradigm to a second element in Paul's subversion of the worldliness at Corinth.

Eloquence

It is hard for those nurtured in a TV—and now internet—culture (where information is constantly available) to perceive the power and significance of public speeches in the ancient world, or to comprehend the attraction of the so-called sophists.[34] The ability to give outstanding public speeches brought honor.[35] A good example is found in Cicero's *Brutus*:

> This is what I wish for my orator: when it is reported that he is going to speak, let every place on the benches be taken, the judges' tribunal full, the clerks busy and obliging in assigning or giving up places, a listening crowd thronging about, the presiding judge erect and attentive; when the speaker rises the whole throng will give a sign for silence, then expressions of assent, frequent applause; laughter when he wills it, or if he wills, tears; so that a mere passerby observing from a distance, though quite ignorant of the case in question, will recognize that he is succeeding and that a Roscius is on the stage. (290)[36]

The audiences for rhetoricians were full participants, including the Athenians when Paul was on the Areopagus and the Corinthians when Paul or Apollos or Peter was speaking. Duane Litfin compiled a list of audience responses from his reading of the last first-century AD orator, Dio Chrysostom, and this is his list: "The audience might cheer and applaud with enthusiasm, or raise an uproar, shouting the speaker down; they might sit, silent and indulgent, or pelt the speaker with stones out of rage; they might listen raptly in awe, or respond with jeering, hissing, derisive laughter or crude jokes. In short, the audience had it in its power to terrify and dominate the speaker if it cared to, a fact that was not lost on speakers."[37] The Corinthians had experienced an unusual diet of good speeches and considered themselves worthy of experiencing only top-level displays of rhetoric. Eloquence was the measure of a man.

But—and this is a big "but"—Paul was not their sort of rhetorician, and the Corinthians let him know. From the list of verbal crucifixions above, I cite again: 2 Corinthians 10:9–10 reads, "I do not want to seem as though I am trying to frighten you with my letters. For they say, 'His letters are weighty and strong, but his bodily presence is weak, and his speech contemptible.'" Or 11:6: "I may be untrained in speech, but not in knowledge." Yet what is Paul's response to these (probably only somewhat accurate) accusations? He gives in, and by giving in, he subverts their rubrics of evaluation:

> When I came to you, brothers and sisters, I did not come proclaiming the mystery of God to you in lofty words or wisdom. For I decided to know nothing among you except Jesus Christ, and him crucified. And I came to you in weakness and in fear and in much trembling. My speech and my proclamation were not with plausible words of wisdom, but with a demonstration of the Spirit and of power, so that your faith might rest not on human wisdom but on the power of God. (1 Cor. 2:1–5)

Furthermore, rather than permitting the Corinthians to provide him with honors and titles for his teaching skills, Paul subverted competitive contests by saying he and Apollos contributed to each other (3:5–15), while Paul saw himself as a *servant* of Christ (4:1), and the term translated as "servant" was hardly an honorific term for the Corinthians! He degrades his eloquence.

Even if we admit that Paul degraded his eloquence, a good reading of any of Paul's letters, not least Philemon, reveals a man who could persuade, which was the very heart of ancient rhetoric.[38] Perhaps in Tarsus or Jerusalem he did not learn the nuances of Greek or Roman rhetoric, but wherever or however he learned it, Paul was a man of persuasion and, at times, of accomplished rhetorical moves (cf. 1 Cor. 4:6a[39]). Yet he degraded himself and his rhetorical skills because he wanted both to subvert the Corinthians' worldly status measurements and to focus on Christ and the cross.

What can we learn here for a Christoform culture? First, that the drive for celebrity through public performance is contrary to Christoformity. Second, it will not wound the pastor to follow Paul in degrading one's status intentionally. Tell them that Andy Stanley's a better preacher; that N. T. Wright's writings are more compelling; tell them you're ordinary and ordinary is OK because God loves the ordinary too. Tell them that your sermons get lots of steam from scholars you often don't mention and that you don't know it all. There is a lot of competition today among preachers and authors, and it's a fools game to try to win it. Be faithful; forget being great.

Now to another element of Paul's subversion of their worldliness.

Manual Labor

Paul's manual labor was an intentional laying aside of his social and cultural capital[40] and at the same time an intentional insult of the Corinthian leaders.[41] Combined, as it was, with refusal of support from Corinth alongside acceptance of support from Philippi, his manual labor aggravated that insult deeply.[42] Even if a rabbi was (later) expected to practice a trade alongside Torah study (m. Avot 2:2; 4:5–7), such was clearly not the custom among Roman and Greek philosophers and teachers. Manual labor was below the status of a teacher. Cicero states our concern:

> Now in regard to trades and other means of livelihood, which ones are to be considered becoming to a gentleman and which ones are vulgar. . . . Unbecoming to a gentleman, too, and vulgar are the means of livelihood of all hired workmen whom we pay for mere manual labour, not for artistic skill; for in their case the very wage they receive is a pledge of their slavery. . . . And all mechanics [*opifices*] are engaged in vulgar trades; *for no workshop can have anything liberal about it.* . . .
>
> But the professions in which either a higher degree of intelligence is required or from which no small benefit to society is derived—medicine and architecture, for example, and *teaching*—these are proper for those whose social position they become. (*On Duties* 1.150–51; italics added)

For a teacher there were a few acceptable forms of income: (1) charge fees for teaching; (2) dwell in the household of someone with status; or even, as with the Cynics especially, (3) beg. But what was not acceptable to those with status was Paul's choice: manual labor.[43]

Did Paul learn the degraded status of this kind of work in Tarsus? In Dio Chrysostom's *Second Tarsic Discourse* (34.21–23) the nonstatus of "linen workers" (*linourgoi*) is discussed. Dio pleads the case of making the linen workers "citizens" (*politai*), though the reputation he is fighting is that the linen workers are known to be "useless rabble." If one connects—and this is more than reasonable—the status of linen workers with that of the Tarsian Paul as a tentmaker (*skēnopoios*, Acts 18:3), one might put some skin on the kind of work Paul chose. He chose something unworthy of citizenship and associated with rabble-rousers. Paul could not have but known the sort of associations made with his manual labor.

Paul chose to degrade his status and to demonstrate to the Corinthians Christoformity. Here are the statements by Paul about his manual labor:

> You remember our labor and toil, brothers and sisters; we worked night and day, so that we might not burden any of you while we proclaimed to you the gospel of God (1 Thess. 2:9).
>
> And we grow weary from the work of our own hands. When reviled, we bless; when persecuted, we endure (1 Cor. 4:12).
>
> Or is it only Barnabas and I who have no right to refrain from working for a living? (9:6).
>
> Here I am, ready to come to you this third time. And I will not be a burden, because I do not want what is yours but you; for children ought not to lay up for their parents, but parents for their children (2 Cor. 12:14).

Add Acts 18:3; 20:34; and probably 28:30, too, and you have abundant evidence that in his Aegean mission and beyond, Paul worked manually while he was on mission for the gospel.

Here's what we have then: Paul was a teacher and that meant Paul had a calling that made him a man of status and honor for the Corinthians. But Paul chose not to indwell status because it was worldly. On one occasion, Paul frames it all in terms of rights and a choice to deny those rights:

> Am I not free? Am I not an apostle? Have I not seen Jesus our Lord? Are you not my work in the Lord? If I am not an apostle to others, at least I am to you; for you are the seal of my apostleship in the Lord. This is my defense to those who would examine me. Do we not have the right to our food and drink? Do we not have the right to be accompanied by a believing wife, as do the other apostles and the brothers of the Lord and Cephas? Or is it only Barnabas and I who have no right to refrain from working for a living? (1 Cor. 9:1–6; cf. v. 12)

He attaches a passage in the Torah that can be read as authorizing support for the rights of a teacher (1 Cor. 9:8–11). But Paul has eschewed his right to "food and drink." Turning the language of the

Corinthians on its head, Paul chooses to boast in his lack of support and therefore in his lack of being dependent or associated with status (vv. 12–17). That is, "What then is my reward? Just this: that in my proclamation I may make the gospel free of charge, so as not to make full use of my rights in the gospel" (v. 18). Turning language again on its head, Paul subverts the Corinthians' status-crazed world: "For though I am free with respect to all, I have made myself a slave to all, so that I might win more of them" (v. 19). He chooses to be a "slave" instead of being "free."[44]

In choosing not to claim rights, in choosing not to live as a free man, and in choosing to work with his hands in a degraded occupation and thus to be a slave to the gospel, Paul subverted the status-and-honor approach of the Corinthians. For sure, he had to explain himself, and his explanations may not have convinced the Corinthians, but what his explanation did was show them that Christoformity pervaded every element of his life. One must consider his manual labor as an embodied parable of the cross of Christ.

That cross also led him to choose titles and images for his calling as another element of subverting the worldliness at Corinth.

Titles and Images

In a world where titles mattered (e.g., Matt. 23:8–10) and one's pecking order on the ladder of status determined how one was spoken to by others, the apostle Paul blew apart such titles. If one's image was shaped by one's title, Paul knocked his own image off its pedestal.[45] Speaking of pedestals, Roman colonies such as Corinth paved the *cursus honorum* with titles that brought a man honor, titles such as those of members of the council of decurions, magistrates or justices, aediles, council members, curators of provisions, quaestors, and the highly regarded organizers of public games. The people of Corinth knew who was who and who did what in the colony, and those in these positions knew they were somebody. Paul envisioned his churches having leaders, *proistēmi* being one of the terms for "to lead" (Rom. 12:8; 1 Thess. 5:12; 1 Tim. 3:4, 5, 12; 5:17; translated as "devote oneself" in Titus 3:8, 14). While gifts and Spirit-prompted ministries run right through the Pauline mission, offices are clearly present in Philippians 1:1 (bishops, deacons) and even more on display in 1 Timothy 3:1–13 and Titus 1:5–9. [46] Alongside these are Paul's pet names for his associates, terms such as *coworkers* and *servants*. Thus, Paul's churches have leaders, they have some kind of hierarchy, he is not averse to titles, but Paul spins around and walks in another direction when it comes to which titles and images he chose for leadership.[47]

There is no reason to discuss at length each of these texts and Paul's in-your-face degrading of titles, but at least the following italicized terms scream for attention as they confront the Corinthians and their worldliness:[48]

"We have become like the *rubbish* of the world, the *dregs* of all things, to this very day" (1 Cor. 4:13).

"But thanks be to God, who always leads us as *captives* in Christ's triumphal procession" (2 Cor. 2:14 NIV).

Paul routinely uses *weakness*, as in 1 Corinthians 2:3, "I came to you in weakness," or 2 Corinthians 11:30's "If I must boast, I will boast of the things that show my weakness" (cf. 12:5, 9–10). Notice how christological this can be for Paul: "For . . . he [Christ] was crucified in weakness, yet he lives by God's power. Likewise, we are weak in him, yet by God's power we will live with him in our dealing with you" (13:4).

"For God's *foolishness* is wiser than human wisdom, and God's weakness is stronger than human strength" (1 Cor. 1:25). "We are *fools* for the sake of Christ, but you are wise in Christ" (4:10). Also, "For the wisdom of this world is *foolishness* with God" (3:19).

"God chose what is *low and despised in the world*, things that are not, to reduce to nothing things that are" (1 Cor. 1:28).

The traditional interpretation of *clay jars* in 2 Corinthians 4:7 is the dramatic contrast of the "treasure" of Christ and the gospel in the utter frailty and destructibility of humans.

Paul refers to Christians as performing menial tasks with words such as *servants* (1 Cor. 3:5), *farming* (3:6), *artisan builder* (3:10).

Paul sees himself as both a *father*[49] (1 Cor. 4:14–17; 2 Cor. 6:13; 12:14–15) and *mother* (1 Cor. 3:1–2; Gal. 4:19; 1 Thess. 2:7). It might be said that it is somewhat condescending for Paul to see himself in maternal terms.[50]

In a world caught up in status, where the Corinthians are verbally crucifying him because of his refusal to play their game of honor, the apostle Paul degrades his titles to press the status question one more time. This assault on titles and images is an intentional provocation to make clear his rejection of their worldly status system.

What to do? It will not hurt a pastor to announce that she is first a Christian, first a disciple, first a follower of Jesus, and only second a pastor in a church. It won't hurt to announce that a pastor is a servant, a slave, a captive, and rubbish when it comes to status in our world. I could go on but need not. Pastors can fill in the blank spaces and complete the paragraph on their own in their own way. To keep this from winding into nonsense, I do not mean by this that pastors ought not to be respected, be respectful, and be nurturers of leadership. Rather, I'm chasing down one element of leadership for Paul: his desire to degrade the status system of the world. One way he did that was to degrade his titles. We may not worry so much about titles, but we do need to worry about worldliness.

Perspectives

Light from Paul's subversiveness can now be directed at what he means in 2 Corinthians 5:16: "From now on, therefore, *we regard no one from a human point of view*; even though we once knew Christ from a human point of view, we know him no longer in that way." At least one dimension of a "human point of view" is the status- and honor-consciousness of the Roman *cursus honorum*, which Paul is rejecting. Paul at one time—prior to his conversion—saw the crucifixion of Christ as a demonstration that Jesus the Galilean lacked status, but once he came to know the Messiah in the power of his resurrection, that perspective on Christ was undone. The same conversion of perspective occurred for Paul with respect to all other humans: what mattered was not the world's perspective but Christ's.

Furthermore, Paul counters the Corinthians' boasting by boasting about his "losses." If they boast in their status, their honors, and their achievements, Paul can boast too. He opens with common boasting:

"But whatever anyone dares to boast of—I am speaking as a fool—I also dare to boast of that. Are they Hebrews? So am I. Are they Israelites? So am I. Are they descendants of Abraham? So am I. Are they ministers of Christ?" (2 Cor. 11:21–23a). But then in 11:23b–33 he subverts common boasting with counter-boasting. The problem for the Corinthians was that Paul had things exactly backward, and it was precisely this backwardness that opened up the door for them to see the Christoformity embodied in Paul's own ministry.

Finally, everything in ministry needs to point to Christ and not to leaders. The personality cult of Corinth was very much like our pastor-as-celebrity culture, but Paul will have none of it: "So let no one boast about human leaders. For all things are yours, whether Paul or Apollos or Cephas or the world or life or death or the present or the future—all belong to you, and you belong to Christ, and Christ belongs to God" (1 Cor. 3:21–23). Any ministry or leadership that does not lead through the Spirit to Christ to the glory of the Father subverts the gospel. Any ministry that subverts human celebrity and status for the glory of the Crucified One is genuine ministry.

Conclusion

In the preface to the 1961 edition of *The Screwtape Letters*, C. S. Lewis surmised that "we must picture Hell as a state where everyone is perpetually concerned about his own dignity and advancement, where everyone has a grievance, and where everyone lives the deadly serious passions of envy, self-importance, and resentment."[51] He could have been describing Corinth, Ephesus, Rome, or even—in its more common elements—Jerusalem. He is describing some pastors, some churches, plenty of businesses and universities. The game of status is played best by the ambitious and envious and jealous, the latter two terms not meaning the same thing.

Once I was in a conversation on the phone with a well-known Roman Catholic theologian and author of many books. He began to reflect on where he had come from, how, when he was a teen, he was in trouble and his future looking at best dim, and without one second of gloating or boasting, he described what he had accomplished—earned a seminary degree and a PhD, published writing, became director of a program at his school, and traveled all over the world, including a few private sessions with a pope. With his accomplishments now on the table he could say what he wanted to say all along: "And I'm nothing but a jackass."

Exactly.

And very Pauline. Why? Because this theologian was devaluing what so many value—his accomplishments—and boasting in nothing less than what God was doing through him, a most unworthy candidate for preaching the gospel.

What Paul does with the Corinthians is not a recipe for all church conflicts. Paul is a penetrating embodiment of Christoformity in a specific situation. More generally, the pastor's responsibility is to perceive where worldliness lurks in our churches and to subvert it with nothing less than the cross of Christ. What drew Paul's ire was a party spirit, or divisiveness; a personality-cult attachment that promoted people into celebrities; valuing people on the basis of their location on the ladder of social scaling or their appropriation of worldly wisdom; and the use and abuse of status and power and wealth and wisdom to diminish radical Christoformity. When the life of Christ—from equality with God to the cross and back to the throne room—becomes our model, we nurture Christoformity.

8

A Culture of Wisdom

When I wrote to a few friends to ask what they had read on Paul as a sage—that is, Paul's pastoral practice of wisdom—there was an odd sort of silence.[1] *Really, no one has written on this topic?*, I thought. This led to, *Why?* Strange, because Paul was Jewish, and if anything characterizes the Jewish understanding of life, it is wisdom—and not a few books in the Bible and what we call Apocrypha and Pseudepigrapha are devoted to wisdom. Even more, many today would say wisdom pervades the whole of the Old Testament, not just those books classified as Wisdom literature.

Why is the Wisdom literature in the Old Testament so widely ignored in the church, and why do so few Pauline scholars address wisdom? Let's push harder: Why is wisdom so little valued in our churches today? One word, and an inelegant one at that: juvenilization.

Juvenilization

Thomas Bergler, in a recent set of studies, has exposed the "juvenilization" or "youthicization" of church culture in the US.[2] I quote Bergler to put the issue on the table with a thump: "Beginning in the 1930s and 1940s, three factors combined to create the juvenilization

of American Christianity." What are these three factors? "First, new
and more powerful youth cultures created distance between adults and
adolescents." Then, second, "Christian adults adapted the faith to
adolescent tastes. As a result of these first two factors, the stereotypical
youth group that combines fun and games with a brief, entertaining
religious message was born." The result? He concludes with a third:
"The journey to adulthood became longer and more confusing, with
maturity now just one among many options." It's one thing to see
juvenilization of the faith among our youth; it's another to see it take
over church culture, and this is what we need to emphasize in a study of
wisdom and the pastor: "The result was juvenilization: the process by
which the religious beliefs, practices, and developmental characteristics
of adolescents *become accepted—or even celebrated—as appropriate
for Christians of all ages.*"[3]

Juvenilization emerges from what Charles Taylor calls "authenticity"[4] and produces what Christian Smith and Melinda Lundquist
Denton call "moralistic therapeutic deism."[5] Ministry in an age of
authenticity and youthfulness requires a special sensitivity.[6] However,
the focus in this chapter is not on that kind of ministry but on the
comparison of authenticity/juvenilization with a wisdom culture. In
her elegant essay "Surprised by Wisdom," Ellen Davis observes that
"we are in a wisdom crisis."[7] I wonder, too, whether this approach
of making everything palatable for the youth isn't part of making us
consumerists. Susan Neiman, in her brilliant book called *Why Grow
Up?*, cuts to the core of what happens when this problem takes root in
our churches: "When consuming goods rather than working becomes
the focus of our culture, we have created (or acquiesced in) a society
of permanent adolescents."[8]

People today care less about growing up or gaining wisdom and
far more about staying young, maintaining relevancy, and dressing according to the latest youth fad. No one wants to get old and weak and
die, but wanting to remain a teenager is a sign of juvenilization and
not wisdom. Any number of observations could be made, but I want
to focus in this chapter on but one: a wisdom culture is necessarily diminished when a youth culture becomes the dominant culture. If how
the young behave is what it means to be "with it," then how the gray
hairs live is "not with it." The issue, I must insist, is not that a single

person or church has become juvenile. The issue is that juvenility has infected our culture—which reminds me of a funny observation by Flannery O'Connor, who raised peacocks. She once said, "The habits of any peachicken left to himself would hardly be noticeable, but multiplied by forty, they become a situation."[9] What we've got in the church today, to use her words, is a "situation."

I have no desire to diminish the faith vibrancy of America's youth, which I often admire, nor do I want to point fingers at youth leaders, whom Bergler is not tossing under the bus, nor am I. No, I want to point to the lack of leadership by the gray hairs when the moment arrived (and continues to arrive). The issue here is the lack of interest *in* and therefore a lack *of* a wisdom culture in the church. In the world of the Bible—Jewish, Greek, Roman—when you needed insight, you went to the elders; in our world, we consult the latest sociological study, and we often also worry if it will be relevant. This is the crisis Ellen Davis is talking about, and it is also a problem of a church not maturing enough to know what it got from the church in its past. In that wonderful cowritten book by father Jim and son Brian Doyle, the son says this of his parents: "Like most children, I loved my parents without qualification until I was a teenager, when I began to hate them for the boundaries they placed about me; and then I woke up from those years, at about age nineteen, I began again to love them without qualification but also with a deepening sense of the thousand ways in which they had given their lives for me, to me."[10] That's a young man, a juvenile, growing into wisdom.

Pastors are called to nurture Christoformity in their congregations, and Christoformity is wisdom, and the pastor is called, then, to nurture a culture of wisdom. Before we get to Paul and wisdom, we need a firm grip on wisdom, because if we want to nurture a culture of wisdom, we need to know what it is.

Wisdom in the Old Testament: Paul's Inheritance[11]

We will dip into four themes, each of which comes into play in Paul's own approach to wise pastoral theology. It would be wise to begin with definitions of *wisdom* (Hebrew *hokmah* and Greek *sophia*), because definitions seek to get to the bottom of ideas and terms.[12]

Definition

Here is my favorite: Old Testament professor and eloquent commentator Ellen Davis says *wisdom* is "living in the world in such a way that God, and God's intentions for the world, are acknowledged in all that we do." This, as she wisely points out, is for all: "The fruit of wisdom, a well-ordered life and a peaceful mind, results not from a high IQ but from a disposition of the heart that the sages (wisdom teachers) of Israel most often called 'fear of the LORD.'" [13] One of my favorite lines of hers, a wise one indeed, is this: "The sages of Israel teach that those who would be wise must aim, not at power, but at goodness." [14] For a brief definition, I offer this: wisdom is living in God's world in God's way.

Wisdom is not the same as education. Wisdom, we will show below, requires emulation and reception out of a relationship with a sage, and this simply cannot be equated with education. Our cultural crisis is exacerbated because we believe education is redemptive. In his wonderful book on Alexis de Tocqueville, Joseph Epstein said, "In our own day, of course, this notion of the redemptive power of education retains great currency; enough education will root out evil, stimulate goodness, show the way, making life better for one and all. Educate, educate, educate—and sweetness and light will follow." [15] Education offers what to know; wisdom offers an acceptable life before God.

Wisdom as Conservative

Wisdom, it is true, is essentially conservative with respect to tradition, or at least wisdom is a preservative. But that does not mean wisdom is resistant to change, even though resistance to change is conservatism's problem. In fact, conservatism is a theory of change—to be a sure, a theory of organic change but not a theory of nonchange. [16] The conservative seeks to preserve the best wisdom of the past and to let that wisdom guide the present in foresight of the future. Environmentalists are society's best example of wise conservatives. How so? Roger Scruton, my favorite conservative, once said, "Environmentalism is the quintessential conservative cause, the most vivid instance in the world as we know it, of that partnership between the dead, the living and the unborn." [17] Precisely: environmentalists respect the past and long for a consistent future, so they choose now in light of that past and future. American Indians combine environmentalism with reverence, and no one expressed this any more incisively than Willa Cather, in *Death Comes for the Archbishop*: "Father Latour judged that, just as it was the white man's way to assert himself in any landscape, to change it, make it over a little (at least to leave some mark of memorial of his sojourn), it was the Indian's way to pass through a country without disturbing anything; to pass and leave no trace, like fish through the water, or birds through the air."[18] A clear image, to be sure: white man and change, American Indian and conserve the environment. One the fool, the other one wise.

If we return to Bergler's descriptions of juvenilization, we discover that wisdom left the room when adaptation of the gospel to culture entered. Instead of preserving, it focused on innovating. When I think of *conservative*, I think of the famous gospel passage in 1 Corinthians 15:1–8. Why? Here we see Paul conserving the gospel by passing it on from one generation to another. Too, Christian theology has its own wisdom tradition about its very substance. The Latin formula *Quod semper, quod ubique, quod ab omnibus*, "what is believed always, everywhere, by everyone," is a conserving of what is deemed wise. Wisdom conserves and adapts judiciously. However, the tradition of wisdom is not resistant to change, nor does it have an unswerving commitment to the past. As Old Testament scholar Joseph Blenkinsopp defines it, "Tradition may be defined as the aggregate of assumptions, beliefs, practices, and ethos that combine to sustain a sense of continuity in a society."[19] He continues by noting the wisdom tradition's capacity to adapt because it is "a body of knowledge or a cluster of themes transmitted orally or in writing over several generations and subject to adaptation, modification, reinterpretation, and possibly refutation in the course of transmission" and "does not rule out innovation."[20]

Of course, at times the problem is the unwillingness of the gray hairs to adjust to new ways, to accommodate new developments, or to listen to the youth. At other times it is the relentless desire of the youth to change. One could throw one's hands up, like the old pastor in Marilynne Robinson's novel *Home*, in argument with his son, Jack, over change. Jack bursts with anger and swears, and the father says people don't talk like that in the house. Jack apologizes, and the father says,

"No need to be sorry, Jack. Young people want the world to change and old people want it to stay the same. And who is to judge between thee and me?"[21] Sometimes that's about as far as one can get, but the aim in the Christian wisdom tradition is to pursue wisdom when the relation of father and son, gray hairs and youthful hairs, is sound enough to listen and learn. When that happens, change can occur, and it can occur in healthy continuity with the past.

Receptive Reverence

Every discussion about wisdom eventually must pass the test of Proverbs 1:1–7:

> The proverbs of Solomon, son of David, king of Israel:
>   For learning about wisdom and instruction,
>   for understanding words of insight,
>   for gaining instruction in wise dealing,
>   righteousness, justice, and equity;
>   to teach shrewdness to the simple,
>   knowledge and prudence to the young—
>   let the wise also hear and gain in learning,
>   and the discerning acquire skill,
>   to understand a proverb and a figure,
>   the words of the wise and their riddles.
>
> The fear of the LORD is the beginning of knowledge;
>   fools despise wisdom and instruction.

Proverbs does not define wisdom so much as describe it and declare its value. What do we find in this description of wisdom? First, a wise person "gains" instruction, or correction, in wise dealing (1:3a); second, the wise person has the attributes of righteousness, justice, and equity (*tsedeq, mishpat, meshar*; 1:3b); third, the wise person is prudent and has discretion (*ormah, mezimmah*; 1:4; cf. 8:12); and, fourth, the wise person possesses skill to know as well as practice these various attributes (1:5b).[22]

Wisdom is characterized by "receptive reverence."[23] One of the most important terms in wisdom texts is *listen*. So "receptive reverence" has become my summary translation of the Hebrew *laqahath musar haskel* in Proverbs 1:3a: "to take, or receive, or absorb the instruction/correction of insight [or discipline]."[24] Scholars study the ancient context for Israel's wisdom, but here's something I have observed: this hunt for ancient parallels is sometimes not accompanied by a focus on the posture of receptivity by the young man or young woman acquiring wisdom from the wise.[25] More directly, I put it like this: a wise person is receptive, malleable, and submissive in a reverent and respectful manner before the wisdom of their teachers. Which is to say, the sage is wise, and the wise student is receptive to the sage. That is how wisdom works: it works from a sage to a student, from a student to a sage. Wisdom is relational all the way down. It is learned at the feet of one who walks in the tradition, not just one who talks the tradition.

Fear of God

Reverent receptivity, I must emphasize, begins not with observation of nature or with intelligent deductions but with the "fear of YHWH."[26] Receptive reverence makes possible wise observations of nature and the power of learning from experience (6:6–8); receptive reverence involves learning, memorizing, absorbing, and living out the tradition in which one is nurtured (4:1–4; 22:17–21); receptive reverence includes learning from one's mistakes and correction (10:17); and finally, receptive reverence knows it needs to respond to God's Word as revelation—and that is why it all begins with the fear of YHWH (1:7).[27]

It has become customary in wisdom studies to see even biblical wisdom as a secularization of Torah or of the ways of God. That is, wisdom is discerned by all humans as they examine creation and make sense of created orders. However, Longman disagrees, concluding this:

> Let's begin with the obvious. We have seen that the central theme of wisdom repeated over and over again with slight variations and taught in a multitude of ways is "the fear of the Lord is the beginning of wisdom." This is the fundamental lesson of Proverbs, Job, Ecclesiastes, the wisdom psalms, and Deuteronomy.
>
> The fear of the Lord is the beginning of wisdom. Whether beginning is taken temporally or foundationally, the clear point is that unless one fears the Lord, there is no wisdom. And it is the Lord, Yahweh, Israel's deity, not the "common God," who is to be feared.[28]

A life shaped by the fear of YHWH becomes a life of wisdom, a life in which decisions and judgments and discernments organically embody the wisdom of the sages and, like them, bring it to life in new contexts. J. de Waal Dryden complements Ellen Davis's definition (above) and the conclusions we have just drawn about wisdom with his own clear definition of how Scripture can become wisdom: *wisdom* is "a skill of discernment active in moral deliberations to perceive the right course of action by applying general principles within a teleological frame of reference." With this, Dryden points us to the kingdom of God, while also promoting moral progress through the development of habits of virtue.[29]

Paul inherited wisdom from the Bible and its Jewish tradition. Conservation? Yes. Adaptation? Yes. Perhaps revolutionary.

Paul and Wisdom

What then do we mean when we say Paul was a sage or a wise man, and in what does his wisdom consist? What does it mean to say Paul as a pastor was a sage? What does it mean to nurture wisdom in a Christoform culture or to nurture Christoform wisdom?

Wisdom by nature is needed for all of life. Thus one needs wisdom to lead a nation; one needs it to discern the right decision at the right time, and sometimes such wisdom comes to be expressed in a proverb; at other times wisdom is required for a particular skill, as when an artisan has wisdom to work with wood. Since wisdom is needed for all of life, wisdom can be understood as encyclopedic knowledge of nature and creation.[30] We are concerned in this chapter with Paul's pastoral skill at knowing how to live in God's world in God's way and, because he's a pastor and letter writer, what to say to his siblings in Christ. To comprehend Paul as a sage we must first get a grip on Paul's fundamental message. Above, we observed that Jewish wisdom begins with the fear of YHWH. That fear of YHWH was expressed paradigmatically, if not quintessentially, in Torah observance, so that wisdom gets firmly connected to Torah in the Jewish tradition. But the earliest followers of Jesus reframed wisdom from Torah to Christ and Spirit. Hence, for them wisdom becomes Christ; Christ is Wisdom; the crucified and resurrected Jesus is the Wisdom of God. Wisdom is a substance-based discernment. The practice of wisdom is determined by its content, the content for Paul is the gospel, and the gospel reshapes Israel's wisdom into Christoformity.

Nurturing Wisdom as Christ-Wisdom: Paul's Statements

Proverbs emphasizes the fear of YHWH as the beginning of wisdom, and the Jewish scribal tradition turns that more toward Torah observance. The apostle Paul shifts wisdom into Christoformity.

Nothing in Paul's writings expresses how he understands wisdom more clearly than the following statements:

> For the message about the *cross is foolishness* [the opposite of wisdom] to those who are perishing, but to us who are being saved it is the power of God (1 Cor. 1:18).

> For since, in the wisdom of God, the world did not know God through wisdom, God decided, through the foolishness of our proclamation, to save those who believe. For Jews demand signs and Greeks desire wisdom, but we proclaim Christ crucified, a stumbling block to Jews and foolishness to Gentiles, but to those who are the called, both Jews and Greeks, *Christ the power of God and the wisdom of God*. For God's foolishness is wiser than human wisdom, and God's weakness is stronger than human strength (1:21–25).

> He [God] is the source of your life in *Christ Jesus, who became for us wisdom from God*, and righteousness and sanctification and redemption (1:30).

> For I want you to know how much I am struggling for you, and for those in Laodicea, and for all who have not seen me face to face. I want their hearts to be encouraged and united in love, so that they may have all the riches of assured understanding and have the knowledge of God's mystery, that is, *Christ himself, in whom are hidden all the treasures of wisdom and knowledge* (Col. 2:1–3).

God's wisdom is Christ, this wisdom at the practical level is Christoformity, and Christ-as-Wisdom is Paul's pastoral starting point. Wisdom, thus, is not an intellectual structure nor a philosophical pursuit, and wisdom is not reducible to discernment. Wisdom is Christ, and Christian wisdom looks to Christ to perceive what wisdom is.

Wisdom Is a Person

For Paul, Wisdom is Christ. Wisdom is a person. This was not altogether a new idea in Paul's Jewish world, so I will sketch how wisdom was personified in the Jewish wisdom tradition.[31] (1) Wisdom has its origin in God. (2) Wisdom—and here we begin to see personifications—preexisted and played a role in the work of creation. (3) Wisdom is infused in creation, accounting for its coherence and endurance. (4) Wisdom is identified with the divine spirit and is immanent in the world. (5) Wisdom comes to the human world with a distinctive mission: (a) the mission entails personally addressing the world, and (b) Wisdom offers life, sometimes prosperity, and a panoply of other blessings. (6) Wisdom is especially associated with Israel: (a) by divine order Wisdom dwells in Israel, (b) Wisdom can be identified with Torah, and (c) Wisdom was at work in Israel's history. (7) Wisdom, while a gift from God, is simultaneously acquired by disciplined effort (e.g., *musar*).[32] In these ways, then, the Jewish wisdom tradition personified wisdom. When Paul says "Christ is wisdom," he is altogether Jewish, but at the same time he is making a messianic claim for Christ. Hence, Paul takes one step beyond the Jewish personification of Wisdom.

Again, the big idea must be kept in mind: Paul locates this Jewish personification of Wisdom in Christ, so that Christ is himself Wisdom. Wisdom is not merely personified: Wisdom is a person. As both Colossians 1:15–20 and 2:9 also clarify, for Paul the wisdom tradition finds its fulfillment in Christ, and from Christ on, Christian pastoral wisdom begins with Christ.

Wisdom and Spirit

One doesn't acquire wisdom simply by attending a seminary or by reading a great book about wisdom; wisdom is more than knowledge and intellectual growth. Pastoral wisdom in Paul is Spirit prompted, for in his list of Spirit-prompted gifts, we read, "To one is given *through the Spirit* the utterance of wisdom, and to another the utterance of

knowledge *according to the same Spirit*" (1 Cor. 12:8). Paul's understanding of wisdom is thus Pneumacentric too.[33] Wisdom is a gift of
God for which Paul is praying for his churches (Eph. 1:8–9, 17; Col.
1:9, 28). As a gift, it is not something acquired by discipline, no matter
how vital that was in the Jewish wisdom tradition. I want to make this
clear. The Christ-Wisdom of Paul is something God grants to people
through God's Spirit, and hence we will see the Spirit-Wisdom of Paul
in the passages I will now cite. Wisdom is an apocalyptic mystery, "the
mystery that has been hidden throughout the ages and generations but
has now been revealed to his saints. To them God chose to make known
how great among the Gentiles are the riches of the glory of this mystery, which is Christ in you, the hope of glory" (Col. 1:26–27). Paul's
storytelling begins with Christ, and it is because he begins with Christ
that, through God's Spirit, he can see God's wisdom in this apocalyptic
mystery. As Paul contemplates this wisdom-mystery-gospel, the Spirit
suddenly prompts him to praise God by drawing from a variety of
scriptural and extrascriptural Jewish sources:

> O the depth of the riches and wisdom and knowledge of God!
>   How unsearchable are his judgments and how inscrutable
>   his ways!
> "For who has known the mind of the Lord?
>   Or who has been his counselor?"
> "Or who has given a gift to him,
>   to receive a gift in return?"
> For from him and through him and to him are all things.
> To him be the glory forever. Amen. (Rom. 11:33–36; cf.
>   16:25–27)

It is this gospel-centered and Christ-shaped and Spirit-prompted wisdom that permits Paul to find Christ in the Jewish Shema: "Indeed,
even though there may be so-called gods in heaven or on earth—as in
fact there are many gods and many lords—yet for us there is one God,
the Father, from whom are all things and for whom we exist, and one
Lord, Jesus Christ, through whom are all things and through whom
we exist" (1 Cor. 8:5–6). The more often I read this text, the more
stunning it has become for me. As Paul sees Christ as the wisdom of
God (1 Cor. 1:24, 30; Col. 2:3) and sees Christ as creator (1:15–20), so

Paul identifies "one Lord" from Deuteronomy 6:4 with "Jesus Christ" and identifies him as the creator (1 Cor. 8:6). This, in my judgment, is Christian pastoral wisdom on display. Again, however, one doesn't discern this by an intellectual deduction or clarification but through a Spirit-prompted moment of insight that only those who know God in Christ—the wisdom of God—will see.

Briefly, what can pastors do to nurture a Christ-Wisdom Christoformity? What happens if we choose to think of the origins of creation as an act of God, however it happened?[34] What happens, then, if we see God's act in terms of Christ, as Paul does in Colossians 1:15–20? What happens to our understanding of creation if we define our Creator-Christ in terms of incarnation, death, resurrection, and rule? I am confident that this set of questions, when pondered by pastors who are indwelled by the Spirit, can lead us to perceive all of creation in terms of Christoformity. Enough of that. What if we ponder in the Spirit all things churchy— meetings, worship, preaching, evangelism, missions—in terms of Christ-Wisdom? These are the sorts of moves that Paul made, and each of my chapters in this book is an illustration of Paul's own Spirit-prompted Christ-Wisdom becoming pastoral wisdom.

Nurturing Christ-Wisdom as Down on Worldly Wisdom

Because wisdom is Christ and because worldly wisdom is foolishness (1 Cor. 1:18–25), Paul is down on worldly wisdom (see the previous chapter). One of wisdom's deepest themes is that it is theological: it begins with the fear of God. It is, then, more than observation of creation or a natural skill. Of course, many have been quick to point out that Scripture is not against reason and careful thinking—read the narrative art of Genesis; the careful-thinking of Leviticus; the brilliant, patient questions and ponderings of Job; the visions of Isaiah; Jesus's Sermon on the Mount; John's verbal dexterity; the writer of Hebrews on the relation of Old Testament to the New Testament; and don't ignore the profound symbolic architecture of Revelation. In fact, Paul's own letter to the Romans is a grand exercise in reason and careful thinking. Philemon is an orchestrated act of persuasion, so Paul's problem is not simply rhetoric. The Bible is zippered up with brilliant thinkers and thinking.

But Paul is against worldliness masked as wisdom and against preaching captured by rhetorical eloquence:

When I came to you, brothers and sisters, I did not come proclaiming the mystery of God to you *in lofty words or wisdom* (1 Cor. 2:1).

My speech and my proclamation were not *with plausible words of wisdom*, but with a demonstration of the Spirit and of power, so that your faith might rest not on *human wisdom* but on the power of God. Yet among the mature we do speak wisdom, though it is *not a wisdom of this age or of the rulers of this age*, who are doomed to perish. But we speak God's wisdom, secret and hidden, which God decreed before the ages for our glory (vv. 4–7).

And we speak of these things in words *not taught by human wisdom* but taught by the Spirit, interpreting spiritual things to those who are spiritual (v. 13).

He opens the second letter to the Corinthians on the same note: "Indeed, this is our boast, the testimony of our conscience: we have behaved in the world with frankness and godly sincerity, *not by earthly wisdom* but by the grace of God—and all the more toward you" (2 Cor. 1:12). And when Epaphras informs Paul of the problems at Colossae, Paul's answer is that Christ is the embodied wisdom of God (Col. 2:2–3) and that worldly wisdom won't help: "I am saying this so that no one may deceive you *with plausible arguments*" (v. 4). The same two-note theme reverberates on and on:

Do not let anyone disqualify you, insisting on self-abasement and worship of angels, dwelling on visions, puffed up without cause by a human way of thinking, and not holding fast to the head, from whom the whole body, nourished and held together by its ligaments and sinews, grows with a growth that is from God (vv. 18–19).

These have indeed *an appearance of wisdom* in promoting self-imposed piety, humility, and severe treatment of the body, but they are of no value in checking self-indulgence (v. 23).

Any intellectual effort that does not begin with Christ and end with Christ is not Christian wisdom. "True wisdom," Kavin Rowe observes, "is the repair of reason by trust in the trustworthiness of the Crucified Christ—what looks to the world's way of knowing to be pure folly."[35] So central is Christ to Paul's pastoral wisdom that he told the Corinthians this: "But we do not wage war *according to human standards*; for the weapons of our warfare are *not merely human*, but they have divine power to destroy strongholds. We destroy *arguments and every proud obstacle* raised up against the knowledge of God, and we take every thought captive to obey Christ" (2 Cor. 10:3–5).

Wisdom in Paul also developed an iconic flair. That is, what the world saw as beauty or intelligent or natural Paul saw as an *eikōn*, a window, on the truth of God in Christ. He did not see—to use words from Homer—the broad-backed Aegean; he saw the creation of God, the *tohu va bohu* ("formless void," Gen. 1:2; see also Jer. 4:23) of demons and the doom of death that is overcome by Christ's resurrection. He was not impressed with the Acropolis of Athens, the library in Ephesus, or the Forum spreading out in Rome. No, what he saw was The Powers seizing control of the orders established by God. Indeed, he saw through them to see Christ on the throne as the exalted Lord of Jews and gentiles. He did not see Israel according to the flesh but the Messiah who had redeemed that people and who now had a claim on their allegiance. He did not see the Old Testament as Josephus read it or as Philo read it or as the Essenes read it; rather, he saw the old covenant as a witness to Christ, whose life, death, resurrection, and ascension clarified the whole of the Old Testament as a witness to him. He was not impressed, finally, with the intelligentsia of the Areopagus, but instead he saw men and women groping for what Christ had to offer, the true wisdom of God, Wisdom embodied. All their efforts in intellectual curiosity, he was preaching, were aimed at Christ himself.

Pastors who pastor people toward Christ, who nurture a Christ-Wisdom Christoformity, show one and all how present Christ is in all places and how all things witness to the glory of Christ. Often enough pastors do this by what they do and not by what they say, by their touch, by their compassion, by their clarity, by their presence and faithful embodiment of the gospel. But this they do: they see through this world to the glory of God in Christ. Alexander Schmemann called this world "the chalice of eternity."[36] That's Christ-Wisdom to the core: to see through this world into the eternity of God. How can one establish a wisdom culture that leads us into Christoformity?

Nurturing the Establishment of Wisdom

Christ-Wisdom is established and conserved in a culture most purely and deeply by personal embodiment. Wisdom is not established by going through a course on spiritual formation, though that may help. Wisdom is not established by reading the Bible or by praying or by fasting, though again these will help. Wisdom—and this echoes pastoral nurture as emulation and imitation (chap. 1)—is established by reverent reception of wisdom in the ageless chain of wisdom. Here is how I see this chain of wisdom, and it all begins with (the fear of) God:

God (Father, Son, Spirit)

apostles, prophets

wisdom from the church's history

wise leaders in a local church

Wisdom cultures know this chain of wisdom, and a good example is found in the classic rabbinic text Mishnah Avot 1:1:

A. Moses received Torah at Sinai and handed it on to Joshua, Joshua to elders, and elders to prophets, and
B. prophets handed it on to the men of the great assembly.
C. They said three things: (1) "Be prudent in judgment." (2) "Raise up many disciples." (3) "Make a fence for the Torah."

What we see here is the famous chain of tradition in Judaism.

The Christian Chain of Wisdom

Wisdom in the Christian tradition begins with God revealing himself as Wisdom in Christ. That Christ-Wisdom is "passed on" truly only through the Spirit of God, who regenerates and illumines the heart, soul, mind, and body of those in the body of Christ. That Christ-Wisdom, then, is embodied in imperfect but real ways in human beings. Since Wisdom is Christ, the apostles form the first link after Christ to the church as witnesses and authorized teachers of the true Wisdom. The prophets, Paul tells us, come next (Eph. 2:20). With Christ as the foundation, they are but the first blocks built, and they extend that wisdom to the body of Christ. This theme of traditioned and conserved wisdom, and therefore of reverent reception by those in the body of Christ, is expressed clearly in Ephesians 4:11–13: "The gifts he gave were that some would be apostles, some prophets, some evangelists, some pastors and teachers, to equip the saints for the work of ministry, for building up the body of Christ, *until all of us come to the unity of the faith and of the knowledge of the Son of God, to maturity, to the measure of the full stature of Christ.*" The verses in italics demonstrate the wisdom-tradition theme. Notice, too, that the wisdom tradition here is developed by focusing on those who "tradition" that wisdom—that is, the leaders.

Gospel and Wisdom

The theme of tradition was not only important in Judaism but also fundamental to the gospel itself. Notice these verses emphasizing "tradition" or "passing on" the gospel tradition:

> But thanks be to God that you, having once been slaves of sin, have become obedient from the heart *to the form of teaching to which you were entrusted* (Rom. 6:17).

> I commend you because you remember me in everything and *maintain the traditions just as I handed them on to you* (1 Cor. 11:2).

> For *I received from the Lord what I also handed on to you*, that the Lord Jesus on the night when he was betrayed took a loaf of bread (v. 23).

> For *I handed on to you* as of first importance *what I in turn had received*: that Christ died for our sins in accordance with the scriptures (15:3).

> Now we command you, beloved, in the name of our Lord Jesus Christ, to keep away from believers who are living in idleness and not *according to the tradition that they received from us* (2 Thess. 3:6).

The wisdom tradition of the apostolic faith countered both the non-messianic Jewish tradition (Gal. 1:14) and the gentile pagan tradition (Col. 2:8). This tradition had within it the beginnings of what became the creeds (Rom. 10:9–10; 1 Cor. 15:3–8; Phil. 2:6–11; Col. 1:15–20; 1 Tim. 3:16; 2 Tim. 2:11–13; 1 Pet. 3:18–22), and any examination of these pro-tocreedal statements clearly reveals their Christ-Wisdom. It is the responsibility of the wise pastor to pass on and nurture the Christocentric nature of our faith: we confess Jesus as Lord and as God to the glory of God the Father, and we can only do this through the anointing of the Spirit. Pastors, like Paul, are stewards of the mysteries, and mystery is connected to Christ-as-Wisdom. Thus, to the Corinthians: "Think of us in this way, as servants of Christ and stewards of God's mysteries. Moreover, it is required of stewards that they be found trustworthy" (1 Cor. 4:1–2).

To summarize where we are: We establish wisdom through personal embodiment. Jesus was and is Wisdom in person; the Spirit is the Advocate for Christ; the apostles, prophets, evangelists, pastors, and teachers are those who (are supposed to) have received this wisdom reverently. These leaders are called to transmit and to nurture that wisdom to those in their care.

Our culture, captured as it is in juvenilization, either is irritated by the wisdom chain or goes beyond irritation to rebellion. So many want revolution and are trashing the deep traditions of the church's wisdom and are put off by the patience of the gray hairs and so reject the wisdom tradition. The gray hairs are part of the problem, for they either have surrendered church cultures to relevance or have not become worthy of emulation. The solution to this is not revolution or rebellion but repentance, turning back to the wisdom of the church, and seeking it with the gray hairs.

Elders and Wisdom

This is where elders now come into play. We have been so hog-tied to debates about the relationship of elders and bishops/overseers and pastors and teachers that we miss the basic sense of *elder* in the Jewish and Greco-Roman world. Here is Joseph Blenkinsopp's condensed summary:[37]

Tribal elders functioned as a deliberative body in matters concerning the tribe as a whole, especially in emergency situations. At the local level, the elder exercised authority in the individual household or village settlement, a situation somewhat analogous to the role of the *mukhtar* in Palestinian Arab villages today. Patriarchs or elders exercised a judicial function, both individually and collectively, in such matters as undetected homicide (Deut. 21:1–9), ungovernable sons (Deut. 21:18–21), sanctuary (Josh. 20:1–6), charges of sexual misconduct directed against wives (Deut. 22:13–21), and disputes concerning marriage and property in general (Deut. 25:5–10; 1 Kings 21:8–14; Ruth 4:2). The elders were also the depositaries, custodians, and transmitters of the group ethos and the shared traditions that helped to constitute the group's identity. They would also have presided over family rituals, especially concerning the ancestors, that did not call for the presence of a cultic specialist.

Elders had a responsibility that can be summarized like this: knowing the past and thinking toward the future, they rendered judgment in the present in order to keep the present and the future consistent with the wise past. I hope that's not too convoluted, but the point is that decisions now need to be based on the organic wisdom of the past so that the future will form a continuity over time. Continuity over time is wisdom. Elders are responsible for this kind of wisdom.

Andrew Clarke, a New Testament specialist on all things pertaining to early Christian leadership, also sees elders in the New Testament in terms of their wisdom function. I quote extensively:

> Accordingly, "eldership" is not an individual office, but an honoured status, bringing with it membership of an influential and respected body. Such a council of elders would give wise counsel, and each elder would need to display the kind of qualities provided in the short list in Titus 1.6. Throughout the synoptic gospels and Acts, the elders are characterized as a powerful and decisive, even formidable, group. 1 Tim. 5.17–19 insists that elders are honoured appropriately, and are not subject to accusation without at least two witnesses; but if an elder is found to have been at fault, his rebuke should be handled publicly. The Pastoral Epistles add nothing further about how they were or should be perceived.[38]

Those Pauline contexts where there were a significant number of house-churches may well also have had a council of elders—a group that only acted collegially, and would have comprised the overseers together with an additional number of respected men who were not qualified to teach and did not have their own house-church (and were therefore not overseers), but were nonetheless heads of their family. The duties and responsibilities of the eldership, as distinct from the overseers, are not spelled out in the Pastoral Epistles. However, in the Jewish context of the synoptic Gospels and Acts, they were an authoritative group, whose role was predominantly to make decisions and pass judgements from a community-wide perspective.[39]

In other words, Christian elders looked like Ephesian or Corinthian or Roman secular elders. They were gray heads and baldheads who on the basis of their life had become functional sages in their society. They knew the past, and they rendered judgments in the present for the sake of the future.

The download is this: elders were responsible for passing on and maintaining the wisdom of the community. In our case, this means passing on and maintaining Christoform wisdom for the church. Pastors are to nurture a culture in which Christ-Wisdom is supreme, and they nurture such a culture by maintaining consistency with the wisdom tradition in their Spirit-Wisdom.

Nurturing the Expressions of Wisdom

Wisdom is expressed in two ways: by behaving wisely and by speaking wisely. Paul told the Colossians, after he had leveled the claims of the opponents who were probably leading some Colossian Christians into a kind of halakic mysticism,[40] this: "Conduct yourselves wisely toward outsiders, making the most of the time. Let your speech always be gracious, seasoned with salt, so that you may know how you ought to answer everyone" (Col. 4:5–6). Noticeably, here Paul speaks of behavior and of speech. Wisdom embodied is the best apologetic for the substance of wisdom, in this case a Christ-centered gospel that transcends the claims of the emperor and offers redemption to all in a new community encompassing Jews and gentiles, male and female, slave and free, and all ethnicities and languages. It is one of the strongest features of Kavin Rowe's *One True Life* that he speaks of both the Stoic and Christian traditions as lived traditions. "Stoicism and Christianity," he concludes, "are claims to the truth of life, and knowing the things they teach requires a life that is true."[41] Rowe favors Kierkegaard and says, "No matter how many criteria we find for living in one way or another, we cannot make them add up to a judgment about a true life before we live it."[42] I agree, mostly. What concerns me is that a lived life is an embodiment of something, and that something—namely Christ-Wisdom—is distinguishable from that life. Hence, yes, I agree: behavior embodies the gospel, but it is the separable gospel that it embodies.

With verbal expressions of wisdom, which accompany behavior, one could offer a running commentary on Paul's letters. Here is a brief sampling of moments of wisdom. In 1 Corinthians 8 Paul addresses food sacrificed to idols. To eat or not to eat? Idolatrous or adiaphora? Here are Paul's opening words from 8:1, beginning with his quotation (probably) from the letter from Chloe: "We know that 'all of us possess knowledge.'" Paul's response: "Knowledge puffs up, but love builds up." This same cycle of citation and response is found in 1 Corinthians 10:23–24:

> "All things are lawful," but not all things are beneficial.
> "All things are lawful," but not all things build up.
> Do not seek your own advantage, but that of the other.

When doing his dead-level best to exhort and even cajole the Corinthians to be generous with their resources for the sake of the saints in Jerusalem, Paul says this: "The point is this: the one who sows sparingly will also reap sparingly, and the one who sows bountifully will also reap bountifully" (2 Cor. 9:6). These are proverbial statements by Paul, by form connected to the wisdom tradition of Judaism, but there's more there: these are proverbs dipped deeply in Christ-Wisdom and therefore in Christoformity. What matters is love, not knowledge (which was the height of honor in Corinth); what matters is what is beneficial to all, what builds up, and what is good for the other. These are instances of a life shaped like Christ's by the giving of oneself for the sake of others. For all the chatter today about "incarnational" living, this is what the incarnation truly is: a life of sacrifice for the sake of the redemption of others (e.g., Phil. 2:6–11).[43]

As I said, we could exegete each letter. I will shutter this chapter now by looking at random wisdom moments of discernment—where Christ-Wisdom, Spirit-Wisdom, and pastoral wisdom converge—in Colossians. In 1:7 Paul reminds the Colossians that they learned the gospel "from Epaphras," who embodies "fellow servant" and "faithful minister" because he reverently receives Christ-as-Wisdom from the apostle Paul. Therefore Paul says, "We have not ceased praying . . . that you may be filled with the knowledge of God's will in all spiritual wisdom and understanding, so that you may lead lives worthy of the Lord, fully pleasing to him, as you bear fruit in every good work and as you grow in the knowledge of God" (1:9–10). Wisdom as a gift from God generates a life "worthy of the Lord." Paul's pastoral response to the halakic mystics of Colossae, before he mentions them, is Christocentricity, made famous in the hymn of 1:15–20, where I highlight only these words: "He is the image of the invisible God, the firstborn of all creation; for in him all things . . . were created. . . . All things have been created through him and for him. He himself is before all things, and in him all things hold together. He is the head of the body, the church . . . so that he might come to have first place in everything. For in him all the fullness of God was pleased to dwell, and through him God was pleased to reconcile to himself all things . . . through the blood of his cross." If that isn't Christocentricity nothing is, and since it is, we learn here the pastoral strategy of Christian wisdom in the moment: the way to fight false teaching is to present Christ in all his glory and compare Christ to what is being offered by the false teachers (who embody false wisdom).

The Colossians are instructed about their co-death and their co-resurrection (2:12–15; 2:20–3:11), which is to say, the moral life in Pauline wisdom is Christoformity. Paul doesn't enter into how they too might find mystical experiences or what practices are needed to become habits that can generate worship with the angels. No, he points them time and time again to the cross and to the resurrection, thereby framing the Christian life as one shaped by Christ-Wisdom. In that famous household regulation passage we find a subversion of the Roman way of family and household life, for in this section it is the subordinates (wives, children, slaves) who are empowered, while the superordinates (husbands, parents, slave owners) are taught the way of the cross. Nothing is more revolutionary than teaching masters to treat their slaves "justly and fairly," and the term *fairly* is *isotēs*, meaning "as an equal." This is precisely what Paul will tell Philemon about how to treat his new brother Onesimus (Philem. 16). One might say the subordinates are given resurrection and the superordinates the cross, and in that way the household embodies Christian wisdom. What is most important here is the pastoral wisdom we find in this moment of instruction. I could go on, but I offer the foregoing examples only to illustrate the right substance (Christocentricity, Christoformity) at the right time for the right people and in the right manner.

Wisdom is embodied, and the embodiments establish Christ-Wisdom in local churches. Pastors are to nurture Christ-Wisdom to nurture Christoform cultures. How will it be gained if not by the receptive reverence toward wisdom from the sages of the church? Those sages need to be both local—older, gray-haired pastors and elders in the community—and global, and under global I include sage writers, such as John Stott and Tim Keller and Eugene Peterson and Marilynne Robinson and Fleming Rutledge and . . . over to you.

Final Thoughts:
Nurturing Christoformity

Since this book will be of particular interest to pastors and I am not one of them, a simple idea from early in this book needs a short revival: I have no desire to tell pastors how to do their job, nor do I think I could. Nor have I sought a sparkling new theory about pastoring that we've all missed since the days of Jesus but that now finally can see the light of day. Pastors have tried everything, and I have no new ideas, nor would pastors be wise to listen to me on how to pastor. What I have attempted to do is explain what pastoring was for Paul and to shed light on pastoring in a way consistent with Paul. I have offered not a comprehensive pastoral theology of Paul but only examples of a theme, Christoformity.

The best part of this book was writing it. I loved the pondering of texts about Paul's pastoral life, I loved reading what so many pastors say about Paul the pastor, but most of all I loved the process of thinking my way into this book by writing. I am a fan of Joseph Epstein, and his ever-witty line about the labor of writing is worth repeating: "If the drama of writers is even minimally true, why, one wonders, would anyone take up such a hard calling? I have myself always thought that it had something to do with the notion that writing, whatever its complications and difficulties, still beats working, though I could be wrong."[1] If it was work to write this book, I never noticed.

191

As I read pastors who discussed pastoring or Paul as a pastor, time and time again I noticed how people-oriented pastors are in their ruminations. I don't see the same in the professors who talk about pastoring or Paul pastoring or Paul in general. The professor's supposed distance and theories of objectivity blunt the pastoral themes of Paul into the negligible and at times unnoticed. When I read *Death in Holy Orders*, therefore, this pastoral moment of pastoring real people stood up for more attention:

> [The pastor] had returned from two hours of visiting long-term sick and housebound parishioners. As always he had tried conscientiously to meet their individual and predictable needs: blind Mrs. Oliver, who liked him to read a passage of scripture and pray with her; old Sam Possinger, who on every visit re-fought the Battle of Alamein; Mrs. Poley, caged in her Zimmer frame, avid for the latest parish gossip; Carl Lomas, who had never set foot in St. Botolph's but liked discussing theology and the defects of the Church of England. Mrs. Poley, with his help, had edged her way painfully into the kitchen and made tea, taking from the tin the gingerbread cake she had baked for him. He had unwisely praised it four years ago, on his first visit, and was now condemned to eat it weekly, finding it impossible to admit that he disliked gingerbread. But the tea, hot and strong, had been welcome and would save him the trouble of making it at home.[2]

I read passages like this and I wonder whether I could handle the pastor's handholding and routine visitations. Pastors who pastor people have my admiration for their pastoring, for this kind of Christo-formity.

Taking Paul as our guide, we have seen that Paul understands the pastoral task to be one of nurturing Christoformity. That is, Paul and each one of us and each pastor are called to be conformed to the image of Christ, and pastors are nurturers of Christoformity as it appears in every facet of Jesus's life: called to be conformed to, and to nurture people by, Jesus's life, death, resurrection, and ascension. To once again use the Greek terms no one uses (mentioned in chap. 1): *bio*-formity, *cruci*-formity, and *anastasi*-formity. Add those together and you get Christoformity. You get what Paul was working at among his coworkers and their churches.

Christoformity, to remind us, is rooted in Jesus's own words and life. Hence Jesus said,

> A disciple is not above the teacher, nor a slave above the master; it is enough for the disciple to be like the teacher, and the slave like the master. If they have called the master of the house Beelzebul, how much more will they malign those of his household! (Matt. 10:24–25).
>
> For the Son of Man came not to be served but to serve, and to give his life a ransom for many (Mark 10:45).

If we take the second text first, we see that the mission of Jesus was to serve and give himself for others, and the first text says it's enough for us to be like Jesus. That's Christoformity. If the Christian life is about Christoformity, then pastoring is about nurturing Christoformity in ourselves and in others.

Christoformity is not the inevitable consequence of forming the right habits, nor is it simply the result of intentions and willpower. Rather, Christ is present in our world at its core through the Spirit, and the grace of God operating through the Spirit is the only path of Christoformity. Speaking theologically, Christocentricity is only possible through Pneumacentricity: we can only find Christ at the center if we are open to the Spirit taking us there. Gordon Fee, our generation's "expert" on all things Holy Spirit, takes us home with this:

> We have been invaded by the living God himself, in the person of his Spirit, whose goal is to infect us thoroughly with God's own likeness. Paul's phrase for this infection is the fruit of the Spirit. The coming of the Spirit, with the renewing of our minds, gives us a heavenly appetite for this fruit. The growing of this fruit is the long way on the journey of Christian conversion, the "long obedience in the same direction," and it is altogether the work of the Spirit in our lives.[3]

Once in a conversation with Dallas Willard I asked him, "Dallas, are you an Aristotelian virtue ethicist? Or a virtue ethicist?" His response was unforgettable: "Aristotle was so cold." He continued, "Well, I believe the spiritual practices are the means by which we make ourselves available to and open to God's grace, to the Spirit of God working in us to transform us." So, let's make this clear: Christoformity in us and in others only happens through the Spirit.

Nurturing Christoformity is a full-time challenge. Pastors have more than enough to do today, and often more than they can possibly do. Models for successful churches too often are measured by "butts in seats" and "budgets at the end of the year." They work together: the more people we get into our Sunday services, the more money we will have and the more ministry we can accomplish. Not so, I have learned from Paul and many wise pastors. Homogeneous church principles— where we focus on one type of person in one kind of community—and the church-growth movement are not found in the New Testament and are but another version of Corinthianizing the church. These principles are worldly. Measuring success by numbers—butts or budgets—is also worldly. What mattered to Paul was presenting his churches complete in Christ. Maturity for Paul was Christoformity, so the only metric Paul knew for pastoral ministry was this question: "How Christoform is she or he? How Christoform is the church of Ephesus?" Christoformity countered the ways of Rome and embodied the life of Christ in a congregation and in individuals.

There are many more examples of Paul nurturing Christoformity, but the seven examples provided in chapters 2–8 will serve, I pray, to remind pastors of all they have done and perhaps even whet their appetite to take up the challenge of nurturing Christoformity as the essence of pastoring. Pastors who pastor people will recognize the moment, will know the person in need of pastoring, and will nurture Christoformity in the moment, like the old priest in Willa Cather's *Death Comes for the Archbishop*. The priest, Father Joseph, was being asked to leave his church and serve the bishop in another context, and here is the interchange:

[Father Joseph:] "A word, a prayer, a service, is all that is needed to set free those souls in bondage. I confess I am covetous of that mission. I desire to be the man who restores these lost children to God. It will be the greatest happiness of my life."

The Bishop did not reply at once to this appeal. At last he said gravely, "You must realize that I have need of you here, Father Joseph. My duties are too many for one man."

"But you do not need me so much as they do!" Father Joseph threw off his coverings and sat up in his cassock, putting his feet to the ground. "Any one of our good French priests from Montferrand can serve you here. It is work that can be done by intelligence. But down there it is work for the heart, for a particular sympathy, and none of our new priests understand those poor natures as I do. I have almost become a Mexican! I have learned to like *chili colorado* and mutton fat. Their foolish ways no longer offend me, their very faults are dear to me. I am *their man*!"

[Bishop] ". . . you must follow the duty that calls loudest."[4]

Christoformity is the loudest, in a quiet way.

Notes

Series Preface

1. John Wesley, "Catholic Spirit," sermon 39, in *Bicentennial Edition of the Works of John Wesley* (Nashville: Abingdon, 1985), 2:79–95. We know, however, that his public ties with Anglicanism were at some points in his life anything but tender and close.

Preface

1. Mary Karr, *The Art of Memoir* (New York: HarperCollins, 2015), 1.

Chapter 1 Pastors as Culture Makers

1. Philip L. Culbertson and Arthur Bradford Shippee, *The Pastor: Readings from the Patristic Period* (Minneapolis: Augsburg Fortress, 2009); William H. Willimon, *Pastor: A Reader for Ordained Ministry* (Nashville: Abingdon, 2002); Willimon, *Pastor: The Theology and Practice of Ordained Ministry*, rev. ed. (Nashville: Abingdon, 2016).

2. Eugene H. Peterson, *The Contemplative Pastor: Returning to the Art of Spiritual Direction* (Grand Rapids: Eerdmans, 1993), 89.

3. Eugene H. Peterson, *Working the Angles: The Shape of Pastoral Integrity* (Grand Rapids: Eerdmans, 1993), 3.

4. For a solid but unflinching book on this see Graham Buxton, *An Uncertain Certainty: Snapshots in a Journey from "Either-Or" to "Both-And" in Christian Ministry* (Eugene, OR: Pickwick, 2014).

5. Karl Barth, *Church Dogmatics, III.4: The Doctrine of Creation*, trans. G. W. Bromiley (Edinburgh: T&T Clark, 1961), xi. I have been unable to find this in the study edition.

6. Taken from Michael J. Gorman, *Becoming the Gospel: Paul, Participation, and Mission* (Grand Rapids: Eerdmans, 2015), 26–36.

7. For an academic study on this see Colin Kruse, *New Testament Models for Ministry: Jesus and Paul* (Nashville: Thomas Nelson, 1983), 34–51.

8. Paul Barnett, *Paul: A Pastor's Heart in Second Corinthians* (Sydney, Australia: Aquila, 2012), 114.

9. Graham Buxton, *Dancing in the Dark: The Privilege of Participating in God's Ministry in the World*, rev. ed. (Eugene, OR: Cascade, 2016), 19.

10. Beverly Gaventa, "The Mission of God in Paul's Letter to the Romans," in *Paul as Missionary: Identity, Activity, Theology, and Practice*, ed. Trevor J. Burke and Brian S. Rosner, LNTS 420 (London: T&T Clark, 2011), 65–75. See also L. L. Morris, "The Theme of Romans," in *Apostolic History and the Gospel: Biblical and Historical Essays Presented to F. F. Bruce on His 60th Birthday*, ed. W. W. Gasque and R. P. Martin (Grand Rapids: Eerdmans, 1970), 249–63.

11. For a solid discussion, see Trevor J. Burke, "The Holy Spirit as the Controlling Dynamic in Paul's Role as Missionary to the Thessalonians," in Burke and Rosner, *Paul as Missionary*, 142–57.

12. See Kruse, *New Testament Models for Ministry*, 52–64.

13. James W. Thompson, *Pastoral Ministry according to Paul: A Biblical Vision* (Grand Rapids: Baker Academic, 2006), 19–20 (italics original).

14. Haley Goranson Jacob, *Conformed to the Image of His Son: Reconsidering Paul's Theology of Glory in Romans* (Downers Grove, IL: IVP Academic, 2018). For the theme of God's glory in Paul's missionary practice see Brian S. Rosner, "The Glory of God in Paul's Missionary Theology and Practice," in Burke and Rosner, *Paul as Missionary*, 158–68.

15. C. Kavin Rowe, *One True Life: The Stoics and Early Christians as Rival Traditions* (New Haven: Yale University Press, 2016), 215.

16. Willimon, *Pastor: The Theology and Practice of Ordained Ministry*, 203.

17. C. S. Lewis, *Mere Christianity* (New York: Macmillan, 1956), 155. I am grateful to Kevin Vanhoozer for reminding me of this famous line in Lewis.

18. Peggy Noonan, *When Character Was King: A Story of Ronald Reagan* (New York: Penguin, 2002), 303.

19. Emmanuel Y. Lartey, *Pastoral Theology in an Intercultural World*, repr. (Eugene, OR: Wipf & Stock, 2013), 149.

20. What follows develops what I have learned from Diane J. Chandler, "The Perfect Storm of Leaders' Unethical Behavior: A Conceptual Framework," *International Journal of Leadership Studies* 5 (2009): 69–93. I am grateful that Diane pointed me to this excellent study.

21. Peterson, *Contemplative Pastor*, 112–16.

22. Eugene H. Peterson, "Pastor Paul," in *Romans and the People of God: Essays in Honor of Gordon D. Fee on the Occasion of His 65th Birthday*, ed. Sven K. Soderlund and N. T. Wright (Grand Rapids: Eerdmans, 1999), 291.

23. Margaret Whipp, *Pastoral Theology*, SCM Studyguide (London: SCM, 2013), 1.

24. Barna Group, *The State of Pastors: How Today's Faith Leaders Are Navigating Life and Leadership in an Age of Complexity* (Ventura, CA: Barna, 2017), 96.

25. On Paul's life, see the biographies by two of the foremost Pauline scholars of our day: Douglas A. Campbell, *Paul: An Apostle's Journey* (Grand Rapids: Eerdmans, 2018); N. T. Wright, *Paul: A Biography* (San Francisco: HarperOne, 2018).

26. On Paul as pastor, see Anthony Tyrrell Hanson, *The Pioneer Ministry: The Relation of Church and Ministry*, Library of History and Doctrine (Philadelphia: Westminster, 1961); Kruse, *New Testament Models for Ministry*; Ernest Best, *Paul and His Converts*, Sprunt Lectures 1985 (Edinburgh: T&T Clark, 1988); Abraham J. Malherbe, *Paul and the Thessalonians: The Philosophic Tradition of Pastoral Care*

(repr., Eugene, OR: Wipf & Stock, 2011); J. Thompson, *Pastoral Ministry*; Victor A. Copan, *Saint Paul as Spiritual Director: An Analysis of the Concept of the Imitation of Paul with Implications and Applications to the Practice of Spiritual Direction*, Paternoster Biblical Monographs (repr., Eugene, OR: Wipf & Stock, 2008); Timothy Laniak, *Shepherds after My Own Heart: Pastoral Traditions and Leadership in the Bible* (Downers Grove, IL: IVP Academic, 2006); Brian S. Rosner, Andrew S. Malone, and Trevor J. Burke, eds., *Paul as Pastor* (New York: Bloomsbury T&T Clark, 2017); Michael B. Thompson, *Owned by God: Paul's Pastoral Strategy in 1 Corinthians* (Cambridge: Grove Books, 2017). Another volume, with numerous important observations about Paul and the Corinthians, is unfortunately either willfully misrepresenting or woefully misunderstanding the new perspective: Barnett, *Paul*, 47–54. Barnett somehow manages to find new perspective people in the opponents of Paul in Corinth.

27. Best, *Paul and His Converts*, 29–58; Trevor J. Burke, "Mother, Father, Infant, Orphan, Brother: Paul's Variegated Pastoral Strategy towards His Thessalonian Church Family," in Rosner, Malone, and Burke, *Paul as Pastor*, 123–41.

28. Henri J. M. Nouwen, *The Wounded Healer: Ministry in Contemporary Society* (New York: Doubleday, 1990).

29. J. Thompson, *Pastoral Ministry*, 153.

30. M. Thompson, *Owned by God*, 17.

31. There is a cottage industry of clever categories for pastors and not a few critics of all the new categories. A good sketch of some of these comes from Will Willimon: media star, political negotiator, therapist, manager, resident activist, preacher, servant, and rebel. See Willimon, *Pastor: The Theology and Practice of Ordained Ministry*, 56–70.

32. Barbara Brown Taylor, *The Preaching Life* (Plymouth, UK: Cowley, 1992), 30.

33. Cf. Josh. 22:5; Ruth 1:14; 2:8, 21, 23; 2 Kings 18:6; Pss. 63:8; 119:31.

34. Nouwen, *Wounded Healer*, 37–38.

35. One wonderful reference for pastors is a book about the pastoral ideal—namely, the Zaddik—in Hasidic Judaism: Samuel H. Dresner, *The Zaddik: The Doctrine of the Zaddik according to the Writings of Rabbi Yaakov Yosef of Polnoy* (Northvale, NJ: Jason Aronson, 1994).

36. Pope Gregory 1, *The Book of Pastoral Rule* 2.1, quoted in Culbertson and Shippee, *Pastor*, 202–3.

37. *Book of Pastoral Rule* 2.1, quoted in Culbertson and Shippee, *Pastor*, 202–3.

38. Sondra Wheeler, *The Minister as Moral Theologian: Ethical Dimensions of Pastoral Leadership* (Grand Rapids: Baker Academic, 2017), xiii–xiv.

39. Copan, *Saint Paul as Spiritual Director*, 2. Copan offers careful descriptions and solid evaluations of the terms (and nonsense) as well as the individualism at work in some theologies of spiritual direction; see pp. 7–39. Copan looks at the following terms: *spiritual direction, spiritual guidance, spiritual friend, discipler*, and *mentor*.

40. See Copan's sketch in *Saint Paul as Spiritual Director*, 45–69. See further Best, *Paul and His Converts*, 59–72; Jason B. Hood, *Imitating God in Christ: Recapturing a Biblical Pattern* (Downers Grove, IL: IVP Academic, 2013).

41. D. Campbell, *Paul: An Apostle's Journey*, 69.

42. Georges Bernanos, *The Diary of a Country Priest: A Novel* (Cambridge: Da Capo Press, 2002).

43. Bernanos, *Diary of a Country Priest*, 28.

44. Bernanos, *Diary of a Country Priest*, 83–84.

45. Many emphasize this element of pastoring; see Ritva H. Williams, *Stewards, Prophets, Keepers of the Word: Leadership in the Early Church* (Peabody, MA: Hendrickson, 2006); Rosner, Malone, and Burke, *Paul as Pastor*.

46. J. Thompson, *Pastoral Ministry*, 159.

47. A point made often by Graham Buxton; see his *Dancing in the Dark*, 249–82.

48. Mandy Smith, *The Vulnerable Pastor: How Human Limitations Empower Our Ministry* (Downers Grove, IL: IVP Books, 2015), 175.

49. Thomas G. Long, *The Witness of Preaching*, 3rd ed. (Louisville: Westminster John Knox, 2016); B. Taylor, *Preaching Life*; Timothy Keller, *Preaching: Communicating Faith in an Age of Skepticism* (New York: Penguin, 2016); John Stott, *Between Two Worlds* (repr., Grand Rapids: Eerdmans, 2017); Ellen F. Davis, *Preaching the Luminous Word: Biblical Sermons and Homiletical Essays*, ed. Austin McIver Dennis (Grand Rapids: Eerdmans, 2016); Frederick Buechner, *Telling the Truth: The Gospel as Tragedy, Comedy, and Fairy Tale* (San Francisco: Harper & Row, 1977); Haddon W. Robinson, *Biblical Preaching: The Development and Delivery of Expository Messages*, 3rd ed. (Grand Rapids: Baker Academic, 2014); Fred B. Craddock, *Craddock on the Craft of Preaching* (St. Louis: Chalice Press, 2013). My friend Joe Modica and I have recently coedited a book designed to aid in the preaching of Romans by sorting out four views of interpreting Paul as well as offering sample sermons illustrating each view; see Scot McKnight and Joseph B. Modica, *Preaching Romans: Four Perspectives* (Grand Rapids: Eerdmans, 2019).

50. Buechner, *Telling the Truth*, 34–35.

51. Richard B. Hays, *Echoes of Scripture in the Letters of Paul* (New Haven: Yale University Press, 1993); Hays, *The Conversion of the Imagination: Paul as Interpreter of Israel's Scripture* (Grand Rapids: Eerdmans, 2005); Hays, *Echoes of Scripture in the Gospels* (Waco: Baylor University Press, 2016); J. Ross Wagner, "The Heralds of Isaiah and the Mission of Paul: An Investigation of Paul's Use of Isaiah 51–55 in Romans," in *Jesus and the Suffering Servant: Isaiah 53 and Christian Origins*, ed. William H. Bellinger Jr. and William R. Farmer (Harrisburg, PA: Trinity Press International, 1998), 193–222.

52. Davis, *Preaching the Luminous Word*, 71.

53. For a brief sketch of salient points, see also Gordon Fee, "Paul's Conversion as Key to His Understanding of the Spirit," in *The Road from Damascus: The Impact of Paul's Conversion on His Life, Thought, and Ministry*, ed. Richard N. Longenecker (Grand Rapids: Eerdmans, 1997), 168–69.

54. Whipp, *Pastoral Theology*, 12.

55. Alec Guinness, *Blessings in Disguise* (New York: Knopf, 1986), 36.

56. B. Taylor, *Preaching Life*, 32.

57. On this topic, see esp. Bryan A. Stewart, *Priests of My People: Levitical Paradigms for Early Christian Ministers*, Patristic Studies 11 (New York: Peter Lang, 2015). He develops with finesse a religio-political understanding of Christian priesthood—that is, he sees the church as an alternative polis in the Roman Empire, with a priestly responsibility to the world. Importantly, this development occurred when Christians appropriated the story of Israel with its Levitical priests for the church and its material culture (sacred buildings) and so began to see their pastors as priests who guarded the holiness of sacred space. Stewart's study, focused as it is on the origins of priestly

language in the church, could have developed a pastoral theology of priesthood more. I offer a few observations in this section.

58. Willimon uses an eightfold breakdown of the church at worship from Justin Martyr's famous section in the *First Apology* to describe the priestly role of the pastor in leading worship. See Willimon, *Pastor: The Theology and Practice of Ordained Ministry*, 77–90.

59. Eugene H. Peterson, *As Kingfishers Catch Fire: A Conversation on the Ways of God Formed by the Words of God* (Colorado Springs: WaterBrook, 2017), 119.

60. J. R. R. Tolkien, *Tree and Leaf* (Boston: Houghton Mifflin, 1989).

61. Christopher J. H. Wright, ed., *Portraits of a Radical Disciple: Recollections of John Stott's Life and Ministry* (Downers Grove, IL: IVP Books, 2011), 143.

62. For a good discussion, see Andrew D. Clarke, *A Pauline Theology of Church Leadership* (London: Bloomsbury T&T Clark, 2008), 95–102.

63. Michael J. Gorman, *Cruciformity: Paul's Narrative Spirituality of the Cross* (Grand Rapids: Eerdmans, 2001); Gorman, *Inhabiting the Cruciform God: Kenosis, Justification, and Theosis in Paul's Narrative Soteriology* (Grand Rapids: Eerdmans, 2009); Gorman, *Becoming the Gospel*.

64. Robert K. Greenleaf and Stephen R. Covey, *Servant Leadership: A Journey into the Nature of Legitimate Power and Greatness*, ed. Larry C. Spears, 25th anniversary ed. (New York: Paulist Press, 2002); Kent M. Keith, *The Case for Servant Leadership*, 2nd ed. (Westfield, IN: Greenleaf Center, 2015); Keith, *Jesus Did It Anyway* (New York: Putnam Adult, 2005); Keith, *Do It Anyway: Finding Personal Meaning and Deep Happiness by Living the Paradoxical Commandments* (Novato, CA: New World Library, 2008).

65. John N. Collins, *Diakonia: Re-Interpreting the Ancient Sources* (New York: Oxford University Press, 1990).

66. Andrew D. Clarke, *Serve the Community of the Church: Christians as Leaders and Ministers*, First Century Christians in the Graeco-Roman World (Grand Rapids: Eerdmans, 2000), 233–45.

67. Brian Harris, *The Tortoise Usually Wins: Biblical Reflections on Quiet Leadership for Reluctant Leaders* (Milton Keynes, UK: Paternoster / Authentic Media, 2013).

68. Ernst Käsemann, "Paul and Early Catholicism," in *New Testament Questions of Today*, trans. W. J. Montague (Philadelphia: Augsburg Fortress, 1979), 236–51; James D. G. Dunn, *Unity and Diversity in the New Testament: An Inquiry into the Character of Earliest Christianity*, 3rd ed. (London: SCM, 2006), 112–34, 135–63, 372–400.

69. Joseph Epstein, *Pertinent Players: Essays on the Literary Life* (New York: Norton, 1993), 35.

70. Discussed briefly in the pages cited here but appearing throughout the work of Clarke, *Pauline Theology*, 11–16.

71. See Kevin Giles, *Patterns of Ministry among the First Christians*, 2nd ed. (Eugene, OR: Cascade, 2017).

72. Wayne Meeks, *The First Urban Christians: The Social World of the Apostle Paul*, 2nd ed. (New Haven: Yale University Press, 2003), 111. See 111–39 for a full discussion. See also Todd G. Still, "Organizational Structures and Relational Struggles among the Saints: The Establishment and Exercise of Authority within Pauline Assemblies," in *After the First Urban Christians: The Social-Scientific Study of Pauline*

Christianity Twenty-Five Years Later, ed. Todd G. Still and David G. Horrell (London: T&T Clark, 2009), 79–98.

73. In my definition I combine charismatic, institutional, and moral authority. Pastor and historian John Dickson explains four elements in leaders, with the third and fourth most important: ability, authority, persuasion, and example. See John Dickson, *Humilitas: A Lost Key to Life, Love, and Leadership* (Grand Rapids: Zondervan, 2011), 37–42. A leader shapes these elements in herself by setting her direction in holiness and mission and, I would add, love; so writes David I. Starling in *UnCorinthian Leadership: Thematic Reflections on 1 Corinthians* (Eugene, OR: Cascade, 2014), 41–42. Victor Copan writes, "Spiritual direction is the (variegated) means by which one person intentionally influences another person or persons in the development of his [or her] life as a Christian with the goal of developing his [or her] relationship to God and His purposes for that person in the world." So Copan, *Saint Paul as Spiritual Director*, 39.

74. B. Harris, *Tortoise Usually Wins*, 18–19.

75. Wheeler, *Minister as Moral Theologian*, xiv.

76. Willimon, *Pastor: The Theology and Practice of Ordained Ministry*, 57.

77. Carl Trueman, foreword to Starling, *UnCorinthian Leadership*, ix.

78. David Foster Wallace, *This Is Water: Some Thoughts, Delivered on a Significant Occasion, about Living a Compassionate Life* (New York: Little, Brown, 2009), 109.

79. Jerry Useem, "Power Causes Brain Damage," *The Atlantic*, July/August 2017, https://www.theatlantic.com/magazine/archive/2017/07/power-causes-brain-damage /528711/.

80. Adams, quoted in Useem, "Power Causes Brain Damage."

81. Wallace, *This Is Water*, 110.

82. This entire book was written prior to the public accusations against an internationally known pastor in Chicagoland. None of what is written in this chapter or this book, therefore, alludes to or was based on that story. Even more recently, a new story about another Chicagoland pastor has gone public. Celebrity and power were involved in both of these stories.

Chapter 2 A Culture of Friendship

1. Edward Gibbon, *The Decline and Fall of the Roman Empire* (New York: Everyman's Library, 1993), 1:168–69.

2. The Barna Group, *The State of Pastors: How Today's Faith Leaders Are Navigating Life and Leadership in an Age of Complexity* (Ventura, CA: Barna, 2017), 96.

3. Barna Group, *State of Pastors*, 38–42.

4. Al Gini, *The Importance of Being Lazy: In Praise of Play, Leisure, and Vacation* (New York: Routledge, 2003). On reading essays, see Phillip Lopate, ed., *The Art of the Personal Essay: An Anthology from the Classical Era to the Present* (New York: Anchor Doubleday, 1994).

5. Robert N. Bellah et al., *Habits of the Heart: Individualism and Commitment in American Life* (New York: Harper & Row, 1985); Robert D. Putnam, *Bowling Alone: The Collapse and Revival of American Community* (New York: Simon & Schuster, 2000).

6. See the wide-ranging and enjoyable D. J. Enright and David Rawlinson, eds., *The Oxford Book of Friendship* (New York: Oxford University Press, 1991). A charming

jaunt through some of the literature can be found in Joseph Epstein, *Friendship: An Exposé* (Boston: Houghton Mifflin, 2006).

7. The literature on friendship in the classical world continues to grow, but the place to start is with David Konstan, *Friendship in the Classical World* (New York: Cambridge University Press, 1997).

8. See books 8 and 9. Aristotle's (probably) earlier *Eudemian Ethics* also has a section on friendship, but it will not be discussed here.

9. For a good sketch of various approaches among the philosophers, see Abraham J. Malherbe, *Paul and the Thessalonians: The Philosophic Tradition of Pastoral Care*, repr. (Eugene, OR: Wipf & Stock, 2011), 81–88.

10. Of course, Plato, *Symposium*. For discussion, see Konstan, *Friendship in the Classical World*, 44–47.

11. Konstan, *Friendship in the Classical World*, 71–72.

12. Joseph Blenkinsopp, *Sage, Priest, Prophet: Religious and Intellectual Leadership in Ancient Israel* (Louisville: Westminster John Knox, 1995), 32–37.

13. Sappho and Alcaeus, *Greek Lyric: Sappho and Alcaeus*, trans. David A. Campbell, LCL 142 (Cambridge: Harvard University Press, 1982).

14. I think here also of Martin Buber, *I and Thou*, trans. Ronald Gregor Smith, 2nd ed. (New York: Charles Scribner's, 1958).

15. For a brief comparison of these three kinds of friends with similar classifications in the Old Testament, see Saul M. Olyan, *Friendship in the Hebrew Bible*, ABRL (New Haven: Yale University Press, 2017), 107.

16. Peggy Noonan, *The Time of Our Lives: Collected Writings* (New York: Twelve, 2015), 217.

17. Epstein, *Friendship*, 23.

18. Trust, or a "reliable comrade/friend," is characteristic as well of the elegiac poetry of Theognis. See Tyrtaeus et al., *Greek Elegiac Poetry: From the Seventh to the Fifth Centuries B.C.*, trans. Douglas E. Gerber, LCL 258 (Cambridge: Harvard University Press, 1999).

19. See the discussion in Adrian Goldsworthy, *Pax Romana: War, Peace and Conquest in the Roman World* (New Haven: Yale University Press, 2016), 63–70.

20. The case that Paul renamed some closely associated with church planting has been argued by Richard G. Fellows, "Renaming in Paul's Churches: The Case of Crispus-Sosthenes Revisited," *TynBul* 56 (2005): 111–30; Fellows, "Name Giving by Paul and the Destination of Acts," *TynBul* 67 (2016): 247–68. For example, on the basis of Acts 18:8 (Crispus) and 18:17 (evidently Sosthenes), it appears Crispus was renamed.

21. Olyan, *Friendship in the Hebrew Bible*.

22. "Love (n.)," *Merriam-Webster.com Dictionary*, https://www.merriam-webster.com/dictionary/love.

23. "Love (v.)," *Samuel Johnson's Dictionary*, https://johnsonsdictionaryonline.com/page-view/?i=1228.

24. This section is a revision of Scot McKnight, *A Fellowship of Differents: Showing the World God's Design for Life Together* (Grand Rapids: Zondervan, 2014), 51–63.

25. Olyan, *Friendship in the Hebrew Bible*, 62–69.

26. Olyan, *Friendship in the Hebrew Bible*, 69–77.

27. See Lev. 26:12; Jer. 7:23; 11:4; Ezek. 14:11; Zech. 8:8.

28. Missy Franklin, with D. A. Franklin and Dick Franklin, *Relentless Spirit: The Unconventional Raising of a Champion* (New York: Dutton, 2016), 205.

29. Eugene H. Peterson, *As Kingfishers Catch Fire: A Conversation on the Ways of God Formed by the Words of God* (Colorado Springs: WaterBrook, 2017), 20.

30. Henry David Thoreau, "Walking," quoted in Lopate, *Art of the Personal Essay*, 483.

31. John Goldingay, *Old Testament Theology: Israel's Gospel* (Downers Grove, IL: IVP Academic, 2015), 332–43.

32. David A. deSilva, *Transformation: The Heart of Paul's Gospel* (Bellingham, WA: Lexham Press, 2014).

33. Fully explored in Jon D. Levenson, *The Love of God: Divine Gift, Human Gratitude, and Mutual Faithfulness in Judaism* (Princeton: Princeton University Press, 2016).

34. Levenson, *Love of God*, 13.

35. Levenson, *Love of God*, 21–48.

36. John Goldingay translates Psalm 91:14 as, "Because he's attracted to me" and Isaiah 38:17 as, "But you yourself delighted in me." See John Goldingay, *The First Testament: A New Translation* (Downers Grove, IL: IVP Academic, 2018).

37. The texts on which I base the following narrative are Acts 11:19–30; 12:12; 13:13; 15:36–41; 1 Cor. 9:6; Col. 4:10; Philem. 24; 2 Tim. 4:11.

38. A recent exposition of the centrality of reconciliation in Paul's theology is Stanley E. Porter, "Reconciliation as the Heart of Paul's Missionary Theology," in *Paul as Missionary: Identity, Activity, Theology, and Practice*, ed. Trevor J. Burke and Brian S. Rosner, LNTS 420 (London: T&T Clark, 2011), 169–79.

39. Robert Jewett, *Romans: A Commentary*, Hermeneia (Minneapolis: Fortress, 2007), 941–48; Lynn H. Cohick, *Women in the World of the Earliest Christians: Illuminating Ancient Ways of Life* (Grand Rapids: Baker Academic, 2009), 285–320; Joan Cecelia Campbell, *Phoebe: Patron and Emissary* (Collegeville, MN: Michael Glazier, 2009).

40. Cohick, *Women in the World of the Earliest Christians*, 303–7.

41. On the importance of reciprocity among the benevolent, see John M. G. Barclay, *Paul and the Gift* (Grand Rapids: Eerdmans, 2015).

42. What follows strings together Col. 1:7–8; 2:1; 4:12; Philem. 23.

43. See Scot McKnight, *The Letter to the Colossians*, NICNT (Grand Rapids: Eerdmans, 2018), 18–34.

44. Here are the texts behind my brief sketch of Timothy's life: Acts 14:19–20; 16:1–3; 17:14–16; 18:5; 19:22; 20:4; 1 Thess. 1:1; 3:1–6; 2 Thess. 1:1; 1 Cor. 4:17; 16:10–11; 2 Cor. 1:1, 19; 11:9; Rom. 16:21; Col. 1:1; Philem. 1; Phil. 1:1; 2:19, 22–23; 1 Tim. 1:3, 18; 4:12, 14; 2 Tim. 1:5–6; 3:11, 15; 4:13, 21; Heb. 13:23.

45. E. Randolph Richards, *The Secretary in the Letters of Paul*, WUNT 2.42 (Tübingen: Mohr Siebeck, 1991); Richards, *Paul and First-Century Letter Writing: Secretaries, Composition and Collection* (Downers Grove, IL: InterVarsity, 2004). Some of Richards has been challenged recently; see Jeffrey A. D. Weima, *Paul the Ancient Letter Writer: An Introduction to Epistolary Analysis* (Grand Rapids: Baker Academic, 2016).

Chapter 3 A Culture of Siblings

1. P. D. James, *Death in Holy Orders* (New York: Knopf, 2001), 94–95.

2. Richard S. Ascough, *The Formation of Pauline Churches* (New York: Paulist Press, 1998); Philip Harland, *Associations, Synagogues, and Congregations: Claiming*

a Place in Ancient Mediterranean Society (Minneapolis: Fortress, 2003); Richard S. Ascough, Philip A. Harland, and John S. Kloppenborg, *Associations in the Greco-Roman World: A Sourcebook* (Waco: Baylor University Press, 2012); Richard S. Ascough, "What Are They *Now* Saying about Christ Groups and Associations?," *CurBR* 13 (2015): 207–44.

3. This word is used in the New Testament only in Matt. 20:13; 22:12; 26:50, and never as a term describing Jesus's relations with his disciples or their relations with one another. It is used in unremarkable, typical ways in two parables and then in 26:50 for Judas. Jesus uses *philoi* at times (John 11:11; 15:13–15; see also Matt. 11:19; Luke 11:5, 8; 12:4; 14:10, 12; 15:6, 9, 29; 16:9; 21:16), and in Acts, Luke twice speaks of Paul's *philoi* (19:31; 27:3). All the more reason, then, for us to take note of the absence of *philoi* in Paul.

4. Developed throughout the small book by J. Neusner, *Fellowship in Judaism: The First Century and Today* (London: Vallentine and Mitchell, 1963).

5. The emphasis on food for Pharisees draws me into the orbit of Neusner and away from some of the claims of E. P. Sanders, though I don't line up with everything Neusner says on this issue. He overdoes the priestly feel of the Pharisees but does get their concern for purity right. This debate once raged, but many today are unaware of it. See Jacob Neusner, *The Rabbinic Traditions about the Pharisees Before 70*, 3 vols. (repr., Eugene, OR: Wipf & Stock, 2005); E. P. Sanders, *Judaism: Practice and Belief, 63 BCE–66 CE* (Minneapolis: Fortress, 2016); E. P. Sanders, *Jewish Law from Jesus to the Mishnah: Five Studies* (Minneapolis: Fortress, 2016), 183–354. For a good discussion, see R. Deines, "Pharisees," in *Eerdmans Dictionary of Early Judaism*, ed. J.J. Collins and D. C. Harlow (Grand Rapids: Eerdmans, 2010), 1061–63.

6. Neusner, *Fellowship in Judaism*, 12.

7. H. Richard Niebuhr, *Christ and Culture* (San Francisco: HarperSanFrancisco, 2001), 190–229.

8. E.g., Luke 12:4; 14:12; 16:9; John 3:29; 11:11; 15:13–15; see also Acts 27:3; 3 John 15.

9. See Paul S. Minear, *Images of the Church in the New Testament* (Philadelphia: Westminster John Knox, 1960). See also, Paul Trebilco, *Self-Designations and Group Identity in the New Testament* (Cambridge: Cambridge University Press, 2012)—p. 14 alone contains much of Minear! A wider study is Avery Dulles, *Models of the Church*, 2nd ed. (New York: Image, 1991).

10. The dominance of *adelphos*/sibling language for the Pauline mission churches in some ways reveals that Paul's churches are not simply to be identified as *collegia*, or associations, inasmuch as *adelphos*/sibling language was used much less in reference to such groups. But see Harland, *Associations, Synagogues, and Congregations*, 31–33.

11. Saul M. Olyan, *Friendship in the Hebrew Bible*, ABRL (New Haven: Yale University Press, 2017), 37.

12. For a broader but still useful sketch, see the discussion of body, fellowship, and siblingship in Ernest Best, *Paul and His Converts*, Sprunt Lectures 1985 (Edinburgh: T&T Clark, 1988), 125–37.

13. Reidar Aasgaard, *"My Beloved Brothers and Sisters!" Christian Siblingship in Paul*, JSNTSup 265 (London: T&T Clark, 2004), 3. On siblingship, David G. Horrell, "From *adelphoi* to *oikos*: Social Transformation in Pauline Christianity," *JBL* 120 (2001): 293–311; Mary Katherine Birge, *The Language of Belonging: A Rhetorical*

Analysis of Kinship Language in First Corinthians, CBET 31 (Leuven: Peeters, 2002); Aasgaard, *"My Beloved Brothers and Sisters!"*; Andrew D. Clarke, "Equality or Mutuality? Paul's Use of 'Brother' Language," in *The New Testament in Its First Century Setting: Essays in Honour of B. W. Winter on His 65th Birthday*, ed. P. J. Williams et al. (Grand Rapids: Eerdmans, 2004), 151–64; Trebilco, *Self-Designations and Group Identity*; David G. Horrell, *Solidarity and Difference: A Contemporary Reading of Paul's Ethics*, 2nd ed. (London: Bloomsbury T&T Clark, 2015), 121–26.

14. "Body" (*sōma*) is used for the church some thirty times, with eighteen times in 1 Cor. 12:12–27; "saints," again about thirty times; "fellowship," about a dozen times. "Church" is used about sixty times.

15. John M. G. Barclay, "The Family as the Bearer of Religion in Judaism and Early Christianity," in *Constructing Early Christian Families: Family as Social Reality and Metaphor*, ed. Halvor Moxnes (London: Routledge, 1997), 66–80. Also, Stephen C. Barton, "The Relativisation of Family Ties in the Jewish and Graeco-Roman Traditions," in Moxnes, *Constructing Early Christian Families*, 81–100. Not denying the tension in some early Christian families, one must also consider both the common reality that religions were not ordinarily chosen but handed down to the family by the family's traditions and that "household" baptisms often maintained family ties.

16. Did Paul see himself as a sibling among siblings, or was his relationship asymmetrical? The latter is true without denying the former. If Paul can call someone "my" brother (e.g., Rom. 7:4; 15:14; 1 Cor. 8:13; 11:33; 15:58; 2 Cor. 1:1; 2:13; 8:22–23; Phil. 3:1; 4:1; Col. 1:1–2; 4:7, 9; 1 Thess. 3:2), he makes himself a sibling among siblings. The address "brothers (and sisters)" then makes no sense if Paul is not one of them. Just as Paul can sustain various hierarchies among siblings (in accordance with antiquity), so asymmetrical authority will not delete Paul's own sense of siblingship. See Clarke, "Equality or Mutuality?," 156–64. Contra Horrell, "From *adelphoi* to *oikos*."

17. "Sibling" is not the same as "family," though they are obviously connected. For a wide-ranging series of studies by a number of scholars on family in early Christianity and its contexts, see Moxnes, *Constructing Early Christian Families*.

18. Greg Mamula, "Welcome to the Family Table," https://welcometothefamily table.wordpress.com/welcome-to-the-family-table/.

19. John Sanders, *Theology in the Flesh: How Embodiment and Culture Shape the Way We Think about Truth, Morality, and God* (Minneapolis: Fortress, 2016), 45–77.

20. For now see Beverly Gaventa, *Our Mother Saint Paul* (Louisville: Westminster John Knox, 2007). Estimates for the ancient world are always a bit speculative, but experts contend 80 percent of children had a living father at birth; at twenty that number decreases to 50 percent; at thirty, to 20 percent; at forty, 10 percent; and by fifty most had no living father. See Aasgaard, *"My Beloved Brothers and Sisters!,"* 37.

21. Developed in Trevor J. Burke, "Mother, Father, Infant, Orphan, Brother: Paul's Variegated Pastoral Strategy towards His Thessalonian Church Family," in *Paul as Pastor*, ed. Brian S. Rosner, Andrew S. Malone, and Trevor J. Burke (New York: Bloomsbury T&T Clark, 2017), 123–41.

22. George Lakoff and Mark Johnson, *Metaphors We Live By* (Chicago: University of Chicago Press, 2003); J. Sanders, *Theology in the Flesh*.

23. Aasgaard, *"My Beloved Brothers and Sisters!,"* 61–92, 93–106.

24. Joseph Epstein, *Life Sentences: Literary Essays* (New York: Norton, 1997), 207.

25. Murray J. Harris, *The Second Epistle to the Corinthians*, NIGTC (Grand Rapids: Eerdmans, 2005), 486–521.

26. Aasgaard, *"My Beloved Brothers and Sisters!,"* 75–78, 285–95; Trebilco, *Self-Designations and Group Identity*, 20–21.

27. (Quintus Caecilius) Metellus (Macedonicus) was a Roman general and opposed Scipio, but when the latter died, Metellus urged his sons to carry the bier; see Plutarch, *Sayings of the Romans* 202.1–3.

28. On the importance of differences, see Larry W. Hurtado, *Destroyer of the Gods: Early Christian Distinctiveness in the Roman World* (Waco: Baylor University Press, 2016).

29. Again, I recommend Greg Mamula, "Shaped by the Story," https://shapedby thenarrative.wordpress.com/welcome-to-the-family-table/.

30. Robert Jewett, *Romans: A Commentary*, Hermeneia (Minneapolis: Fortress, 2007), 953.

31. Larry W. Hurtado, *At the Origins of Christian Worship: The Context and Character of Earliest Christian Devotion* (Grand Rapids: Eerdmans, 1999), 39–62.

32. Explored in P. F. Esler, "Family Imagery and Christian Identity in Galatians 5:13 to 6:10," in Moxnes, *Constructing Early Christian Families*, 121–49. The nuanced difference between family and siblings, however, shifts the group identity slightly. Such is explored in the same volume by Karl Olav Sandnes, "Equality within Patriarchal Structures: Some New Testament Perspectives on the Christian Fellowship as a Brother- or Sisterhood and a Family," in Moxnes, *Constructing Early Christian Families*, 150–65. In the same volume, Aasgaard's early work appears, but I have used throughout this chapter his later study, *"My Beloved Brothers and Sisters!"*

33. On honor, Aasgaard, *"My Beloved Brothers and Sisters!,"* 51–53.

34. On this passage, see Andrew D. Clarke, *Secular and Christian Leadership in Corinth: A Socio-Historical and Exegetical Study of 1 Corinthians 1–6*, Paternoster Biblical Monographs (Milton Keynes, UK: Paternoster, 2006), 59–71.

35. For an excellent commentary on this passage, see Roy E. Ciampa and Brian S. Rosner, *The First Letter to the Corinthians* (Grand Rapids: Eerdmans, 2010), 237–45. For a study, see Roy E. Ciampa, "'Flee Sexual Immorality': Sex and the City of Corinth," in *The Wisdom of the Cross: Exploring 1 Corinthians*, ed. Brian S. Rosner (Nottingham, UK: Apollos/Inter-Varsity, 2011), 100–133. For one man's journey in life with this text, see Wesley Hill, *Washed and Waiting: Reflections on Christian Faithfulness and Homosexuality* (Grand Rapids: Zondervan, 2010).

36. See Scot McKnight, *The Letter to Philemon*, NICNT (Grand Rapids: Eerdmans, 2017). See also the sibling themes developed in Aasgaard, *"My Beloved Brothers and Sisters!,"* 237–60.

37. Roger Scruton, *Gentle Regrets: Thoughts from a Life* (London: Continuum, 2006), 85.

38. Norman R. Petersen, *Rediscovering Paul: Philemon and the Sociology of Paul's Narrative World* (Philadelphia: Fortress, 1985), 93–124.

39. Aasgaard, *"My Beloved Brothers and Sisters!,"* 107–16.

40. Trebilco, *Self-Designations and Group Identity*, 39–42; Scot McKnight, *A New Vision for Israel: The Teachings of Jesus in National Context* (Grand Rapids: Eerdmans, 1999), 179–87.

41. Dietrich Bonhoeffer, *"Life Together" and "Prayerbook of the Bible,"* ed. Eberhard Bethge, trans. G. L. Müller, Dietrich Bonhoeffer Works 5 (Minneapolis: Fortress, 1996), 27–47.

Chapter 4 A Culture of Generosity

1. Marilynne Robinson, *Gilead* (New York: Farrar, Straus and Giroux, 2004), 39.

2. Anthony Trollope, *The Warden* (repr., Harmondsworth, UK: Penguin Classics, 1984), 67–68.

3. E. Earle Ellis, *Pauline Theology: Ministry and Society* (Grand Rapids: Eerdmans, 1989), 154–55.

4. Ellis, *Pauline Theology*, 17–25, 122–59. In comparing Paul to contemporary philosophers, Malherbe thinks Paul (and his churches) chose not to take the withdrawal options of either the Cynics or the Epicureans, but was more socially engaged: see Abraham J. Malherbe, *Paul and the Thessalonians: The Philosophic Tradition of Pastoral Care* (repr., Eugene, OR: Wipf & Stock, 2011), 95–107.

5. Bruce W. Longenecker, *Remember the Poor: Paul, Poverty, and the Greco-Roman World* (Grand Rapids: Eerdmans, 2010), 5–6.

6. Verlyn D. Verbrugge and Keith R. Krell, *Paul and Money: A Biblical and Theological Analysis of the Apostle's Teachings and Practices* (Grand Rapids: Zondervan, 2015). I cannot move on without paying homage to Verlyn, not only for his career of editing for Zondervan but also for his exemplary Christian character.

7. Alistair C. Stewart, *The Original Bishops: Office and Order in the First Christian Communities* (Grand Rapids: Baker Academic, 2014).

8. R. Alastair Campbell, *The Elders: Seniority within Earliest Christianity*, SNTW (Edinburgh: T&T Clark, 1994), 246.

9. Edwin Hatch, *The Organization of the Early Christian Churches*, The Bampton Lectures 1880 (repr., Eugene, OR: Wipf & Stock, 1999).

10. For a brief review, see Kevin Giles, *Patterns of Ministry among the First Christians*, 2nd ed. (Eugene, OR: Cascade, 2017), 75–77.

11. B. Longenecker, *Remember the Poor*, 36–59, 317–32. He places Paul in what he calls "ES4" (= economic scale number 4), which puts Paul in the "moderate surplus" level and above ES5s, persons whose economic condition was stable and near subsistence with reasonable hope of staying there; ES6s, those living at the subsistence level and often below minimum level; and ES7s, those living below subsistence levels. Three percent of those in the Roman Empire were above Paul's level, while Paul's level (ES4) had about 15 percent, ES5 had 27 percent, ES6 was at 30 percent, and 25 percent were at ES7. Our capacity to grade demographics and economic levels entails both sophisticated analysis and a moderate amount of speculation. Scholars today generally agree with the conclusions of this scale.

12. Gary A. Anderson, *Charity: The Place of the Poor in the Biblical Tradition* (New Haven: Yale University Press, 2013); David J. Downs, *Alms: Charity, Reward, and Atonement in Early Christianity* (Waco: Baylor University Press, 2016).

13. Ernest Best, *Paul and His Converts*, Sprunt Lectures 1985 (Edinburgh: T&T Clark, 1988), 97–106; Stephan Joubert, *Paul as Benefactor: Reciprocity, Strategy and Theological Reflection in Paul's Collection*, WUNT 2.124 (Tübingen: Mohr Siebeck, 2000); David J. Downs, *The Offering of the Gentiles: Paul's Collection for Jerusalem*

in Its Chronological, Cultural, and Cultic Contexts (Grand Rapids: Eerdmans, 2016); B. Longenecker, *Remember the Poor*; Verbrugge and Krell, *Paul and Money*. Long ago I wrote "Collection for the Saints," in *DPL*, 143–47, and I make use of that piece at times in this chapter.

14. Joubert makes much of this event as an act that obligated Paul to collect funds for the poor in Jerusalem; see Joubert, *Paul as Benefactor*, 73–115. Some think Gal. 6:6–10 echoes the collection; see Larry W. Hurtado, "The Jerusalem Collection and the Book of Galatians," *JSNT* 5 (1979): 46–62.

15. So B. Longenecker, *Remember the Poor*; Verbrugge and Krell, *Paul and Money*, 107–29; Downs, *Offering of the Gentiles*, 30–72.

16. For a summary analysis, S. Hafemann, "Letters to the Corinthians," *DPL*, 175–77.

17. The best recent sketch of the options is Downs, *Offering of the Gentiles*, 3–26.

18. The desire to find a theological explanation is criticized by Joubert, *Paul as Benefactor*, 3–5.

19. Verbrugge and Krell, *Paul and Money*, 130–46.

20. For discussion, see Keith Fullerton Nickle, *The Collection: A Study in Paul's Strategy*, SBT 48 (Naperville, IL: Allenson, 1966), 129–42; Downs, *Offering of the Gentiles*, 3–9. In a recent study, Seyoon Kim has argued the collection was designed to spur the Jews to jealousy, faith, and to witness to the wealth of the gentiles flowing to Zion; see his "Paul as an Eschatological Herald," in *Paul as Missionary: Identity, Activity, Theology, and Practice*, ed. Trevor J. Burke and Brian S. Rosner, LNTS 420 (London: T&T Clark, 2011), 9–24. The term meaning "fullness" (*plēroma*) in the collection passage in Rom. 15:29 as well as in the jealousy passage in 11:11–12 and hardening passage in 11:25 supports such a connection (see also 2 Cor. 9:12–14).

21. Klaus Berger, "Almosen für Israel," *NTS* 23 (1977): 180–204; Joubert, *Paul as Benefactor*. Berger connects almsgiving to entrance into the covenant, whereas Joubert masterfully expounds the benefit exchange inherent to the Roman practices of friendship. He has a clear outline of how benefaction worked in practice on pp. 70–72. An earlier study on the theme is G. W. Peterman, *Paul's Gift from Philippi: Conventions of Gift Exchange and Christian Giving*, SNTSMS 92 (Cambridge: Cambridge University Press, 1997), 22–89. All of this has been enhanced now by the full study of John M. G. Barclay, *Paul and the Gift* (Grand Rapids: Eerdmans, 2015).

22. Joubert, *Paul as Benefactor*, 132 (italics original).

23. The consistency of Paul's practice of receiving support has been called into question (Why not Corinth? Why Philippi?), and the best explanations I have seen are found in these two studies: Peterman, *Paul's Gift from Philippi*, 90–194; David E. Briones, *Paul's Financial Policy: A Socio-Theological Approach*, LNTS 494 (London: Bloomsbury T&T Clark, 2013). For Peterman, Paul avoided gifts that were still too formed by the social conventions of reciprocity and obligation; for Briones, Paul had a two-step policy: as he established a church, he did not receive funds, but upon relocating to another city, he could receive support if the church was sufficiently Christoform. A view similar to Briones's is found in Verbrugge and Krell, *Paul and Money*.

24. B. Longenecker, *Remember the Poor*, 216.

25. Bruce W. Winter, *Seek the Welfare of the City: Christians as Benefactors and Citizens*, First Century Christians in the Graeco-Roman World (Grand Rapids: Eerdmans, 1994), 11–40, esp. 19–20. But see also B. Longenecker, *Remember the Poor*, 157–82.

26. For full discussions, see B. Longenecker, *Remember the Poor*, 60–107, 108–31; Anderson, *Charity*; Downs, *Alms*. For a wide-ranging study on Ephesus and wealth, see Gary G. Hoag, *Wealth in Ancient Ephesus and the First Letter to Timothy: Fresh Insights from "Ephesiaca" by Xenophon of Ephesus* (Winona Lake, IN: Eisenbrauns, 2015).

27. On this theme, which clashes in Protestant ears, see Anderson, *Charity*; Downs, *Alms*.

28. Jeanne E. Arnold et al., *Life at Home in the Twenty-First Century: Thirty-Two Families Open Their Doors* (Los Angeles: The Cotsen Institute of Archaeology Press, 2017), 23–51.

29. I find wisdom in David Roseberry, *Giving Up: How Giving to God Renews Hearts, Changes Minds, and Empowers Ministry* (Franklin, TN: New Vantage, 2017). Two standard books, recommended to me by pastors, on this theme that might help pastors teach congregations financial integrity and responsibility, and especially learning to avoid debt and overspending, are Dave Ramsey, *The Total Money Makeover, Classic Edition: A Proven Plan for Financial Fitness* (Nashville: Thomas Nelson, 2013); Randy Alcorn, *Managing God's Money: A Biblical Guide* (Carol Stream, IL: Tyndale House, 2011). A friend of mine whom we consult about all things financial, Scott Wagoner, recommends Eric Ravenscraft's blog post "How to Start Managing Your Money, for Those Who Never Learned Growing Up," Lifehacker, May 12, 2015, https://lifehacker .com/how-to-manage-your-money-for-those-who-never-learned-g-1703892260.

30. Roseberry, *Giving Up*, 25, 37–50, 53–59.

31. Roseberry, *Giving Up*, 158.

32. The thesis of Joubert, *Paul as Benefactor*.

33. This has been fully explored by David Downs, and in what follows I rely on Downs, *Offering of the Gentiles*, 120–60.

34. Downs, *Offering of the Gentiles*, 129–31. He cites evidence from inscriptions.

35. Initial research was done by Richard S. Ascough, "The Completion of a Religious Duty: The Background of 2 Cor. 8.1–15," *NTS* 42 (1996): 584–99. See the summary of Downs, *Offering of the Gentiles*, 135–37.

36. This is the thesis especially of Downs, *Offering of the Gentiles*.

37. This is emphasized by many, including Peterman, *Paul's Gift from Philippi*; Joubert, *Paul as Benefactor*; B. Longenecker, *Remember the Poor*; Downs, *Offering of the Gentiles*.

38. One who has not neglected this, though it came to my attention after I had come to this conclusion myself, is David G. Horrell, *Solidarity and Difference: A Contemporary Reading of Paul's Ethics*, 2nd ed. (London: Bloomsbury T&T Clark, 2015), 254–65. Another study with some focus on 2 Cor. 8:13–14 is Justin Meggitt, *Paul, Poverty and Survival*, SNTW (Edinburgh: T&T Clark, 1998).

39. Surely something that could have attracted nonbelievers. Developed by B. Longenecker, *Remember the Poor*, 259–78.

40. BDAG, 481.

41. Spicq, *TLNT* 2:223–32.

42. The numbers in parentheses indicate section numbers in "Letter of Aristeas," trans. R. J. H. Shutt, in *The Old Testament Pseudepigrapha*, vol. 2, ed. James H. Charlesworth, 7–34 (New York: Doubleday, 1985).

43. Deut. 8:3 reimagines the manna story in a direction different from Exod. 16 and Paul; for Deut. 8 the "manna" becomes code for learning to trust the word of

God. This won't work for Paul. John interprets manna christologically in John 10, and neither is this enough for Paul, who wants something to take place at the socioeconomic level.

44. *Seneca: On Benefits*, trans. Miriam Griffin and Brad Inwood (Chicago: University of Chicago Press, 2011), 2.17.3–5.

45. In Ephesus at the time of Paul's ministry a fishing cartel raised funds to build a customs building near the harbor, and the monument listed the names of the donors. Such public honor commonly attended gifts in the first century. See *NewDocs*, 5:95–114.

46. An illustration of this sense of *isotēs* can be found in an inscription from the southeastern port of the Peloponnesus, where we learn of a doctor named Damidas who gave to those in need "so that there might be equality for all." See *IG* V.1 1145, *Laconia et Messenia*, line 19: εἰς τὸ πᾶσιν ἴσος εἶναι (https://epigraphy.packhum.org/text /31559?&bookid=11&location=1699).

47. Horrell, *Solidarity and Difference*, 264.

48. Murray J. Harris, *The Second Epistle to the Corinthians*, NIGTC (Grand Rapids: Eerdmans, 2005), 588, 592.

49. Willimon, *Pastor: The Theology and Practice of Ordained Ministry*, 85.

50. B. Longenecker, *Remember the Poor*, 1. Better is p. 219, where caring for the poor is connected to the cruciform life. Even more should it be connected to what I call the Jesus creed: loving God and loving others (see Mark 12:28–32).

51. Stated at B. Longenecker, *Remember the Poor*, 12.

52. B. Longenecker, *Remember the Poor*, 291.

53. Downs, *Offering of the Gentiles*, 21, 22.

Chapter 5 A Culture of Storytellers

1. Richard N. Longenecker, *Biblical Exegesis in the Apostolic Period*, rev. ed. (Grand Rapids: Eerdmans, 1999), 91–98.

2. Eugene H. Peterson, "Pastor Paul," in *Romans and the People of God: Essays in Honor of Gordon D. Fee on the Occasion of His 65th Birthday*, ed. Sven K. Soderlund and N. T. Wright (Grand Rapids: Eerdmans, 1999), 286, 287 (italics original).

3. Peggy Noonan, *The Time of Our Lives: Collected Writings* (New York: Twelve, 2015), 199–200.

4. I focused on racism in Scot McKnight, *A Fellowship of Differents: Showing the World God's Design for Life Together* (Grand Rapids: Zondervan, 2014).

5. On which I have yet to read de Tocqueville, *Democracy in America*, trans. Harvey C. Mansfield and Delba Winthrop (Chicago: University of Chicago Press, 2000).

6. An important set of studies here is by Randall Balmer: *Thy Kingdom Come: How the Religious Right Distorts Faith and Threatens America* (New York: Basic Books, 2007); *God in the White House: A History; How Faith Shaped the Presidency from John F. Kennedy to George W. Bush* (New York: HarperOne, 2008).

7. Abraham Kuyper, *Lectures on Calvinism* (Grand Rapids: Eerdmans, 1931); H. Richard Niebuhr, *Christ and Culture* (San Francisco: HarperSanFrancisco, 2001); Francis A. Schaeffer, *How Should We Then Live? The Rise and Decline of Western Thought and Culture* (Wheaton: Crossway, 2005); David T. Koyzis, *Political Visions and Illusions: A Survey and Christian Critique of Contemporary Ideologies* (Downers

Grove, IL: InterVarsity, 2003); David R. Swartz, *Moral Minority: The Evangelical Left in an Age of Conservatism* (Philadelphia: University of Pennsylvania Press, 2012); Craig G. Bartholomew, *Contours of the Kuyperian Tradition: A Systematic Introduction* (Downers Grove, IL: IVP Academic, 2017).

8. There is a movement, mostly in the US, called dominion theology or dominionists or Christian Reconstructionism or Theonomy, which takes its cues from folks such as R. J. Rushdoony or David Barton or Gary North and others, and which believes in influentialism to the degree that it is striving for America as a Christian state.

9. Marilynne Robinson, *What Are We Doing Here? Essays* (New York: Farrar, Straus and Giroux, 2018), 36.

10. Daniel L. Dreisbach, *Reading the Bible with the Founding Fathers* (New York: Oxford University Press, 2016).

11. Brent A. Strawn, *The Old Testament Is Dying: A Diagnosis and Recommended Treatment* (Grand Rapids: Baker Academic, 2017).

12. Henri J. M. Nouwen, *The Wounded Healer: Ministry in Contemporary Society* (New York: Doubleday, 1990), 9–12.

13. The idea of a storied core is rooted in R. Bauckham, "Reading Scripture as a Coherent Story," in Ellen F. Davis and Richard B. Hays, *The Art of Reading Scripture* (Grand Rapids: Eerdmans, 2003), 38–52. For scholarship on Scripture's summaries, see Jason B. Hood and Matthew Y. Emerson, "Summaries of Israel's Story: Reviewing a Compositional Category," *CurBR* 11 (2013): 328–48. They provide a comprehensive listing of all the canonical and noncanonical passages on pp. 340–43. Here, I'll suggest the following: Exod. 15; Lev. 26:4–13; Deut. 6:20–24; 26:5–9; 29; 32; Josh. 23:2–4; 24:2–13; 1 Sam. 12:7–15; 1 Kings 8; 1 Chron. 1–9; 16:8–36; Ezra 5:11–27; Neh. 9:6–37; Pss. 78; 105; 106; 135:8–12; 136; Isa. 5:1–7; Jer. 2:2–9; Ezek. 16; 20; 23; Dan. 9:1–27; Hab. 3:1–16; Matt. 1:1–17; Acts 7:2–50; 10:36–43; 13:17–41; Rom. 9–11; Heb. 11; Rev. 12:1–12. How can one not also include 1 Cor. 15:1–28 and Rev. 21–22?

For historical context, one must add to this at least Josephus's various books, most especially *Antiquities of the Jews* and the *Jewish War*, which bring to the surface his worldview and story. If we begin reading the Dead Sea Scrolls with 1QM or CD, we will find a rudimentary narrative, and yet again we have another worldview, more like the Old Testament and the New Testament than like Josephus. The Maccabean narratives float on a narrative of Israel that informs each of the texts, and they too take what is found in various Old Testament narratives and reimagine them into a new worldview. Beyond the New Testament, early Christian literature also got in on the act of summarizing Israel's story as it had come to fulfillment in Jesus: 1 Clement 4–6; 9–12; 17:1–19:2; 31:1–32:4; Athanasius, *Letter to Marcellinus* 2–8; Origen, *First Homily*; and perhaps pride of place goes to Irenaeus, *On the Apostolic Preaching*. For a complete listing, see Hood and Emerson, "Summaries of Israel's Story," 343.

14. David Steinmetz, *Taking the Long View: Christian Theology in Historical Perspective* (New York: Oxford University Press, 2011), 15–26.

15. See esp. James D. G. Dunn, "The Narrative Approach to Paul: Whose Story?," in *Narrative Dynamics in Paul: A Critical Assessment*, ed. Bruce W. Longenecker (Louisville: Westminster John Knox, 2002), 217–30.

16. The various grand, assumed, and hermeneutically exploited narratives of some scholarship today have been put through the ringer by A. Andrew Das, *Paul and the Stories of Israel: Grand Thematic Narratives in Galatians* (Minneapolis: Fortress,

2016). He examines and finds serious criticisms of the major theories: the gentile influx to Zion, covenant, the Aqedah, exodus, the Spirit in the cloud, and the imperial cult.

17. In making this move I am agreeing with the formidable study of Matthew Bates about the apostolic proclamation of the gospel as the basis of Paul's hermeneutics: Matthew W. Bates, *The Hermeneutics of the Apostolic Proclamation: The Center of Paul's Method of Scriptural Interpretation* (Waco: Baylor University Press, 2012). He sketches a variety of approaches to Paul's hermeneutics on pp. 9–41.

18. Many today would contend that Paul didn't write the Pastoral Epistles (1–2 Timothy, Titus) and that they are pseudonymously attributed to him. Such discussions can be found in any New Testament introduction or in a commentary on the Pastorals.

19. Scot McKnight, *The King Jesus Gospel: The Original Good News Revisited*, 2nd ed. (Grand Rapids: Zondervan, 2015).

20. For a christological narrative rooted in Rom. 8, see Douglas A. Campbell, "The Story of Jesus in Romans and Galatians," in B. Longenecker, *Narrative Dynamics in Paul*, 97–124. His narrative is outlined into descent and ascent motifs on p. 108. His analysis is critiqued in the same volume by Graham N. Stanton, "'I Think, When I Read That Sweet Story of Old,'" in B. Longenecker, *Narrative Dynamics in Paul*, 125–32.

21. On Nero, see David Shotter, *Nero Caesar Augustus: Emperor of Rome* (New York: Routledge, 2008).

22. On Petronius and Seneca, see *Petronius: Satyricon; Seneca: Apocolocyntosis*, trans. Michael Heseltine and W. H. D. Rouse, revised by E. H. Warmington, rev. ed., LCL 15 (Cambridge: Harvard University Press, 1975). On Seneca, see James Romm, *Dying Every Day: Seneca at the Court of Nero* (New York: Knopf, 2014).

23. At this point a long and energetic discussion about how Paul read the Bible—forward? backward? forward and backward? backward and forward?—could overwhelm this chapter. In an earlier version of the chapter, it did. By admitting the gospel as a "second" narrative, I have admitted, too, that a Christian forward reading of the Old Testament or a forward reading of Israel's story is ultimately based on the gospel itself. For this discussion, one needs to engage at least the following top-notch scholarship: John Goldingay, *Do We Need the New Testament? Letting the Old Testament Speak for Itself* (Downers Grove, IL: IVP Academic, 2015); Goldingay, *Reading Jesus's Bible: How the New Testament Helps Us Understand the Old Testament* (Grand Rapids: Eerdmans, 2017); N. T. Wright, *Paul and the Faithfulness of God*, 2 vols., Christian Origins and the Question of God 4 (Minneapolis: Fortress, 2013); Douglas A. Campbell, *The Quest for Paul's Gospel* (London: T&T Clark, 2005); D. Campbell, *The Deliverance of God: An Apocalyptic Rereading of Justification in Paul* (Grand Rapids: Eerdmans, 2013); D. Campbell, *Paul: An Apostle's Journey* (Grand Rapids: Eerdmans, 2018); Richard B. Hays, *Echoes of Scripture in the Letters of Paul* (New Haven: Yale University Press, 1993); Hays, *The Conversion of the Imagination: Paul as Interpreter of Israel's Scripture* (Grand Rapids: Eerdmans, 2005); Hays, *Echoes of Scripture in the Gospels* (Waco: Baylor University Press, 2016); Hays, *Reading Backwards: Figural Christology and the Fourfold Gospel Witness* (Waco: Baylor University Press, 2014); Hans Boersma, *Scripture as Real Presence: Sacramental Exegesis in the Early Church* (Grand Rapids: Baker Academic, 2017).

24. We could at this point dwell, too, on 2 Cor. 3:17–4:6 as another instance of how Jesus as Lord reshapes Israel's story. For discussions, see Hays, *Echoes of Scripture*

in the Letters of Paul, 131–49; Bates, *Hermeneutics of the Apostolic Proclamation*, 160–81.

25. Matthew E. Gordley, *Teaching through Song in Antiquity: Didactic Hymnody among Greeks, Romans, Jews, and Christians*, WUNT 2.302 (Tübingen: Mohr Siebeck, 2011).

26. For the debate, see James D. G. Dunn, *Christology in the Making: A New Testament into the Origins of the Doctrine of the Incarnation*, 2nd ed. (Philadelphia: Westminster John Knox, 1989); Larry W. Hurtado, *Lord Jesus Christ: Devotion to Jesus in Earliest Christianity* (Grand Rapids: Eerdmans, 2003); Larry W. Hurtado, *How on Earth Did Jesus Become a God? Historical Questions about Earliest Devotion to Jesus* (Grand Rapids: Eerdmans, 2005); James D. G. Dunn, *Did the First Christians Worship Jesus? The New Testament Evidence* (Louisville: Westminster John Knox, 2010).

27. Michael J. Gorman, *Inhabiting the Cruciform God: Kenosis, Justification, and Theosis in Paul's Narrative Soteriology* (Grand Rapids: Eerdmans, 2009).

28. For more on this theme, concentrating especially on Rom. 8, see Edward Adams, "Paul's Story of God and Creation: The Story of How God Fulfils His Purposes in Creation," in B. Longenecker, *Narrative Dynamics in Paul*, 19–43. For a royal interpretation of Col. 1:15–20, see Joshua W. Jipp, *Christ Is King: Paul's Royal Ideology* (Minneapolis: Fortress, 2015), 100–127.

29. Matthew Croasmun, *The Emergence of Sin: The Cosmic Tyrant in Romans* (New York: Oxford University Press, 2017).

30. See, e.g., Scot McKnight, *A Community Called Atonement* (Nashville: Abingdon, 2007).

31. Simeon R. Burke, "'Render to Caesar the Things of Caesar and to God the Things of God': Recent Perspectives on a Puzzling Command (1945–Present)," *CurBR* 16 (2018): 157–90.

32. David A. deSilva, *Transformation: The Heart of Paul's Gospel* (Bellingham, WA: Lexham Press, 2014), 2 (italics original).

33. This section is a condensed and revised version of Scot McKnight, *The Letter to the Colossians*, NICNT (Grand Rapids: Eerdmans, 2018), 251–61.

34. Andrew T. Lincoln, "Liberation from the Powers: Supernatural Spirits or Societal Structures?," in *The Bible in Human Society: Essays in Honour of John Rogerson*, ed. M. Daniel Carroll R., David J. A. Clines, and Philip R. Davies, JSOTSup 200 (Sheffield: Sheffield Academic Press, 1995), 348.

35. See Dan. 11:40–12:3; 1QM.

36. Tremper Longman III and Daniel G. Reid, *God Is a Warrior*, Studies in Old Testament Biblical Theology (Grand Rapids: Zondervan, 1995), 136–37.

37. See the good study on this text by John K. Goodrich, "After Destroying Every Rule, Authority, and Power: Paul, Apocalyptic, and Politics in 1 Corinthians," in *Paul and the Apocalyptic Imagination*, ed. Ben C. Blackwell, John K. Goodrich, and Jason Maston (Minneapolis: Fortress, 2016), 275–95.

38. So Walter Wink: "What we are arguing is that *the Powers are simultaneously the outer and inner aspects of one and the same indivisible concretion of power*" (italics original; see Walter Wink, *Naming the Powers: The Language of Power in the New Testament* [Minneapolis: Fortress, 1984], 107). Hence Wink's project is a desupernaturalizing and a politicizing of the powers into mythic, indeed supernatural, proportions!

39. Joseph Conrad, *Heart of Darkness*, Everyman's Library (New York: Knopf, 1993), 68.

40. A delightful emphasis in John C. Nugent, *Endangered Gospel: How Fixing the World Is Killing the Church* (Eugene, OR: Cascade, 2016).

41. Dietrich Bonhoeffer, *"Life Together" and "Prayerbook of the Bible,"* ed. Eberhard Bethge, trans. G. L. Müller, Dietrich Bonhoeffer Works 5 (Minneapolis: Fortress, 1996), 27–47.

42. This bumps a hornet's nest on the meaning of "head" (*kephalē*). Does it mean authority, source, or preeminence? For discussion, see Philip Barton Payne, *Man and Woman, One in Christ: An Exegetical and Theological Study of Paul's Letters* (Grand Rapids: Zondervan, 2009), 113–39; Cynthia Long Westfall, *Paul and Gender: Reclaiming the Apostle's Vision for Men and Women in Christ* (Grand Rapids: Baker Academic, 2016), 61–105.

Chapter 6 A Culture of Witness

1. Fred B. Craddock, *The Collected Sermons of Fred B. Craddock* (Louisville: Westminster John Knox, 2011); Barbara Brown Taylor, *The Preaching Life* (Plymouth, UK: Cowley, 1992); Fleming Rutledge, *Not Ashamed of the Gospel: Sermons from Paul's Letter to the Romans* (Grand Rapids: Eerdmans, 2007); Ellen F. Davis, *Preaching the Luminous Word: Biblical Sermons and Homiletical Essays*, ed. Austin McIver Dennis (Grand Rapids: Eerdmans, 2016); Eugene H. Peterson, *As Kingfishers Catch Fire: A Conversation on the Ways of God Formed by the Words of God* (Colorado Springs: WaterBrook, 2017); John Stott, *Between Two Worlds* (repr., Grand Rapids: Eerdmans, 2017).

2. An exceptional book on Christian witness and testimony is Alan Jacobs, *Looking Before and After: Testimony and the Christian Life*, Stob Lectures (Grand Rapids: Eerdmans, 2008).

3. The Greek terms in the New Testament behind the English term *witness* are *martyreō, martyria, martys*, etc., and they are all terms of *verbal* witness. This is confirmed in all the standard word-study books; e.g., BDAG, 617–20. Some uses of these terms in the New Testament are Rom. 10:2; 1 Cor. 15:15; 2 Cor. 8:3; Gal. 4:15; Col. 4:13; 1 Tim. 6:13. To be a reliable witness means to live a life that is consistent with the verbal witness.

4. Spicq, *TLNT* 2:447–52.

5. B. Taylor, *Preaching Life*, 110–11.

6. Kent Haruf, *Eventide* (New York: Vintage, 2005), 19.

7. Jacobs, *Looking Before and After*, 13–17.

8. Dietrich Bonhoeffer, *Discipleship*, Dietrich Bonhoeffer Works 4 (Minneapolis: Fortress, 2001), 148.

9. Eberhard Bethge, *Dietrich Bonhoeffer: A Biography*, rev. ed. (Minneapolis: Fortress, 2000).

10. Peterson, *As Kingfishers Catch Fire*, 301.

11. Brian Dodd, *Paul's Paradigmatic "I": Personal Example as Literary Strategy*, JSNTSup 177 (Sheffield: Bloomsbury T&T Clark, 1999), 221–34.

12. This chapter draws on Scot McKnight, "Was Paul a Convert?," *Ex Auditu* 25 (2009): 110–32. See also Scot McKnight, *Turning to Jesus: The Sociology of Conversion in the Gospels* (Louisville: Westminster John Knox, 2002).

13. Krister Stendahl, *Paul among Jews and Gentiles, and Other Essays* (Philadelphia: Fortress, 1976), 7–23.

14. For a good survey, see B. Corley, "Interpreting Paul's Conversion—Then and Now," in *The Road from Damascus: The Impact of Paul's Conversion on His Life, Thought, and Ministry*, ed. Richard N. Longenecker (Grand Rapids: Eerdmans, 1997), 1–17.

15. A major pushback came from W. G. Kümmel, *Römer 7 und die Bekehrung des Paulus* (Leipzig: Hinrichs, 1929). Recent attempts to revive the older Lutheran reading of Paul can be found in R. H. Gundry, "The Moral Frustration of Paul before His Conversion: Sexual Lust in Romans 7.7–25," in *Pauline Studies: Essays Presented to F. F. Bruce*, ed. D. A. Hagner and M. J. Harris (Grand Rapids: Eerdmans, 1980), 228–45. For a recent good sketch of the issues, see R. Jewett, *Romans: A Commentary*, Hermeneia (Minneapolis: Fortress, 2007), 441–45, which contends that the autobiographical reading cannot be dismissed. The "I" refers to Paul's pre-Christian Jewish stance, and for Jewett, Paul before he was a Christian was a "zealot," but now that former stance is to be seen through the lens of his Christian theology. Perhaps the most readable critique of the whole approach can be found in K. Stendahl, *Paul among Jews and Gentiles*, 78–96.

16. What "new" means in the new perspective is determined by which scholar one chooses. My professor, James D. G. Dunn, was the original architect of the new perspective, so I cite his own studies on this topic: *The Theology of Paul the Apostle* (Grand Rapids: Eerdmans, 1998); Dunn, *The New Perspective on Paul*, rev. ed. (Grand Rapids: Eerdmans, 2008). Alongside Dunn, and using "new perspective" prior to Dunn making it a category of thought, see N. T. Wright, *Pauline Perspectives: Essays on Paul, 1978–2013* (Minneapolis: Fortress, 2013); N. T. Wright, *Paul and the Faithfulness of God*, 2 vols., Christian Origins and the Question of God 4 (Minneapolis: Fortress, 2013); N. T. Wright, *Paul and His Recent Interpreters* (Minneapolis: Fortress, 2015).

17. Stendahl, *Paul among Jews and Gentiles*, 13.

18. Beverly Gaventa, *From Darkness to Light: Aspects of Conversion in the New Testament*, OBT (Philadelphia: Fortress, 1986), 36–37.

19. Stendahl, *Paul among Jews and Gentiles*, 7, 10–11. One of the more interesting observations by Stendahl is how Paul's name change (from Saul to Paul) occurs only after "Paul's first encounter with Roman officials" (p. 11; see also Acts 13:9).

20. Other studies on Paul that have been sensitive to conversion theory include Gaventa, *From Darkness to Light*; A. F. Segal, *Paul the Convert: The Apostolate and Apostasy of Saul the Pharisee* (New Haven: Yale University Press, 1990). What distinguishes my chapter from these two important studies is the work of Lewis Rambo, whose consensus report put the entire set of issues on a new shelf. See Lewis R. Rambo, *Understanding Religious Conversion* (New Haven: Yale University Press, 1993); also, McKnight, *Turning to Jesus*.

21. Rambo, *Understanding Religious Conversion*; Lewis R. Rambo and Charles E. Farhadian, eds., *The Oxford Handbook of Religious Conversion* (New York: Oxford University Press, 2014).

22. Rambo, *Understanding Religious Conversion*, 7.

23. Nancy Mairs, *Ordinary Time: Cycles in Marriage, Faith, and Renewal* (Boston: Beacon Press, 1993), 89.

24. Segal, *Paul the Convert*, 29 (italics added). See also Jacobs, *Looking Before and After*, 35–39.

25. Jacobs, *Looking Before and After*, 35.

26. J. S. Fowler, *Stages of Faith: The Psychology of Human Development and the Quest for Meaning* (San Francisco: HarperSanFrancisco, 1981), 282.

27. J. S. Fowler, *Becoming Adult, Becoming Christian: Adult Development and Christian Faith* (San Francisco: Jossey-Bass, 2000), 115 (italics original).

28. Peggy Noonan, *The Time of Our Lives: Collected Writings* (New York: Twelve, 2015), 399–400.

29. Abraham J. Malherbe, *Paul and the Thessalonians: The Philosophic Tradition of Pastoral Care* (repr., Eugene, OR: Wipf & Stock, 2011), 21–33.

30. Malherbe, *Paul and the Thessalonians*, 25–26.

31. Malherbe, *Paul and the Thessalonians*, 36–37.

32. Malherbe, *Paul and the Thessalonians*, 38–39. But the whole chapter shows the importance of community; see esp. pp. 34–60.

33. Malherbe, *Paul and the Thessalonians*, 26.

34. From a variety of angles, see esp. R. Longenecker, *Road from Damascus*.

35. Matthew W. Bates, *Salvation by Allegiance Alone: Rethinking Faith, Works, and the Gospel of Jesus the King* (Grand Rapids: Baker Academic, 2017).

36. See 1 Cor. 4:6, 16; 7:7; 11:1; Gal. 4:12; Phil. 3:17; 4:9; 1 Thess. 1:5–6.

37. Dodd, *Paul's Paradigmatic "I."*

38. B. Taylor, *Preaching Life*, 84.

39. A beautiful collection of such essays can be found in Phillip Lopate, ed., *The Art of the Personal Essay: An Anthology from the Classical Era to the Present* (New York: Anchor Doubleday, 1994).

40. Beverly R. Gaventa, "Galatians 1 and 2: Autobiography as Paradigm," *NovT* 28 (1986): 309–26.

41. John M. G. Barclay, "Paul's Story: Theology as Testimony," in, *Narrative Dynamics in Paul: A Critical Assessment*, ed. Bruce W. Longenecker (Louisville: Westminster John Knox, 2002), 137.

42. Peterson, *As Kingfishers Catch Fire*, 169.

43. B. Longenecker, *Narrative Dynamics in Paul*, 141.

44. The following summarizes what is found in the commentary on Col. 1:24 in Scot McKnight, *The Letter to the Colossians*, NICNT (Grand Rapids: Eerdmans, 2018), 184–92, and a bibliography is provided there.

45. E.g., Dan. 7:21–22, 25–27; 12:1–3; Hab. 3:15; Zeph. 1:15; Matt. 24:4–8; Mark 13:5–8; Luke 21:8–11.

46. See also Rom. 8:17; 2 Cor. 1:5; 4:10–11; Phil. 3:10–11.

47. More than two decades ago N. T. Wright contended that "so that in him we might become the righteousness of God" (2 Cor. 5:21) did not mean personal redemption so much as entrance into God's own covenant faithfulness, and one wonders whether Col. 1:24 might take on that sense of covenant faithfulness here. See N. T. Wright, *Pauline Perspectives*, 68–76, now also strengthened in his *Paul and the Faithfulness of God*, 881–85.

48. Bonhoeffer, *Discipleship*, 222.

Chapter 7 A Culture of World Subversion

1. Eugene H. Peterson, *The Contemplative Pastor: Returning to the Art of Spiritual Direction* (Grand Rapids: Eerdmans, 1993), 28–29.

2. James W. Thompson, *Pastoral Ministry according to Paul: A Biblical Vision* (Grand Rapids: Baker Academic, 2006), 155.

3. Craig C. Hill, *Servant of All: Status, Ambition, and the Way of Jesus* (Grand Rapids: Eerdmans, 2016), 76.

4. In my circles of discussion, the term *Constantinianism* is often used to refer to discussions between the church and the dominant culture. Constantinianism was significant in the fourth century not simply because of Constantine's combination of church and state, which is itself a fatal mistake, but because the Roman Empire from the end of the republic on combined head of state (emperor) with the army. The former balance of the republic's people and senate, which was sustained when all citizens served in the army, was upended through wedding the ruler with the army, for then the people and the senate were under the thumb of militarism. That kind of militarism is the heart of Constantinianism. For one who brings this centralization of powers to the surface carefully, see Mary Beard, *SPQR: A History of Ancient Rome* (New York: Liveright, 2015).

5. The volume and intricacies of scholarship on the Corinthian correspondence are beyond the scope of this chapter. For a scholarly and then a brief study of Paul and his pastoral relation to Corinth, see Bruce W. Winter, *After Paul Left Corinth: The Influence of Secular Ethics and Social Change* (Grand Rapids: Eerdmans, 2001); Hans Urs von Balthasar, *Paul Struggles with His Congregation: The Pastoral Message of the Letters to the Corinthians* (San Francisco: Ignatius Press, 1992). In 146 BC Rome sacked and destroyed both Carthage and Corinth, and Corinth had to begin all over again to establish itself in the shadow of its new dominant ruler. It was reestablished as a Roman colony in 44 BC, turning its back in important ways on its Greek connections and maximizing its Roman ones; see Winter, *After Paul Left Corinth*, 7–25. Arguing from this general context to specific lines in Paul's letters is hazardous but so also is ignoring this general context.

6. Many have argued for the unity of 2 Corinthians, though such a view usually entails the belief that a new situation arose between chapters 9 and 10–13. Others have argued that the letter is composite, made up of at least 2 Cor. 1–7; 8–9; and 10–13. Some have found another letter at work in 2:14–6:13 with 7:2–4; yet others, two separate letters in chapters 8 and 9. I'm inclined to think 10–13 is a separate letter attached to the previous chapters because of the tonal changes to these volatile chapters. For recent discussion, see Ralph P. Martin, *2 Corinthians*, 2nd ed., WBC 40 (Nashville: Zondervan, 2014), 42–63; Margaret Thrall, *2 Corinthians 1–7*, ICC (London: Bloomsbury T&T Clark, 1994), 3–49.

7. For a general study of how Paul met opposition, both from his own churches and from intruders, see Ernest Best, *Paul and His Converts*, Sprunt Lectures 1985 (Edinburgh: T&T Clark, 1988), 107–24.

8. For the context, see Winter, *After Paul Left Corinth*, 1–28.

9. Winter, *After Paul Left Corinth*, 25–28.

10. For an exceptional canvassing of the whole, see Paul Barnett, "Paul as Pastor in 2 Corinthians," in *Paul as Pastor*, ed. Brian S. Rosner, Andrew S. Malone, and Trevor J. Burke (London: Bloomsbury T&T Clark, 2017), 55–69.

11. On *boasting*, see Mark T. Finney, *Honour and Conflict in the Ancient World: 1 Corinthians in Its Greco-Roman Social Setting*, LNTS 460 (London: T&T Clark, 2012).

12. Ellen F. Davis, *Preaching the Luminous Word: Biblical Sermons and Homiletical Essays*, ed. Austin McIver Dennis (Grand Rapids: Eerdmans, 2016), 191.

13. Dio Chrysostom, Oration 31, *To the People of Rhodes*, in *Discourses 31–36*, trans. J. W. Cohoon and H. Lamar Crosby, LCL 358 (Cambridge: Harvard University Press, 1940), 1–169.

14. Bruce J. Malina, *Christian Origins and Cultural Anthropology: Practical Models for Biblical Interpretation* (Atlanta: John Knox, 1986); David A. deSilva, *Honor, Patronage, Kinship and Purity: Unlocking New Testament Culture* (Downers Grove, IL: IVP Academic, 2000).

15. Gore Vidal, "Some Memories of the Glorious Bird and an Earlier Self," in *The Art of the Personal Essay: An Anthology from the Classical Era to the Present*, ed. Phillip Lopate (New York: Anchor Doubleday, 1994), 627.

16. For brief discussion, see Joseph H. Hellerman, *Reconstructing Honor in Roman Philippi: Carmen Christi as* Cursus Pudorum, SNTSMS 132 (Cambridge: Cambridge University Press, 2005), 11–32.

17. Hellerman, *Reconstructing Honor.*

18. David I. Starling, *UnCorinthian Leadership: Thematic Reflections on 1 Corinthians* (Eugene, OR: Cascade, 2014), 11–13.

19. Starling, *UnCorinthian Leadership*, 12.

20. For a good discussion, see Andrew D. Clarke, *Secular and Christian Leadership in Corinth: A Socio-Historical and Exegetical Study of 1 Corinthians 1–6*, Paternoster Biblical Monographs (Milton Keynes, UK: Paternoster, 2006), 41–45.

21. Alison E. Cooley, *Res Gestae Divi Augusti: Text, Translation, and Commentary* (Cambridge: Cambridge University Press, 2009). For studies of Augustus, see Anthony Everitt, *Augustus: The Life of Rome's First Emperor* (New York: Random House, 2006); Karl Galinsky, *Augustus: Introduction to the Life of an Emperor* (New York: Cambridge University Press, 2012); J. S. Richardson, *Augustan Rome, 44 BC to AD 14: The Restoration of the Republic and the Establishment of the Empire* (Edinburgh: Edinburgh University Press, 2012). For an example from Cicero, see *Letters to Friends* 22.

22. A good brief commentary is found in Beard, *SPQR*, 360–67. There are, she observes, nearly one hundred self-references in this egocentric record of success (see p. 368).

23. Winter, *After Paul Left Corinth*, 40–43; Clarke, *Secular and Christian Leadership*, 59–107.

24. So, too, David G. Horrell, *Solidarity and Difference: A Contemporary Reading of Paul's Ethics*, 2nd ed. (London: Bloomsbury T&T Clark, 2015), 136; Matthew R. Malcolm, "Paul's Pastoral Sensitivity in 1 Corinthians," in Rosner, Malone, and Burke, *Paul as Pastor*, 43–54. The same upside-down world is demonstrated for the narrative of Acts in C. Kavin Rowe, *World Upside Down: Reading Acts in the Graeco-Roman Age* (New York: Oxford University Press, 2009).

25. At much greater depth, see Finney, *Honour and Conflict in the Ancient World*, 69–109. See also chap. 1 above, under "Pastor as Culture Maker."

26. Barnett, "Paul as Pastor." His sketch of Paul's self-defense can be found on pp. 58–61 (sincerity, integrity, authority).

27. Andrew D. Clarke, *Serve the Community of the Church: Christians as Leaders and Ministers*, First Century Christians in the Graeco-Roman World (Grand Rapids: Eerdmans, 2000), 217.

28. Gordon D. Fee, *The First Epistle to the Corinthians*, NICNT, rev. ed. (Grand Rapids: Eerdmans, 2014), 180 (italics original).

29. For the importance of grace as a subversive power that becomes mutual empowerment, see esp. Kathy Ehrensperger, *Paul and the Dynamics of Power: Communication and Interaction in the Early Christ-Movement*, LNTS 325 (London: T&T Clark, 2007), 63–80. In addition, see John M. G. Barclay, *Paul and the Gift* (Grand Rapids: Eerdmans, 2015).

30. Finney, *Honour and Conflict in the Ancient World*, 145.

31. Michael J. Gorman, *Inhabiting the Cruciform God: Kenosis, Justification, and Theosis in Paul's Narrative Soteriology* (Grand Rapids: Eerdmans, 2009). Unlike so many New Testament scholars, Gorman defines his terms with rigor.

32. Gorman, *Inhabiting the Cruciform God*, 12.

33. Gorman, *Inhabiting the Cruciform God*, 24–25.

34. For an excellent study, Bruce W. Winter, *Philo and Paul among the Sophists: Alexandrian and Corinthian Responses to a Julio-Claudian Movement*, 2nd ed. (Grand Rapids: Eerdmans, 2002).

35. The literature on the subject continues to grow, so I mention only these: George A. Kennedy, *Classical Rhetoric and Its Christian and Secular Tradition from Ancient to Modern Times*, 2nd ed. (Chapel Hill: University of North Carolina Press, 1999); Winter, *After Paul Left Corinth*, 31–43; Thomas Habinek, *Ancient Rhetoric and Oratory* (Malden, MA: Wiley-Blackwell, 2004); Ben Witherington III, *New Testament Rhetoric: An Introductory Guide to the Art of Persuasion in and of the New Testament* (Eugene, OR: Wipf & Stock, 2009); Duane Litfin, *Paul's Theology of Preaching: The Apostle's Challenge to the Art of Persuasion in Ancient Corinth*, 2nd ed. (Downers Grove, IL: IVP Academic, 2015), 57–116.

36. Also, Aristotle, *Rhetoric* 1.1.1, 14; Quintilian, *Institutio oratoria* 12.10.72; Cicero, *De inventione rhetorica* 1.6; *Brutus* 59; Dio Chrysostom, *Discourses* 34.6. On the topic, see Litfin, *Paul's Theology of Preaching*, 95–102.

37. Litfin, *Paul's Theology of Preaching*, 103.

38. In our generation, no one has been more intent on demonstrating this than Witherington, *New Testament Rhetoric*, 94–176.

39. Ben Witherington III, *Jesus the Sage: The Pilgrimage of Wisdom* (Minneapolis: Fortress, 1994), 306.

40. Well explained in Douglas A. Campbell, *Paul: An Apostle's Journey* (Grand Rapids: Eerdmans, 2018), 56–59.

41. On Paul as tentmaker, see Ronald F. Hock, *The Social Context of Paul's Ministry: Tentmaking and Apostleship* (Minneapolis: Fortress, 2007). On how Paul was supported, see Steve Walton, "Paul, Patronage, and Pay: What Do We Know about the Apostle's Financial Support?," in *Paul as Missionary: Identity, Activity, Theology, and Practice*, ed. Trevor J. Burke and Brian S. Rosner, LNTS 420 (London: T&T Clark, 2011), 220–33. Walton argues that consistency is found along two lines: Paul's desire to make the gospel free of charge for all and his Christocentricity and theocentricy transforming all relations.

42. There is much discussion on whether Paul accepted funds while church planting, and if so, when; and a recent good study is Walton, "Paul, Patronage and Pay." See also G. W. Peterman, *Paul's Gift from Philippi: Conventions of Gift Exchange and Christian Giving*, SNTSMS 92 (Cambridge: Cambridge University Press, 1997).

43. Hock, *Social Context of Paul's Ministry*, 52–59.

44. While others point to different reasons—to make the gospel free of charge, to avoid suggestion of other itinerant teachers, his disapproval of idleness—I am led by Paul's language in the context of Corinthian status to see his commitment to embodying Christoformity as his primary reason for eschewing financial support.

45. Andrew D. Clarke, *A Pauline Theology of Church Leadership* (London: Bloomsbury T&T Clark, 2008), 118–26.

46. For discussion, see Clarke, *Pauline Theology*, 42–78.

47. For a good example of how Paul picks up the title "administrator" (Greek *oikonomos*) for his role among his churches—among other titles or names or images he appropriates—and gives that title nuances in such a way as to show it to be both a degrading and an empowering role, see John Goodrich, *Paul as an Administrator of God in 1 Corinthians*, SNTSMS 152 (Cambridge: Cambridge University Press, 2012).

48. For a sketch of images Paul uses for his own ministry, see Stephen C. Barton, "Paul as Missionary and Pastor," in *The Cambridge Companion to St. Paul*, ed. James D. G. Dunn (Cambridge: Cambridge University Press, 2003), 35–39.

49. Clarke, *Serve the Community of the Church*, 218–23; Ehrensperger, *Paul and the Dynamics of Power*, 126–35.

50. For the image, see Beverly Gaventa, *Our Mother Saint Paul* (Louisville: Westminster John Knox, 2007). Gaventa's work is echoed in Ehrensperger, *Paul and the Dynamics of Power*, 126–34.

51. C. S. Lewis, *The Screwtape Letters: Annotated Edition* (New York: HarperOne, 2013), xxxv, xxxvii.

Chapter 8 A Culture of Wisdom

1. Two Paul-scholar friends pointed me to the following book, and it was the only resource I had been able to find on this topic. This scarcity was the reason I had consulted them: Ben Witherington III, *Jesus the Sage: The Pilgrimage of Wisdom* (Minneapolis: Fortress, 1994), 295–333. I am happy to say a new, wide-ranging book, which arrived too late to help with the formation and substance of this chapter, has taken a huge leap forward for Paul and wisdom with its two chapters on the epistles of the New Testament and wisdom. See J. de Waal Dryden, *A Hermeneutic of Wisdom: Recovering the Formative Agency of Scripture* (Grand Rapids: Baker Academic, 2018).

2. Thomas E. Bergler, *The Juvenilization of American Christianity* (Grand Rapids: Eerdmans, 2012); Bergler, *From Here to Maturity: Overcoming the Juvenilization of American Christianity* (Grand Rapids: Eerdmans, 2014). It is easier to find studies on the perpetual adolescence of Americans than it is on the perpetual adolescence of the church, which Bergler's work accomplishes in part. The literature on young adults is beyond my expertise, though the following work is considered standard and is undeniably enlightening, if not at times disheartening: Jeffrey Jensen Arnett, *Emerging Adulthood: The Winding Road from the Late Teens through the Twenties*, 2nd ed. (New York: Oxford University Press, 2014). For significant studies on young adults and faith, see Christian Smith and Patricia Snell, *Souls in Transition: The Religious and Spiritual Lives of Emerging Adults* (New York: Oxford University Press, 2009); Christian Smith and Melina Lundquist Denton, *Soul Searching: The Religious and Spiritual Lives of American Teenagers* (New York: Oxford University Press, 2009);

Christian Smith et al., *Lost in Transition: The Dark Side of Emerging Adulthood* (New York: Oxford University Press, 2011).

3. Quotations in this paragraph are from Bergler, *From Here to Maturity*, 1–2 (italics added).

4. Charles Taylor, *A Secular Age* (Cambridge: Belknap, 2007), 473–504.

5. Smith and Denton, *Soul Searching*.

6. Explored with nuance and perception by Andrew Root, *Faith Formation in a Secular Age: Responding to the Church's Obsession with Youthfulness* (Grand Rapids: Baker Academic, 2017).

7. Ellen F. Davis, *Preaching the Luminous Word: Biblical Sermons and Homiletical Essays*, ed. Austin McIver Dennis (Grand Rapids: Eerdmans, 2016), 141.

8. Susan Neiman, *Why Grow Up? Subversive Thoughts for an Infantile Age*, rev. ed. (New York: Farrar, Straus and Giroux, 2016), 15.

9. Flannery O'Connor, "The King of Birds," in *The Collected Works of Flannery O'Connor*, ed. Sally Fitzgerald (New York: Library of America, 1988), 832–42.

10. Jim Doyle and Brian Doyle, *Two Voices: A Father and Son Discuss Family and Faith* (Liguori, MO: Liguori Publications, 1996), xiv.

11. This section reworks and updates Scot McKnight, "James' Secret: Wisdom in James in the Mode of Receptive Reverence," in *Preaching Character: Reclaiming Wisdom's Paradigmatic Imagination for Transformation*, ed. David Fleer and David Bland (Abilene, TX: Abilene Christian University Press, 2010), 201–16. For discussion now, see the following new books: Tremper Longman III, *The Fear of the Lord Is Wisdom: A Theological Introduction to Wisdom in Israel* (Grand Rapids: Baker Academic, 2017); Glenn Pemberton, *A Life That Is Good: The Message of Proverbs in a World Wanting Wisdom* (Grand Rapids: Eerdmans, 2018).

12. For sketches of recent studies, see J. Crenshaw, *Old Testament Wisdom: An Introduction* (rev. ed., Louisville: Westminster John Knox, 1998), 1–19; B. K. Waltke and D. Diewert, "Wisdom Literature," in *The Face of Old Testament Studies: A Survey of Contemporary Approaches*, ed. D. W. Baker and B. T. Arnold (Grand Rapids: Baker Academic, 1999), 295–328. I heartily recommend in its entirety Tremper Longman III and Peter Enns, eds., *Dictionary of the Old Testament: Wisdom, Poetry & Writings* (Downers Grove, IL: InterVarsity, 2008), as a tool of much use for the preacher.

13. Ellen F. Davis, *Proverbs, Ecclesiastes, and the Song of Songs*, Westminster Bible Companion (Louisville: Westminster John Knox, 2000), 1.

14. Davis, *Proverbs, Ecclesiastes*, 27.

15. Joseph Epstein, *Alexis de Tocqueville: Democracy's Guide*, Eminent Lives (New York: HarperCollins, 2006), 173.

16. Three important studies of conservatism in theory are Edmund Burke, *Reflections on the Revolution in France, and Other Writings*, ed. Jesse Norman (New York: Everyman's Library, 2015); Roger Scruton, *How to Be a Conservative* (London: Continuum, 2014); Scruton, *The Meaning of Conservatism*, 3rd ed. (South Bend, IN: St. Augustine's Press, 2014).

17. Roger Scruton, *Confessions of a Heretic: Selected Essays* (Honiton, UK: Notting Hill, 2016), 152.

18. Willa Cather, *Death Comes for the Archbishop* (New York: Everyman's Library, 1992), 232–33.

19. Joseph Blenkinsopp, *Sage, Priest, Prophet: Religious and Intellectual Leadership in Ancient Israel* (Louisville: Westminster John Knox, 1995), 14.

20. Blenkinsopp, *Sage, Priest, Prophet*, 14, 15.

21. Marilynne Robinson, *Home* (New York: Farrar, Straus and Giroux, 2008), 98.

22. A good summary can be found at Prov. 9:7–12. It is a pity that the wisdom tradition was ignored in C. Kavin Rowe, *One True Life: The Stoics and Early Christians as Rival Traditions* (New Haven: Yale University Press, 2016).

23. William P. Brown, *Wisdom's Wonder: Character, Creation, and Crisis in the Bible's Wisdom Literature* (Grand Rapids: Eerdmans, 2014), 24. I am grateful to Jeff Blair, who, after I said I had heard this expression somewhere, found it in Brown's book.

24. On "discipline" or "instruction" (*musar*), see also 1:8; 4:13; 8:10; 23:23; 24:32.

25. See Blenkinsopp, *Sage, Priest, Prophet*, 9–65; Leo G. Perdue, *Wisdom Literature: A Theological History* (Louisville: Westminster John Knox, 2007), 1–36.

26. A major theme in Longman, *Fear of the Lord Is Wisdom*.

27. See Tremper Longman III, *Proverbs*, Baker Commentary on the Old Testament (Grand Rapids: Baker Academic, 2006), 74–79.

28. Longman, *Fear of the Lord Is Wisdom*, 161.

29. Dryden, *Hermeneutic of Wisdom*, 228; see also 234–39, sections which summarize earlier chapters.

30. Witherington, *Jesus the Sage*, 4.

31. Rehearsing what is found with full references in Witherington, *Jesus the Sage*, 114–15. Ben is reworking Roland Murphy's own summary (see next note).

32. Murphy's own eighth point deserves to be stated here: "A list of the passages (minimum) where Wisdom is found to be personified: Job 28; Prov 1, 8, 9; Sir 1:9–10; 4:11–19; 6:18–31; 14:20–15:8; 51:13–21; Bar 3:9–4:4; Wis 6:12–11:1." See Roland E. Murphy, *The Tree of Life: An Exploration of Biblical Wisdom Literature*, 3rd ed. (Grand Rapids: Eerdmans, 2002), 146.

33. I am surprised by the lack of Spirit-Wisdom emphasis, though not an absence, in Craig S. Keener, *Spirit Hermeneutics: Reading Scripture in Light of Pentecost* (Grand Rapids: Eerdmans, 2016); Keener, *The Mind of the Spirit: Paul's Approach to Transformed Thinking* (Grand Rapids: Baker Academic, 2016). Much better is John R. Levison, *Filled with the Spirit* (Grand Rapids: Eerdmans, 2009).

34. Dennis R. Venema and Scot McKnight, *Adam and the Genome: Reading Scripture after Genetic Science* (Grand Rapids: Brazos, 2017).

35. Rowe, *One True Life*, 221.

36. Alexander Schmemann, *The Journals of Father Alexander Schmemann, 1973–1983*, trans. Juliana Schmemann (Crestwood, NY: St. Vladimir's Seminary Press, 2000), 78.

37. Blenkinsopp, *Sage, Priest, Prophet*, 25.

38. Andrew D. Clarke, *A Pauline Theology of Church Leadership* (London: Bloomsbury T&T Clark, 2008), 56–57.

39. Clarke, *Pauline Theology*, 59–60.

40. I discuss this in Scot McKnight, *The Letter to the Colossians*, NICNT (Grand Rapids: Eerdmans, 2018), 25–34.

41. Rowe, *One True Life*, 257.

42. Rowe, *One True Life*, 257.

43. See my own development of this understanding of incarnational living in Scot McKnight, *Kingdom Conspiracy: Returning to the Radical Mission of the Local Church* (Grand Rapids: Brazos, 2014), 138–42.

Final Thoughts: Nurturing Christoformity

1. Joseph Epstein, *With My Trousers Rolled: Familiar Essays* (New York: Norton, 1995), 187.

2. P. D. James, *Death in Holy Orders* (New York: Knopf, 2001), 166.

3. Gordon D. Fee, *Paul, the Spirit, and the People of God* (Grand Rapids: Baker, 1996), 112.

4. Willa Cather, *Death Comes for the Archbishop* (New York: Everyman's Library, 1992), 207–8.

Bibliography

Aasgaard, Reidar. *"My Beloved Brothers and Sisters!" Christian Siblingship in Paul.* JSNTSup 265. London: T&T Clark, 2004.

Abasciano, Brian J. "Diamonds in the Rough: A Reply to Christopher Stanley concerning the Reader Competency of Paul's Original Audiences." *NovT* 49 (2007): 153–83.

Adams, Edward. *The Earliest Christian Meeting Places: Almost Exclusively Houses?* Rev. ed. New York: Bloomsbury T&T Clark, 2015.

———. "Paul's Story of God and Creation: The Story of How God Fulfils His Purposes in Creation." In B. Longenecker, *Narrative Dynamics in Paul*, 19–43.

Agrell, Göran. *Work, Toil and Sustenance.* Lund: Håkan Ohlssons, 1976.

Alcorn, Randy. *Managing God's Money: A Biblical Guide.* Carol Stream, IL: Tyndale, 2011.

Anderson, Gary A. *Charity: The Place of the Poor in the Biblical Tradition.* New Haven: Yale University Press, 2013.

———. *Christian Doctrine and the Old Testament: Theology in the Service of Biblical Exegesis.* Grand Rapids: Baker Academic, 2017.

Aristotle. *Nicomachean Ethics.* Translated by H. Rackman. LCL 73. Cambridge: Harvard University Press, 1926.

Arnett, Jeffrey Jensen. *Emerging Adulthood: The Winding Road from the Late Teens through the Twenties.* 2nd ed. New York: Oxford University Press, 2014.

Arnold, Jeanne E., Anthony P. Graesch, Enzo Ragazzini, and Elinor Ochs. *Life at Home in the Twenty-First Century: Thirty-Two Families Open Their Doors.* Los Angeles: Cotsen Institute of Archaeology Press, 2017.

Ascough, Richard S. "The Completion of a Religious Duty: The Background of 2 Cor 8.1–15." *NTS* 42 (1996): 584–99.

———. *The Formation of Pauline Churches.* New York: Paulist Press, 1998.

225

———. "What Are They *Now* Saying about Christ Groups and Associations." *CurBR* 13 (2015): 207–44.

Ascough, Richard S., Philip A. Harland, and John S. Kloppenborg. *Associations in the Greco-Roman World: A Sourcebook*. Waco: Baylor University Press, 2012.

Balmer, Randall. *God in the White House: A History; How Faith Shaped the Presidency from John F. Kennedy to George W. Bush*. New York: HarperOne, 2008.

———. *Thy Kingdom Come: How the Religious Right Distorts Faith and Threatens America*. New York: Basic Books, 2007.

Balthasar, Hans Urs von. *Paul Struggles with His Congregation: The Pastoral Message of the Letters to the Corinthians*. San Francisco: Ignatius Press, 1992.

Barclay, John M. G. "The Family as the Bearer of Religion in Judaism and Early Christianity." In Moxnes, *Constructing Early Christian Families*, 66–80.

———. *Paul and the Gift*. Grand Rapids: Eerdmans, 2015.

———. "Paul's Story: Theology as Testimony." In B. Longenecker, *Narrative Dynamics in Paul*, 133–56.

Barna Group, The. *The State of Pastors: How Today's Faith Leaders Are Navigating Life and Leadership in an Age of Complexity*. Ventura, CA: Barna, 2017.

Barnett, Paul. *Paul: A Pastor's Heart in Second Corinthians*. Sydney, Australia: Aquila Press, 2012.

———. "Paul as Pastor in 2 Corinthians." In Rosner, Malone, and Burke, *Paul as Pastor*, 55–70.

Barth, Karl. *Church Dogmatics, III.4: The Doctrine of Creation*. Translated by G. W. Bromiley. Edinburgh: T&T Clark, 1961.

———. *Church Dogmatics, III.4: The Doctrine of Creation*. Edited by Geoffrey W. Bromiley and T. F. Torrance. Study ed. London: T&T Clark, 2010.

Bartholomew, Craig G. *Contours of the Kuyperian Tradition: A Systematic Introduction*. Downers Grove, IL: IVP Academic, 2017.

Bartlett, David. *Ministry in the New Testament*. Overtures to Biblical Theology. Minneapolis: Fortress, 1993.

Barton, Stephen C. "Paul as Missionary and Pastor." In *The Cambridge Companion to St. Paul*, edited James D. G. Dunn, 34–48. Cambridge: Cambridge University Press, 2003.

———. "The Relativisation of Family Ties in the Jewish and Graeco-Roman Traditions." In Moxnes, *Constructing Early Christian Families*, 81–100.

Bates, Matthew W. "A Christology of Incarnation and Enthronement: Romans 1:3–4 as Unified, Nonadoptionist, and Nonconciliatory." *CBQ* 77 (2015): 107–27.

———. *The Hermeneutics of the Apostolic Proclamation: The Center of Paul's Method of Scriptural Interpretation*. Waco: Baylor University Press, 2012.

———. *Salvation by Allegiance Alone: Rethinking Faith, Works, and the Gospel of Jesus the King*. Grand Rapids: Baker Academic, 2017.

Bauckham, Richard. "Reading Scripture as a Coherent Story." In *The Art of Reading Scripture*, edited by Ellen F. Davis and Richard B. Hays, 38–52. Grand Rapids: Eerdmans, 2003.

Beard, Mary. *The Fires of Vesuvius: Pompeii Lost and Found*. Cambridge, MA: Belknap, 2010.

———. *The Roman Triumph*. Cambridge, MA: Belknap, 2007.

———. *SPQR: A History of Ancient Rome*. New York: Liveright, 2015.

Bellah, Robert N., et al. *Habits of the Heart: Individualism and Commitment in American Life*. New York: Harper & Row, 1985.

Berger, Klaus. "Almosen Für Israel." *NTS* 23 (1977): 180–204.

Bergler, Thomas E. *From Here to Maturity: Overcoming the Juvenilization of American Christianity*. Grand Rapids: Eerdmans, 2014.

———. *The Juvenilization of American Christianity*. Grand Rapids: Eerdmans, 2012.

Berlin, Isaiah. *The Proper Study of Mankind: An Anthology of Essays*. Edited by Henry Hardy and Roger Hausheer. New York: Farrar, Straus and Giroux, 2000.

Berlin, Isaiah, and Michael Ignatieff. *The Hedgehog and the Fox: An Essay on Tolstoy's View of History*. Edited by Henry Hardy. 2nd. ed. Princeton: Princeton University Press, 2013.

Bernanos, Georges. *The Diary of a Country Priest: A Novel*. Cambridge, MA: Da Capo Press, 2002.

Best, Ernest. *Paul and His Converts*. The Sprunt Lectures 1985. Edinburgh: T&T Clark, 1988.

Bethge, Eberhard. *Dietrich Bonhoeffer: A Biography*. Rev. ed. Minneapolis: Fortress, 2000.

———. *Friendship and Resistance: Essays on Dietrich Bonhoeffer*. Grand Rapids: Eerdmans, 1995.

Bird, Michael F. *An Anomalous Jew: Paul among Jews, Greeks, and Romans*. Grand Rapids: Eerdmans, 2016.

———. *Crossing over Sea and Land: Jewish Missionary Activity in the Second Temple Period*. Peabody, MA: Hendrickson, 2010.

Birge, Mary Katherine. *The Language of Belonging: A Rhetorical Analysis of Kinship Language in First Corinthians*. CBET 31. Leuven: Peeters, 2002.

Blenkinsopp, Joseph. *Sage, Priest, Prophet: Religious and Intellectual Leadership in Ancient Israel*. Louisville: Westminster John Knox, 1995.

Boersma, Hans. *Sacramental Preaching: Sermons on the Hidden Presence of Christ*. Grand Rapids: Baker Academic, 2016.

———. *Scripture as Real Presence: Sacramental Exegesis in the Early Church*. Grand Rapids: Baker Academic, 2017.

Bonhoeffer, Dietrich. *Discipleship*. Dietrich Bonhoeffer Works 4. Minneapolis: Fortress, 2001.

———. *"Life Together" and "Prayerbook of the Bible."* Edited by Eberhard Bethge. Translated by G. L. Müller. Dietrich Bonhoeffer Works 5. Minneapolis: Fortress, 1996.

Bradshaw, Paul F., Maxwell E. Johnson, and L. Edward Phillips. *The Apostolic Tradition*. Hermeneia. Minneapolis: Fortress, 2002.

Briones, David E. *Paul's Financial Policy: A Socio-Theological Approach*. LNTS 494. London: Bloomsbury T&T Clark, 2013.

Brown, William P. *Wisdom's Wonder: Character, Creation, and Crisis in the Bible's Wisdom Literature*. Grand Rapids: Eerdmans, 2014.

Bruner, Michael Mears. *A Subversive Gospel: Flannery O'Connor and the Reimagining of Beauty, Goodness, and Truth*. Downers Grove, IL: IVP Academic, 2017.

Buber, Martin. *I and Thou*. Translated by Ronald Gregor Smith. 2nd ed. New York: Scribner's, 1958.

———. *Tales of the Hasidim: The Early Masters*. New York: Schocken Books, 1961.

Buechner, Frederick. *Telling the Truth: The Gospel as Tragedy, Comedy, and Fairy Tale*. San Francisco: Harper & Row, 1977.

Burke, Edmund. *Reflections on the Revolution in France, and Other Writings*. Edited by Jesse Norman. New York: Everyman's Library, 2015.

Burke, Simeon R. "'Render to Caesar the Things of Caesar and to God the Things of God': Recent Perspectives on a Puzzling Command (1945–present)." *CurBR* 16 (2018): 157–90.

Burke, Trevor J. "The Holy Spirit as the Controlling Dynamic in Paul's Role as Missionary to the Thessalonians." In Burke and Rosner, *Paul as Missionary*, 142–57.

———. "Mother, Father, Infant, Orphan, Brother: Paul's Variegated Pastoral Strategy towards His Thessalonian Church Family." In Rosner, Malone, and Burke, *Paul as Pastor*, 123–41.

Burke, Trevor J., and Brian S. Rosner, eds. *Paul as Missionary: Identity, Activity, Theology, and Practice*. LNTS 420. London: T&T Clark, 2011.

Buxton, Graham. *Dancing in the Dark: The Privilege of Participating in God's Ministry in the World*. Rev. ed. Eugene, OR: Cascade, 2016.

———. *An Uncertain Certainty: Snapshots in a Journey from "Either-Or" to "Both-And" in Christian Ministry*. Eugene, OR: Pickwick, 2014.

Campbell, Brian. *The Romans and Their World: A Short Introduction*. New Haven: Yale University Press, 2012.

Campbell, Douglas A. *Paul: An Apostle's Journey*. Grand Rapids: Eerdmans, 2018.

———. *The Quest for Paul's Gospel*. London: T&T Clark, 2005.

———. "The Story of Jesus in Romans and Galatians." In B. Longenecker, *Narrative Dynamics in Paul*, 97–124.

Campbell, Joan Cecelia. *Phoebe: Patron and Emissary*. Collegeville, MN: Michael Glazier, 2009.

Campbell, R. Alastair. *The Elders: Seniority within Earliest Christianity*. SNTW. Edinburgh: T&T Clark, 1994.

Carlson, Kent, and Mike Lueken. *Renovation of the Church: What Happens When a Seeker Church Discovers Spiritual Formation*. Foreword by Dallas Willard. Downers Grove, IL: InterVarsity, 2011.

Cather, Willa. *Death Comes for the Archbishop*. New York: Everyman's Library, 1992.

Chandler, Diane J. "The Perfect Storm of Leaders' Unethical Behavior: A Conceptual Framework." *International Journal of Leadership Studies* 5 (2009): 69–93.

Chester, Stephen J. *Reading Paul with the Reformers: Reconciling Old and New Perspectives*. Grand Rapids: Eerdmans, 2017.

Ciampa, Roy E. "'Flee Sexual Immorality': Sex and the City of Corinth." In *The Wisdom of the Cross: Exploring 1 Corinthians*, edited by Brian S. Rosner, 100–133. Nottingham, UK: Apollos/Inter-Varsity, 2011.

Ciampa, Roy E., and Brian S. Rosner. *The First Letter to the Corinthians*. Grand Rapids: Eerdmans, 2010.

Cicero. *Brutus. Orator*. Translated by G. L. Hendrickson and H. M. Hubbell. LCL 342. Cambridge: Harvard University Press, 1939.

———. *On Friendship*. In *On Old Age. On Friendship. On Divination*. Translated by W. A. Falconer. LCL 154. Cambridge: Harvard University Press, 1923.

———. *Letters to Atticus, Volume IV*. Edited and translated by D. R. Shackleton Bailey. LCL 491. Cambridge: Harvard University Press, 1999.

———. *On Duties*. Translated by Walter Miller. LCL 30. Cambridge: Harvard University Press, 1913.

———. *Tusculan Disputations*. Translated by J. E. King. LCL 141. Cambridge: Harvard University Press, 1913.

Clarke, Andrew D. "Equality or Mutuality? Paul's Use of 'Brother' Language." In *The New Testament in Its First Century Setting: Essays in Honour of B. W. Winter on His 65th Birthday*, edited by P. J. Williams, Andrew D. Clarke, Peter M. Head, and David Instone-Brewer, 151–64. Grand Rapids: Eerdmans, 2004.

———. *A Pauline Theology of Church Leadership*. London: Bloomsbury T&T Clark, 2008.

———. *Secular and Christian Leadership in Corinth: A Socio-Historical and Exegetical Study of 1 Corinthians 1–6*. Paternoster Biblical Monographs. Milton Keynes, UK: Paternoster, 2006.

———. *Serve the Community of the Church: Christians as Leaders and Ministers*. First Century Christians in the Graeco-Roman World. Grand Rapids: Eerdmans, 2000.

Cohick, Lynn H. *Women in the World of the Earliest Christians: Illuminating Ancient Ways of Life*. Grand Rapids: Baker Academic, 2009.

Collins, John N. *Diakonia: Re-Interpreting the Ancient Sources*. New York: Oxford University Press, 1990.

Conrad, Joseph. *Heart of Darkness*. Everyman's Library. New York: Knopf, 1993.

Cooley, Alison E. *Res Gestae Divi Augusti: Text, Translation, and Commentary*. Cambridge: Cambridge University Press, 2009.

Copan, Victor A. *Saint Paul as Spiritual Director: An Analysis of the Concept of the Imitation of Paul with Implications and Applications to the Practice of Spiritual Direction*. Reprint ed. Paternoster Biblical Monographs. Eugene, OR: Wipf & Stock, 2008.

Corley, B. "Interpreting Paul's Conversion—Then and Now." In R. Longenecker, *Road from Damascus*, 1–17.

Craddock, Fred B. *The Collected Sermons of Fred B. Craddock*. Louisville: Westminster John Knox, 2011.

———. *Craddock on the Craft of Preaching*. St. Louis: Chalice Press, 2013.

Crenshaw, J. *Old Testament Wisdom: An Introduction*. Rev. ed. Louisville: Westminster John Knox, 1998.

Croasmun, Matthew. *The Emergence of Sin: The Cosmic Tyrant in Romans*. New York: Oxford University Press, 2017.

Culbertson, Philip L., and Arthur Bradford Shippee. *The Pastor: Readings from the Patristic Period*. Minneapolis: Augsburg Fortress, 2009.

Das, A. Andrew. *Paul and the Stories of Israel: Grand Thematic Narratives in Galatians*. Minneapolis: Fortress, 2016.

Davis, Ellen F. *Preaching the Luminous Word: Biblical Sermons and Homiletical Essays*. Edited by Austin McIver Dennis. Grand Rapids: Eerdmans, 2016.

———. *Proverbs, Ecclesiastes, and the Song of Songs*. Westminster Bible Companion. Louisville: Westminster John Knox, 2000.

Deines, R. "Pharisees." In *Eerdmans Dictionary of Early Judaism*. Edited by J .J. Collins and D. C. Harlow, 1061–63. Grand Rapids: Eerdmans, 2010.

deSilva, David A. *Honor, Patronage, Kinship and Purity: Unlocking New Testament Culture*. Downers Grove, IL: IVP Academic, 2000.

———. *Transformation: The Heart of Paul's Gospel*. Bellingham, WA: Lexham Press, 2014.

Dickson, John. *Humilitas: A Lost Key to Life, Love, and Leadership*. Grand Rapids: Zondervan, 2011.

Dio Chrysostom. *Discourses 1–11*. Translated by J. W. Cohoon. LCL 257. Cambridge: Harvard University Press, 1932.

———. Oration 31, *To the People of Rhodes*. In *Discourses 31–36*. Translated by J. W. Cohoon and H. Lamar Crosby. LCL 358. Cambridge: Harvard University Press, 1940.

———. *Second Tarsic Discourse*. In *Discourses 31–36*. Translated by J. W. Cohoon and H. Lamar Crosby. LCL 358. Cambridge: Harvard University Press, 1940.

Dodd, Brian. *Paul's Paradigmatic "I": Personal Example as Literary Strategy*. JSNTSup 177. Sheffield: Bloomsbury T&T Clark, 1999.

Downs, David J. *Alms: Charity, Reward, and Atonement in Early Christianity*. Waco: Baylor University Press, 2016.

———. *The Offering of the Gentiles: Paul's Collection for Jerusalem in Its Chronological, Cultural, and Cultic Contexts*. Grand Rapids: Eerdmans, 2016.

Doyle, Jim, and Brian Doyle. *Two Voices: A Father and Son Discuss Family and Faith*. Liguori, MO: Liguori, 1996.

Dreisbach, Daniel L. *Reading the Bible with the Founding Fathers*. New York: Oxford University Press, 2016.

Dresner, Samuel H. *The Zaddik: The Doctrine of the Zaddik according to the Writings of Rabbi Yaakov Yosef of Polnoy*. Northvale, NJ: Jason Aronson, 1994.

Dryden, J. de Waal. *A Hermeneutic of Wisdom: Recovering the Formative Agency of Scripture*. Grand Rapids: Baker Academic, 2018.

Dulles, Avery. *Models of the Church*. 2nd ed. New York: Image, 1991.

Dunn, James D. G. *Christology in the Making: A New Testament Inquiry into the Origins of the Doctrine of the Incarnation*. 2nd ed. Philadelphia: Westminster John Knox, 1989.

———. *Did the First Christians Worship Jesus? The New Testament Evidence*. Louisville: Westminster John Knox, 2010.

———. "The Narrative Approach to Paul: Whose Story?" In B. Longenecker, *Narrative Dynamics in Paul*, 217–30.

———. *The New Perspective on Paul*. Rev. ed. Grand Rapids: Eerdmans, 2008.

———. *The Partings of the Ways: Between Christianity and Judaism and Their Significance for the Character of Christianity*. Philadelphia: Trinity Press International, 1991.

———. *The Theology of Paul the Apostle*. Grand Rapids: Eerdmans, 1998.

———. *Unity and Diversity in the New Testament: An Inquiry into the Character of Earliest Christianity*. 3rd ed. London: SCM, 2006.

Edwards, Dennis R. *1 Peter*. Grand Rapids: Zondervan, 2017.

Ehrensperger, Kathy. *Paul and the Dynamics of Power: Communication and Interaction in the Early Christ-Movement*. LNTS 325. London: T&T Clark, 2007.

Ellis, E. Earle. *Pauline Theology: Ministry and Society*. Grand Rapids: Eerdmans, 1989.

Enright, D. J., and David Rawlinson, eds. *The Oxford Book of Friendship*. New York: Oxford University Press, 1991.

Epstein, Joseph. *Alexis de Tocqueville: Democracy's Guide*. Eminent Lives. New York: HarperCollins, 2006.

———. *Friendship: An Exposé*. Boston: Houghton Mifflin, 2006.

———. *Life Sentences: Literary Essays*. New York: Norton, 1997.

———, ed. *The Norton Book of Personal Essays*. New York: Norton, 1997.

———. *With My Trousers Rolled: Familiar Essays*. New York: Norton, 1995.

Esler, P. F. "Family Imagery and Christian Identity in Galatians 5:13 to 6:10." In Moxnes, *Constructing Early Christian Families*, 121–49.

Everitt, Anthony. *Augustus: The Life of Rome's First Emperor*. New York: Random House, 2006.

Fee, Gordon D. *The First Epistle to the Corinthians*. NICNT. Rev. ed. Grand Rapids: Eerdmans, 2014.

———. *New Testament Exegesis: A Handbook for Students and Pastors*. 3rd ed. Louisville: Westminster John Knox, 2002.

———. "Paul's Conversion as Key to His Understanding of the Spirit." In R. Longenecker, *Road from Damascus*, 166–83.

———. *Paul, the Spirit, and the People of God*. Grand Rapids: Baker Academic, 1996.

Fee, Gordon D., and Douglas Stuart. *How to Read the Bible for All Its Worth*. 4th ed. Grand Rapids: Zondervan, 2014.

Fellows, Richard G. "Name Giving by Paul and the Destination of Acts." *TynBul* 67 (2016): 247–68.

———. "Renaming in Paul's Churches: The Case of Crispus-Sosthenes Revisited." *TynBul* 56 (2005): 111–30.

Finney, Mark T. *Honour and Conflict in the Ancient World: 1 Corinthians in Its Greco-Roman Social Setting*. LNTS 460. London: T&T Clark, 2012.

Fowler, J. S. *Becoming Adult, Becoming Christian: Adult Development and Christian Faith*. San Francisco: Jossey-Bass, 2000.

———. *Stages of Faith: The Psychology of Human Development and the Quest for Meaning*. San Francisco: HarperSanFrancisco, 1981.

Franklin, Missy, with D. A. Franklin and Dick Franklin. *Relentless Spirit: The Unconventional Raising of a Champion*. New York: Dutton, 2016.

Galinsky, Karl. *Augustus: Introduction to the Life of an Emperor*. New York: Cambridge University Press, 2012.

Gaventa, Beverly R. *From Darkness to Light: Aspects of Conversion in the New Testament*. OBT. Philadelphia: Fortress, 1986.

———. "Galatians 1 and 2: Autobiography as Paradigm." *NovT* 28 (1986): 309–26.

———. "The Mission of God in Paul's Letter to the Romans." In Burke and Rosner, *Paul as Missionary*, 65–75.

———. *Our Mother Saint Paul*. Louisville: Westminster John Knox, 2007.

Gehring, Roger W. *House Church and Mission: The Importance of Household Structures in Early Christianity*. Peabody, MA: Hendrickson, 2004.

Gibbon, Edward. *The Decline and Fall of the Roman Empire*. 6 vols. New York: Everyman's Library, 1993.

Giles, Kevin. *Patterns of Ministry among the First Christians*. 2nd ed. Eugene, OR: Cascade, 2017.

Gini, Al. *The Importance of Being Lazy: In Praise of Play, Leisure, and Vacation.* New York: Routledge, 2003.

Goldingay, John. *Do We Need the New Testament? Letting the Old Testament Speak for Itself.* Downers Grove, IL: IVP Academic, 2015.

———. *The First Testament: A New Translation.* Downers Grove, IL: IVP Academic, 2018.

———. *Old Testament Theology: Israel's Gospel.* Downers Grove, IL: IVP Academic, 2015.

———. *Reading Jesus's Bible: How the New Testament Helps Us Understand the Old Testament.* Grand Rapids: Eerdmans, 2017.

Goldsworthy, Adrian. *Pax Romana: War, Peace and Conquest in the Roman World.* New Haven: Yale University Press, 2016.

Goodman, Martin. *Mission and Conversion: Proselytizing in the Religious History of the Roman Empire.* New York: Oxford University Press, 1994.

Goodrich, John K. "After Destroying Every Rule, Authority, and Power: Paul, Apocalyptic, and Politics in 1 Corinthians." In *Paul and the Apocalyptic Imagination*, edited by Ben C. Blackwell, John K. Goodrich, and Jason Maston, 275–95. Minneapolis: Fortress, 2016.

———. *Paul as an Administrator of God in 1 Corinthians.* SNTSMS 152. Cambridge: Cambridge University Press, 2012.

Gordley, Matthew E. *Teaching through Song in Antiquity: Didactic Hymnody among Greeks, Romans, Jews, and Christians.* WUNT 2.302. Tübingen: Mohr Siebeck, 2011.

Gorman, Michael J. *Apostle of the Crucified Lord: A Theological Introduction to Paul and His Letters.* 2nd ed. Grand Rapids: Eerdmans, 2016.

———. *Becoming the Gospel: Paul, Participation, and Mission.* Grand Rapids: Eerdmans, 2015.

———. *Cruciformity: Paul's Narrative Spirituality of the Cross.* Grand Rapids: Eerdmans, 2001.

———. *Inhabiting the Cruciform God: Kenosis, Justification, and Theosis in Paul's Narrative Soteriology.* Grand Rapids: Eerdmans, 2009.

Greenleaf, Robert K., and Stephen R. Covey. *Servant Leadership: A Journey into the Nature of Legitimate Power and Greatness.* Edited by Larry C. Spears. 25th anniversary ed. New York: Paulist Press, 2002.

Griffin, Miriam, and Brad Inwood, trans. *Seneca: On Benefits.* Chicago: University of Chicago Press, 2011.

Guinness, Alec. *Blessings in Disguise.* New York: Knopf, 1986.

Gundry, R. H. "The Moral Frustration of Paul before His Conversion: Sexual Lust in Romans 7.7–25." In *Pauline Studies: Essays Presented to F. F. Bruce*, edited by D. A. Hagner and M. J. Harris, 228–45. Grand Rapids: Eerdmans, 1980.

Habinek, Thomas. *Ancient Rhetoric and Oratory*. Malden, MA: Wiley-Blackwell, 2004.

Hanson, Anthony Tyrrell. *The Pioneer Ministry: The Relation of Church and Ministry*. Library of History and Doctrine. Philadelphia: Westminster, 1961.

Harland, Philip. *Associations, Synagogues, and Congregations: Claiming a Place in Ancient Mediterranean Society*. Minneapolis: Fortress, 2003.

Harris, Brian. *The Tortoise Usually Wins: Biblical Reflections on Quiet Leadership for Reluctant Leaders*. Milton Keynes, UK: Paternoster/Authentic Media, 2013.

Harris, Murray J. *The Second Epistle to the Corinthians*. NIGTC. Grand Rapids: Eerdmans, 2005.

Haruf, Kent. *Eventide*. New York: Vintage, 2005.

Hatch, Edwin. *The Organization of the Early Christian Churches*. Reprint ed. The Bampton Lectures 1880. Eugene, OR: Wipf & Stock, 1999.

Hays, Richard B. *The Conversion of the Imagination: Paul as Interpreter of Israel's Scripture*. Grand Rapids: Eerdmans, 2005.

———. *Echoes of Scripture in the Letters of Paul*. New Haven: Yale University Press, 1993.

———. *The Faith of Jesus Christ: The Narrative Substructure of Galatians 3:1–4:11*. 2nd ed. Grand Rapids: Eerdmans, 2002.

———. *Reading Backwards: Figural Christology and the Fourfold Gospel Witness*. Waco: Baylor University Press, 2014.

Hellerman, Joseph H. *Reconstructing Honor in Roman Philippi: Carmen Christi as Cursus Pudorum*. SNTSMS 132. Cambridge: Cambridge University Press, 2005.

Hengel, Martin. *The Pre-Christian Paul*. Translated by John Bowden. Philadelphia: Trinity Press International, 1991.

Henry, Carl F. H. *Confessions of a Theologian: An Autobiography*. Waco: Word Books, 1986.

Henze, Matthias, ed. *A Companion to Biblical Interpretation in Early Judaism*. Grand Rapids: Eerdmans, 2012.

Heschel, Abraham Joshua. *The Prophets*. 2 vols. New York: HarperCollins, 2001.

Hill, Craig C. *Servant of All: Status, Ambition, and the Way of Jesus*. Grand Rapids: Eerdmans, 2016.

Hill, Graham. *Global Church: Reshaping Our Conversations, Renewing Our Mission, Revitalizing Our Churches*. Downers Grove, IL: IVP Academic, 2016.

Hill, Wesley. *Washed and Waiting: Reflections on Christian Faithfulness and Homosexuality*. Grand Rapids: Zondervan, 2010.

Hoag, Gary G. *Wealth in Ancient Ephesus and the First Letter to Timothy: Fresh Insights from "Ephesiaca" by Xenophon of Ephesus*. Winona Lake, IN: Eisenbrauns, 2015.

Hock, Ronald F. *The Social Context of Paul's Ministry: Tentmaking and Apostleship*. Minneapolis: Fortress, 2007.

Honan, Park. *Shakespeare: A Life*. Oxford: Clarendon, 1999.

Hood, Jason B. *Imitating God in Christ: Recapturing a Biblical Pattern*. Downers Grove, IL: IVP Academic, 2013.

Hood, Jason B., and Matthew Y. Emerson. "Summaries of Israel's Story: Reviewing a Compositional Category." *CurBR* 11 (2013): 328–48.

Horrell, David G. "From *adelphoi* to *oikos*: Social Transformation in Pauline Christianity." *JBL* 120 (2001): 293–311.

———. *Solidarity and Difference: A Contemporary Reading of Paul's Ethics*. 2nd ed. London: Bloomsbury T&T Clark, 2015.

Hurtado, Larry W. *At the Origins of Christian Worship: The Context and Character of Earliest Christian Devotion*. Grand Rapids: Eerdmans, 1999.

———. *Destroyer of the Gods: Early Christian Distinctiveness in the Roman World*. Waco: Baylor University Press, 2016.

———. *How on Earth Did Jesus Become a God? Historical Questions about Earliest Devotion to Jesus*. Grand Rapids: Eerdmans, 2005.

———. "The Jerusalem Collection and the Book of Galatians." *JSNT* 5 (1979): 46–62.

———. *Lord Jesus Christ: Devotion to Jesus in Earliest Christianity*. Grand Rapids: Eerdmans, 2003.

Isocrates. *Letter 4, To Antipater*. LCL 373:414–15.

Jacob, Haley Goranson. *Conformed to the Image of His Son: Reconsidering Paul's Theology of Glory in Romans*. Downers Grove, IL: IVP Academic, 2018.

Jacobs, Alan. *Looking Before and After: Testimony and the Christian Life*. Stob Lectures. Grand Rapids: Eerdmans, 2008.

James, P. D. *Death in Holy Orders*. New York: Knopf, 2001.

Jewett, Robert. *Romans: A Commentary*. Hermeneia. Minneapolis: Fortress, 2007.

Jipp, Joshua W. "Ancient, Modern, and Future Interpretation of Romans 1:3–4: Reception History and Biblical Interpretation." *JTI* 3 (2009): 241–59.

———. *Christ Is King: Paul's Royal Ideology*. Minneapolis: Fortress, 2015.

John Chrysostom. *Treatise on the Priesthood*. NPNF[1] 9:33.

Josephus. *The Life. Against Apion*. Translated by H. St. J. Thackeray. LCL 186. Cambridge: Harvard University Press, 1926.

Joubert, Stephan. *Paul as Benefactor: Reciprocity, Strategy and Theological Reflection in Paul's Collection*. WUNT 2.124. Tübingen: Mohr Siebeck, 2000.

Karr, Mary. *The Art of Memoir*. New York: HarperCollins, 2015.

Käsemann, Ernst. "Paul and Early Catholicism." In *New Testament Questions of Today*, translated by W. J. Montague, 236–51. Philadelphia: Augsburg Fortress, 1979.

Keener, Craig S. *The Mind of the Spirit: Paul's Approach to Transformed Thinking*. Grand Rapids: Baker Academic, 2016.

———. *Spirit Hermeneutics: Reading Scripture in Light of Pentecost*. Grand Rapids: Eerdmans, 2016.

Keillor, Garrison. *Life among the Lutherans*. Edited by Holly Harden. Minneapolis: Augsburg Books, 2010.

Keith, Kent M. *The Case for Servant Leadership*. 2nd ed. Westfield, IN: Greenleaf Center, 2015.

———. *Do It Anyway: Finding Personal Meaning and Deep Happiness by Living the Paradoxical Commandments*. Novato, CA: New World Library, 2008.

———. *Jesus Did It Anyway*. New York: Putnam Adult, 2005.

Keller, Timothy. *Preaching: Communicating Faith in an Age of Skepticism*. New York: Penguin, 2016.

Kennedy, George A. *Classical Rhetoric and Its Christian and Secular Tradition from Ancient to Modern Times*. 2nd ed. Chapel Hill: University of North Carolina Press, 1999.

Kim, Seyoon. "Paul as an Eschatological Herald." In Burke and Rosner, *Paul as Missionary*, 9–24.

Kimball, Roger, ed. *Vox Populi: The Perils and Promises of Populism*. New York: Encounter Books, 2017.

Konstan, David. *Friendship in the Classical World*. New York: Cambridge University Press, 1997.

Koyzis, David T. *Political Visions and Illusions: A Survey and Christian Critique of Contemporary Ideologies*. Downers Grove, IL: InterVarsity, 2003.

Kruse, Colin. *New Testament Models for Ministry: Jesus and Paul*. Nashville: Nelson, 1983.

Kümmel, W. G. *Römer 7 und die Bekehrung des Paulus* [Romans 7 and the conversion of Paul]. Leipzig: Hinrichs, 1929.

Kuyper, Abraham. *Lectures on Calvinism*. Grand Rapids: Eerdmans, 1931.

Lakoff, George, and Mark Johnson. *Metaphors We Live By*. Chicago: University of Chicago Press, 2003.

Laniak, Timothy. *Shepherds after My Own Heart: Pastoral Traditions and Leadership in the Bible*. Downers Grove, IL: IVP Academic, 2006.

Lartey, Emmanuel Y. *Pastoral Theology in an Intercultural World*. Reprint ed. Eugene, OR: Wipf & Stock, 2013.

"Letter of Aristeas." Translated by R. J. H. Shutt. In *The Old Testament Pseudepigrapha*, vol. 2. Edited by James H. Charlesworth, 7–34. New York: Doubleday, 1985.

Levenson, Jon D. *The Love of God: Divine Gift, Human Gratitude, and Mutual Faithfulness in Judaism*. Princeton: Princeton University Press, 2016.

Levinskaya, Irina. *The Book of Acts in Its Diaspora Setting.* The Book of Acts in Its First Century Setting 5. Grand Rapids: Eerdmans, 1996.

Levison, John R. *Filled with the Spirit.* Grand Rapids: Eerdmans, 2009.

Lewis, C. S. *Mere Christianity.* New York: Macmillan, 1956.

———. *The Screwtape Letters: Annotated Edition.* New York: HarperOne, 2013.

Lincoln, Andrew T. "Liberation from the Powers: Supernatural Spirits or Societal Structures?" In *The Bible in Human Society: Essays in Honour of John Rogerson,* edited by M. Daniel Carroll R., David J. A. Clines, and Philip R. Davies, 335–54. JSOTSup 200. Sheffield: Sheffield Academic Press, 1995.

Litfin, Duane. *Paul's Theology of Preaching: The Apostle's Challenge to the Art of Persuasion in Ancient Corinth.* 2nd ed. Downers Grove, IL: IVP Academic, 2015.

Long, Thomas G. *The Witness of Preaching.* 3rd ed. Louisville: Westminster John Knox, 2016.

Longenecker, Bruce W., ed. *Narrative Dynamics in Paul: A Critical Assessment.* Louisville: Westminster John Knox, 2002.

———. "Prolegomena to Paul's Use of Scripture in Romans." *BBR* 7 (1997): 1–24.

———. *Remember the Poor: Paul, Poverty, and the Greco-Roman World.* Grand Rapids: Eerdmans, 2010.

Longenecker, Richard N. *Biblical Exegesis in the Apostolic Period.* Rev. ed. Grand Rapids: Eerdmans, 1999.

———, ed. *The Road from Damascus: The Impact of Paul's Conversion on His Life, Thought, and Ministry.* Grand Rapids: Eerdmans, 1997.

Longman, Tremper, III. *The Fear of the Lord Is Wisdom: A Theological Introduction to Wisdom in Israel.* Grand Rapids: Baker Academic, 2017.

———. *Proverbs.* Baker Commentary on the Old Testament Wisdom and Psalms. Grand Rapids: Baker Academic, 2006.

Longman, Tremper, III, and Peter Enns, eds. *Dictionary of the Old Testament: Wisdom, Poetry & Writings.* Downers Grove, IL: InterVarsity, 2008.

Longman, Tremper, III, and Daniel G. Reid. *God Is a Warrior.* Studies in Old Testament Biblical Theology. Grand Rapids: Zondervan, 1995.

Lopate, Phillip, ed. *The Art of the Personal Essay: An Anthology from the Classical Era to the Present.* New York: Anchor/Doubleday, 1994.

Mairs, Nancy. *Ordinary Time: Cycles in Marriage, Faith, and Renewal.* Boston: Beacon Press, 1993.

Malcolm, Matthew R. "Paul's Pastoral Sensitivity in 1 Corinthians." In Rosner, Malone, and Burke, *Paul as Pastor,* 43–54.

Malherbe, Abraham J. *Paul and the Thessalonians: The Philosophic Tradition of Pastoral Care.* Reprint ed. Eugene, OR: Wipf & Stock, 2011.

Malina, Bruce J. *Christian Origins and Cultural Anthropology: Practical Models for Biblical Interpretation.* Atlanta: John Knox, 1986.

Marshall, I. Howard. *Jesus the Saviour: Studies in New Testament Theology*. Downers Grove, IL: InterVarsity, 1990.

Martin, Ralph P. *2 Corinthians*. 2nd ed. WBC 40. Grand Rapids: Zondervan, 2014.

Mbanda, Laurent. *From Barefoot to Bishop: A Rwandan Refugee's Journey*. Howard Beach, NY: Changing Lives Press, 2017.

McKnight, Scot. *A Community Called Atonement*. Nashville: Abingdon, 2007.

———. *A Fellowship of Differents: Showing the World God's Design for Life Together*. Grand Rapids: Zondervan, 2014.

———. "James' Secret: Wisdom in James in the Mode of Receptive Reverence." In *Preaching Character: Reclaiming Wisdom's Paradigmatic Imagination for Transformation*, edited by David Fleer and David Bland, 201–16. Abilene, TX: Abilene Christian University Press, 2010.

———. *Kingdom Conspiracy: Returning to the Radical Mission of the Local Church*. Grand Rapids: Brazos, 2014.

———. *The King Jesus Gospel: The Original Good News Revisited*. 2nd ed. Grand Rapids: Zondervan, 2015.

———. *The Letter to Philemon*. NICNT. Grand Rapids: Eerdmans, 2017.

———. *The Letter to the Colossians*. NICNT. Grand Rapids: Eerdmans, 2018.

———. *A Light among the Gentiles: Jewish Missionary Activity in the Second Temple Period*. Minneapolis: Fortress, 1991.

———. *A New Vision for Israel: The Teachings of Jesus in National Context*. Grand Rapids: Eerdmans, 1999.

———. *Turning to Jesus: The Sociology of Conversion in the Gospels*. Louisville: Westminster John Knox, 2002.

———. "Was Paul a Convert?" *Ex Auditu* 25 (2009): 110–32.

McKnight, Scot, and Joseph B. Modica. *Preaching Romans: Four Perspectives*. Grand Rapids: Eerdmans, 2019.

Meeks, Wayne A. *The First Urban Christians: The Social World of the Apostle Paul*. 2nd ed. New Haven: Yale University Press, 2003.

Meggitt, Justin. *Paul, Poverty and Survival*. SNTW. Edinburgh: T&T Clark, 1998.

Minear, Paul S. *Images of the Church in the New Testament*. Philadelphia: Westminster, 1960.

Moon, Gary W. *Becoming Dallas Willard: The Formation of a Philosopher, Teacher, and Christ Follower*. Downers Grove, IL: IVP Books, 2018.

Moore, Erin. *That's Not English: Britishisms, Americanisms, and What Our English Says about Us*. New York: Avery, 2015.

Morris, L. L. "The Theme of Romans." In *Apostolic History and the Gospel: Biblical and Historical Essays Presented to F. F. Bruce on His 60th Birthday*, edited by W. W. Gasque and R. P. Martin, 249–63. Grand Rapids: Eerdmans, 1970.

Moule, C. F. D. *The Birth of the New Testament*. 3rd ed. BNTC. London: Adam & Charles Black, 1981.

Moxnes, Halvor, ed. *Constructing Early Christian Families: Family as Social Reality and Metaphor*. London: Routledge, 1997.

Murphy, Roland E. *The Tree of Life: An Exploration of Biblical Wisdom Literature*. 3rd ed. Grand Rapids: Eerdmans, 2002.

Neiman, Susan. *Why Grow Up? Subversive Thoughts for an Infantile Age*. Rev. ed. New York: Farrar, Straus and Giroux, 2016.

Neusner, Jacob. *Fellowship in Judaism: The First Century and Today*. London: Vallentine and Mitchell, 1963.

———. *The Rabbinic Traditions about the Pharisees before 70*. Reprint ed. 3 vols. Eugene, OR: Wipf & Stock, 2005.

Nickle, Keith Fullerton. *The Collection: A Study in Paul's Strategy*. SBT 48. Naperville, IL: Allenson, 1966.

Niebuhr, H. Richard. *Christ and Culture*. San Francisco: HarperSanFrancisco, 2001.

Noonan, Peggy. *The Time of Our Lives: Collected Writings*. New York: Twelve, 2015.

———. *When Character Was King: A Story of Ronald Reagan*. New York: Penguin, 2002.

Nouwen, Henri J. M. *The Wounded Healer: Ministry in Contemporary Society*. New York: Doubleday, 1990.

Nugent, John C. *Endangered Gospel: How Fixing the World Is Killing the Church*. Eugene, OR: Cascade, 2016.

O'Connor, Flannery. "The King of Birds." In *The Collected Works of Flannery O'Connor*, edited by Sally Fitzgerald, 832–42. New York: Library of America, 1988.

Olyan, Saul M. *Friendship in the Hebrew Bible*. ABRL. New Haven: Yale University Press, 2017.

Payne, Philip Barton. *Man and Woman, One in Christ: An Exegetical and Theological Study of Paul's Letters*. Grand Rapids: Zondervan, 2009.

Pemberton, Glenn. *A Life That Is Good: The Message of Proverbs in a World Wanting Wisdom*. Grand Rapids: Eerdmans, 2018.

Perdue, Leo G. *Wisdom Literature: A Theological History*. Louisville: Westminster John Knox, 2007.

Peterman, G. W. *Paul's Gift from Philippi: Conventions of Gift Exchange and Christian Giving*. SNTSMS 92. Cambridge: Cambridge University Press, 1997.

Petersen, Norman R. *Rediscovering Paul: Philemon and the Sociology of Paul's Narrative World*. Philadelphia: Fortress, 1985.

Peterson, Eugene H. *As Kingfishers Catch Fire: A Conversation on the Ways of God Formed by the Words of God*. Colorado Springs: WaterBrook, 2017.

———. *The Contemplative Pastor: Returning to the Art of Spiritual Direction*. Grand Rapids: Eerdmans, 1993.

———. "Pastor Paul." In *Romans and the People of God: Essays in Honor of Gordon D. Fee on the Occasion of His 65th Birthday*, edited by Sven K. Soderlund and N. T. Wright, 283–94. Grand Rapids: Eerdmans, 1999.

———. *Working the Angles: The Shape of Pastoral Integrity*. Grand Rapids: Eerdmans, 1993.

Petronius: Satyricon; Seneca: Apocolocyntosis. Translated by Michael Heseltine and W. H. D. Rouse. Revised by E. H. Warmington. Rev. ed. LCL 15. Cambridge, MA: Harvard University Press, 1975.

Plutarch. *How a Man May Become Aware of His Progress in Virtue*. In *Moralia, Volume 1*. LCL 197. Cambridge: Harvard University Press, 1927.

———. *On Brotherly Love*. In *Moralia, Volume 6*. Translated by W. C. Helmbold. LCL 337. Cambridge: Harvard University Press, 1939.

———. *On the Sign of Socrates*. In *Moralia, Volume 7*. Translated by Phillip H. De Lacy. LCL 405. Cambridge: Harvard University Press, 1959.

Porter, Stanley E. "Allusions and Echoes." In *As It Is Written: Studying Paul's Use of Scripture*, edited by Stanley E. Porter and Christopher D. Stanley, 29–40. SBL Symposium 50. Atlanta: SBL, 2008.

———. "Reconciliation as the Heart of Paul's Missionary Theology." In Burke and Rosner, *Paul as Missionary*, 169–79.

Powell, Mark Allan. *What Do They Hear? Bridging the Gap between Pulpit and Pew*. Nashville: Abingdon, 2007.

Provan, Iain. *The Reformation and the Right Reading of Scripture*. Waco: Baylor University Press, 2017.

Putnam, Robert D. *Bowling Alone: The Collapse and Revival of American Community*. New York: Simon & Schuster, 2000.

Rambo, Lewis R. *Understanding Religious Conversion*. New Haven: Yale University Press, 1993.

Rambo, Lewis R., and Charles E. Farhadian, eds. *The Oxford Handbook of Religious Conversion*. New York: Oxford University Press, 2014.

Ramsey, Dave. *The Total Money Makeover, Classic Edition: A Proven Plan for Financial Fitness*. Nashville: Nelson, 2013.

Richards, E. Randolph. *Paul and First-Century Letter Writing: Secretaries, Composition and Collection*. Downers Grove, IL: InterVarsity, 2004.

———. *The Secretary in the Letters of Paul*. WUNT 2.42. Tübingen: Mohr Siebeck, 1991.

Richardson, J. S. *Augustan Rome, 44 BC to AD 14: The Restoration of the Republic and the Establishment of the Empire*. Edinburgh: Edinburgh University Press, 2012.

Robinson, Haddon W. *Biblical Preaching: The Development and Delivery of Expository Messages*. 3rd ed. Grand Rapids: Baker Academic, 2014.

Robinson, Marilynne. *Gilead*. New York: Farrar, Straus and Giroux, 2004.

———. *Home*. New York: Farrar, Straus and Giroux, 2008.

———. *What Are We Doing Here? Essays*. New York: Farrar, Straus and Giroux, 2018.

Romm, James. *Dying Every Day: Seneca at the Court of Nero*. New York: Knopf, 2014.

Root, Andrew. *Faith Formation in a Secular Age: Responding to the Church's Obsession with Youthfulness*. Grand Rapids: Baker Academic, 2017.

Roseberry, David. *Giving Up: How Giving to God Renews Hearts, Changes Minds, and Empowers Ministry*. Franklin, TN: New Vantage, 2017.

Rosner, Brian S. "The Glory of God in Paul's Missionary Theology and Practice." In Burke and Rosner, *Paul as Missionary*, 158–68.

Rosner, Brian S., Andrew S. Malone, and Trevor J. Burke, eds. *Paul as Pastor*. New York: Bloomsbury T&T Clark, 2017.

Rowe, C. Kavin. *One True Life: The Stoics and Early Christians as Rival Traditions*. New Haven: Yale University Press, 2016.

———. *World Upside Down: Reading Acts in the Graeco-Roman Age*. New York: Oxford University Press, 2009.

Rutledge, Fleming. *Not Ashamed of the Gospel: Sermons from Paul's Letter to the Romans*. Grand Rapids: Eerdmans, 2007.

Ryan, Alan. *On Politics: A History of Political Thought; From Herodotus to the Present*. New York: Liveright, 2012.

Sanders, E. P. *Jewish Law from Jesus to the Mishnah: Five Studies*. Minneapolis: Fortress, 2016.

———. *Judaism: Practice and Belief, 63 BCE–66 CE*. Minneapolis: Fortress, 2016.

Sanders, John. *Theology in the Flesh: How Embodiment and Culture Shape the Way We Think about Truth, Morality, and God*. Minneapolis: Fortress, 2016.

Sandnes, Karl Olav. "Equality within Patriarchal Structures: Some New Testament Perspectives on the Christian Fellowship as a Brother- or Sisterhood and a Family." In Moxnes, *Constructing Early Christian Families*, 150–65.

Sappho and Alcaeus. *Greek Lyric: Sappho and Alcaeus*. Translated by David A. Campbell. LCL 142. Cambridge: Harvard University Press, 1982.

Schaeffer, Francis A. *How Should We Then Live? The Rise and Decline of Western Thought and Culture*. Wheaton: Crossway, 2005.

Schmemann, Alexander. *The Journals of Father Alexander Schmemann, 1973–1983*. Translated by Juliana Schmemann. Crestwood, NY: St. Vladimir's Seminary Press, 2000.

Schulz, Kathryn. *Being Wrong: Adventures in the Margin of Error*. New York: Ecco, 2011.

Schweitzer, Albert. *The Quest of the Historical Jesus*. Edited by John Bowden. Minneapolis: Fortress, 2001.

Scruton, Roger. *Confessions of a Heretic: Selected Essays*. Honiton, UK: Notting Hill, 2016.

———. *Gentle Regrets: Thoughts from a Life*. London: Continuum, 2006.

———. *How to Be a Conservative*. London: Continuum, 2014.

———. *The Meaning of Conservatism*. 3rd ed. South Bend, IN: St. Augustine's Press, 2014. First published by Palgrave in 2001.

Segal, A. F. *Paul the Convert: The Apostolate and Apostasy of Saul the Pharisee*. New Haven: Yale University Press, 1990.

Seneca. *Letters to Lucilius*. In *Epistles, Volume I: Epistles 1–65*. Translated by Richard M. Gummere. LCL 75. Cambridge: Harvard University Press, 1917.

Smith, Christian, Kari Christoffersen, Hilary Davidson, and Patricia Snell Herzog. *Lost in Transition: The Dark Side of Emerging Adulthood*. New York: Oxford University Press, 2011.

Smith, Christian, and Melina Lundquist Denton. *Soul Searching: The Religious and Spiritual Lives of American Teenagers*. New York: Oxford University Press, 2009.

Smith, Christian, and Patricia Snell. *Souls in Transition: The Religious and Spiritual Lives of Emerging Adults*. New York: Oxford University Press, 2009.

Smith, James Bryan. *The Good and Beautiful Community: Following the Spirit, Extending Grace, Demonstrating Love*. Downers Grove, IL: IVP Books, 2010.

———. *The Good and Beautiful God: Falling in Love with the God Jesus Knows*. Downers Grove, IL: IVP Books, 2009.

———. *The Good and Beautiful Life: Putting on the Character of Christ*. Downers Grove, IL: IVP Books, 2010.

Smith, Mandy. *The Vulnerable Pastor: How Human Limitations Empower Our Ministry*. Downers Grove, IL: IVP Books, 2015.

Soulen, R. Kendall. *The God of Israel and Christian Theology*. Minneapolis: Fortress, 1996.

Stanley, Christopher D. "'Pearls before Swine': Did Paul's Audiences Understand His Biblical Quotations?" *NovT* 41 (1999): 124–44.

Starling, David I. *UnCorinthian Leadership: Thematic Reflections on 1 Corinthians*. Eugene, OR: Cascade, 2014.

Steinmetz, David. *Taking the Long View: Christian Theology in Historical Perspective*. New York: Oxford University Press, 2011.

Stendahl, Krister. *Paul among Jews and Gentiles, and Other Essays*. Philadelphia: Fortress, 1976.

Stewart, Alistair C. *The Original Bishops: Office and Order in the First Christian Communities*. Grand Rapids: Baker Academic, 2014.

Stewart, Bryan A. *Priests of My People: Levitical Paradigms for Early Christian Ministers*. Patristic Studies 11. New York: Peter Lang, 2015.

Still, Todd G. "Organizational Structures and Relational Struggles among the Saints: The Establishment and Exercise of Authority within Pauline Assemblies." In *After the First Urban Christians: The Social-Scientific Study of Pauline Christianity Twenty-Five Years Later*, edited by Todd G. Still and David G. Horrell, 79–98. London: T&T Clark, 2009.

Stott, John. *Between Two Worlds*. Reprint ed. Grand Rapids: Eerdmans, 2017.

Strabo. *Geography, Volume 6*. Translated by Horace Leonard Jones. LCL 223. Cambridge: Harvard University Press, 1929.

Strawn, Brent A. *The Old Testament Is Dying: A Diagnosis and Recommended Treatment*. Grand Rapids: Baker Academic, 2017.

Sumney, Jerry. *Identifying Paul's Opponents: The Question of Method in 2 Corinthians*. Reprint ed. Bloomsbury Academic Collections. Biblical Studies: The Epistles. London: Bloomsbury Academic, 2015.

Swartz, David R. *Moral Minority: The Evangelical Left in an Age of Conservatism*. Philadelphia: University of Pennsylvania Press, 2012.

Taylor, Barbara Brown. *The Preaching Life*. Plymouth, UK: Cowley, 1992.

Taylor, Charles. *A Secular Age*. Cambridge, MA: Belknap, 2007.

Thompson, James W. *Pastoral Ministry according to Paul: A Biblical Vision*. Grand Rapids: Baker Academic, 2006.

Thompson, Michael B. *Owned by God: Paul's Pastoral Strategy in 1 Corinthians*. Cambridge: Grove Books, 2017.

Thrall, Margaret. *2 Corinthians 1–7*. ICC. London: Bloomsbury T&T Clark, 1994.

———. *2 Corinthians 8–13*. ICC. London: Bloomsbury T&T Clark, 2000.

Tocqueville, Alexis de. *Democracy in America*. Translated by Harvey C. Mansfield and Delba Winthrop. Chicago: University of Chicago Press, 2000.

Tolkien, J. R. R. *Tree and Leaf*. Boston: Houghton Mifflin, 1989.

Trebilco, Paul. *Self-Designations and Group Identity in the New Testament*. Cambridge: Cambridge University Press, 2012.

Trollope, Anthony. *The Warden*. Reprint ed. Harmondsworth, UK: Penguin Classics, 1984.

Tyrtaeus, Solon, Theognis, and Mimnermus. *Greek Elegiac Poetry: From the Seventh to the Fifth Centuries B.C.* Translated by Douglas E. Gerber. LCL 258. Cambridge: Harvard University Press, 1999.

Useem, Jerry. "Power Causes Brain Damage." *The Atlantic*, July/August 2017, https://www.theatlantic.com/magazine/archive/2017/07/power-causes-brain-damage/528711/.

Vance, J. D. *Hillbilly Elegy: A Memoir of a Family and Culture in Crisis*. New York: Harper, 2016.

Venema, Dennis R., and Scot McKnight. *Adam and the Genome: Reading Scripture after Genetic Science*. Grand Rapids: Brazos, 2017.

Verbrugge, Verlyn D., and Keith R. Krell. *Paul and Money: A Biblical and Theological Analysis of the Apostle's Teachings and Practices*. Grand Rapids: Zondervan, 2015.

Vidal, Gore. "Some Memories of the Glorious Bird and an Earlier Self." In Lopate, *Art of the Personal Essay*, 623–39.

Wagner, J. Ross. "The Heralds of Isaiah and the Mission of Paul: An Investigation of Paul's Use of Isaiah 51–55 in Romans." In *Jesus and the Suffering Servant: Isaiah 53 and Christian Origins*, edited by William H. Bellinger Jr. and William R. Farmer, 193–222. Harrisburg, PA: Trinity Press International, 1998.

———. *Heralds of the Good News: Isaiah and Paul in Concert in the Letter to the Romans*. NovTSup 101. Leiden: Brill, 2000.

Wallace, David Foster. *This Is Water: Some Thoughts, Delivered on a Significant Occasion, about Living a Compassionate Life*. New York: Little, Brown, 2009.

Waltke, B. K., and D. Diewert. "Wisdom Literature." In *The Face of Old Testament Studies: A Survey of Contemporary Approaches*, edited by D. W. Baker and B. T. Arnold, 295–328. Grand Rapids: Baker Academic, 1999.

Weima, Jeffrey A. D. *Paul the Ancient Letter Writer: An Introduction to Epistolary Analysis*. Grand Rapids: Baker Academic, 2016.

Wesley, John. "Catholic Spirit." Sermon 39 in vol. 2 of *Bicentennial Edition of the Works of John Wesley*, 79–95. Nashville: Abingdon, 1985.

West, M. L., ed. *Iambi et Elegi Graeci: Ante Alexandrum Cantati*. Volume 1, *Archilochus, Hipponax, Theognidea*. Rev. ed. Oxford: Oxford University Press, 1989.

Westfall, Cynthia Long. *Paul and Gender: Reclaiming the Apostle's Vision for Men and Women in Christ*. Grand Rapids: Baker Academic, 2016.

Wheeler, Sondra. *The Minister as Moral Theologian: Ethical Dimensions of Pastoral Leadership*. Grand Rapids: Baker Academic, 2017.

Whipp, Margaret. *Pastoral Theology*. SCM Studyguide. London: SCM, 2013.

Williams, Ritva H. *Stewards, Prophets, Keepers of the Word: Leadership in the Early Church*. Peabody, MA: Hendrickson, 2006.

Willimon, William H. *Pastor: A Reader for Ordained Ministry*. Nashville: Abingdon, 2002.

———. *Pastor: The Theology and Practice of Ordained Ministry*. Rev. ed. Nashville: Abingdon, 2016.

Wilson, Todd, and Gerald L. Hiestand, eds. *Becoming a Pastor Theologian: New Possibilities for Church Leadership*. Downers Grove, IL: IVP Academic, 2016.

Wink, Walter. *Naming the Powers: The Language of Power in the New Testament*. Minneapolis: Fortress, 1984.

Winter, Bruce W. *After Paul Left Corinth: The Influence of Secular Ethics and Social Change*. Grand Rapids: Eerdmans, 2001.

———. *Philo and Paul among the Sophists: Alexandrian and Corinthian Responses to a Julio-Claudian Movement*. 2nd ed. Grand Rapids: Eerdmans, 2002.

————. *Seek the Welfare of the City: Christians as Benefactors and Citizens.* First Century Christians in the Graeco-Roman World. Grand Rapids: Eerdmans, 1994.

Witherington, Ben, III. *Jesus and Money: A Guide for Times of Financial Crisis.* Reprint ed. Grand Rapids: Brazos, 2012.

————. *Jesus the Sage: The Pilgrimage of Wisdom.* Minneapolis: Fortress, 1994.

————. *New Testament Rhetoric: An Introductory Guide to the Art of Persuasion in and of the New Testament.* Eugene, OR: Wipf & Stock, 2009.

Wright, Christopher J. H., ed. *Portraits of a Radical Disciple: Recollections of John Stott's Life and Ministry.* Downers Grove, IL: IVP Books, 2011.

Wright, N. T. *Paul: A Biography.* San Francisco: HarperOne, 2018.

————. *Paul and His Recent Interpreters.* Minneapolis: Fortress, 2015.

————. *Paul and the Faithfulness of God.* 2 vols. Christian Origins and the Question of God 4. Minneapolis: Fortress, 2013.

————. *Pauline Perspectives: Essays on Paul, 1978–2013.* Minneapolis: Fortress, 2013.

Scripture and Ancient Writings Index

Old Testament

Genesis

1–2 6
1:2 182
2:24 11
3 118
12 42
13:15 114
15 42, 114
17 42
17:8 114
22 42
24:7 114
34:8 45
44:20 46
44:30–31 46

Exodus

15 108n13
15:3 44
16 96n43
16:18 96

Leviticus

26:4–13 108n13
26:12 42n27

Numbers

7:5 93
8:22 93
8:25 93
16:9 93

Deuteronomy

6:4 180
6:20–24 108n13, 113
7:7 45
8:3 96n43
10:15 45
10:20 11
11:22 11
13:4 11
13:6 46
15:4 97
21:1–9 186
21:1–14 46
21:18–21 186
22:13–21 186
25:5–10 186
26:5–9 108n13, 113
29 108n13
30 113

30:20 11
32 108n13, 113
33:2 114

Joshua

20:1–6 186
22:5 11n33
23:2–4 108n13
24:2–13 108n13, 113

Ruth

1:14 11n33
2:8 11n33
2:21 11n33
2:23 11n33
4:2 186

1 Samuel

12:7–15 108n13
14:22 12
18:1 46
18:1–4 42, 46

1 Kings

8 108n13
21:8–14 186

2 Kings

18:6 11n33

1 Chronicles

1–9 108n13
16:8–36 108n13

Ezra

5:11–27 108n13

Nehemiah

9:6–37 108n13, 113

Job

28 178n32
41:17 12

Psalms

8:6 123
20:7 112
55:13–14 42
63:8 11n33
72:1–4 112
78 108n13, 113
91:14 45, 45n36

100:1 123
101:1–3 112
105 108n13, 113
106 108n13
119:31 11n33
119:41 42
119:64 42
119:76 42
119:88 42
119:124 42
119:149 42
119:159 42
135:8–12 108n13,
    113
136 108n13, 113

Proverbs

1 178n32
1:1–7 174
1:3 174, 175
1:4 174
1:5 174
1:7 175
1:8 175n24
4:1–4 175
4:13 175n24
6:6–8 175
8 178n32
8:10 175n24
8:12 174
9 178n32
9:7–12 174n22
10:17 175
12:20 36
17:17 46
18:24 46
22:17–21 175
23:23 175n24
24:32 175n24

Isaiah

5:1–7 108n13
38:17 45, 45n36
58 82
61 80

Jeremiah

2:2–9 108n13
4:23 182
7:23 42, 42n27
11:4 42n27
13:11 12
31 42

Ezekiel

14:11 42n27
16 108n13
20 108n13
23 108n13

Daniel

7:2–8 124
7:21–22 145n45
7:25–27 145n45
7:27 122
9:1–27 108n13
10:13 122, 124
10:20 122
10:20–21 124
11:40–12:3 123,
    123n35
12:1–3 145n45

Habakkuk

3:1–16 108n13
3:15 145n45

Zephaniah

1:15 145n45

Zechariah

8:8 42n27

New Testament

Matthew

1:1–17 108n13
1:23 42
10:24–25 193

11:19 58n3
19:6 74
20:12 96
20:13 58n3
22:12 58n3
23:1–12 27
23:8 76
23:8–10 164
24:4–8 145n45
26:50 58n3

Mark

3:31–35 76
10:29–30 76
10:35–45 148
10:42–45 24
10:45 193
12:13–17 119
12:28–32 45,
    100n50
12:28–34 64
13:5–8 145n45

Luke

1:46–55 80
1:67–79 80
3:10–14 80
4:16–30 80
6:20–26 80
6:34 96
11:5 58n3
11:8 58n3
12:4 58n3, 59n8
14:10 58n3
14:12 58n3, 59n8
15:6 58n3
15:9 58n3
15:21 74
15:29 58n3
16:9 58n3, 59n8
21:8–11 145n45
21:16 58n3
22:24–27 24
22:50 148

John

3:29 59n8
5:18 95
10 96n43
11:11 58n3, 59n8
15:13–15 58n3,
    59n8
18:10 148
18:11 148

Acts (of the Apostles)

2:42–47 80, 97
2:45 97
4:32–36 80, 97
4:34 97
7:2–50 108n13
9 138
10:36–43 108n13
11 83
11:17 95
11:19–30 48n37
11:27–30 83
12 83
12:12 48n37
12:25 83
13:9 134n19
13:13 48n37
13:17–41 108n13
14:19–20 53n44
15:36–41 48n37
16:1 84
16:1–3 53n44
16:12 84
16:16 84
17:14–15 55
17:14–16 53n44
17:15 54
17:26–28 115
18:3 162, 163
18:5 53n44
19:22 53n44
19:31 58n3
20:4 53n44, 84

20:5–6 84
20:34
20:35 83, 89
21:3–4 84
21:7 84
21:16 84
21:17 84
21:17–26 85
22 138
22:3 134
23:6 134
24:17 85, 91
26 138
26:14 133
27:3 58n3, 59n8
28:30 163

Romans

1:3–4 109
1:13 84
5:8–11 49
5:12 118
5:12–21 115, 118
5:17 118
5:18 118
6 119–121
6:1 120
6:2 120
6:3 120
6:4 120
6:6 120
6:9 119
6:11 120
6:17 184
7 133
7:4 61n16
7:4–6 131
7:4–7 130
7:7–25 133, 138
7:8–11 130, 131
8 110n20, 116n28
8:15 77
8:17 145n46
8:18–30 5
8:23 77

8:29 77
8:29–30 77
8:37 123
8:38–39 122, 124
9–11 17, 42,
   108n13
9:6 49
10:2 127n3
10:9–10 110, 185
11:1 134
11:11–12 86n20
11:11–24 91
11:25 86n20
11:33–36 179
12:1–2 23, 120
12:2 120
12:8 26, 164
12:9–13 64
12:13 83, 84
12:16 83
13:1 122, 124
13:10 64
15 17
15:10 118
15:14 61n16
15:14–32 84, 93
15:15 118
15:15–16 22, 93
15:16 93, 118
15:18–19 5
15:19 118
15:21 118
15:25 84
15:25–32 93
15:26 84, 87, 91
15:27 84, 91
15:29 86n20
15:31 84, 87
16 41, 67
16:1–2 50, 67
16:14 67
16:15 67
16:21 53n44, 55
16:22 51
16:25–27 179

1 Corinthians

1–4 27
1:12 155
1:18 177
1:18–25 158, 180
1:21–25 177
1:22 156
1:23 156
1:24 179
1:25 165
1:26 153
1:26–31 156
1:28 165
1:30 177, 179
2:1 181
2:1–5 161
2:3 165
2:4–7 181
2:6–8 124
2:8 122
2:13 181
3:1–2 62, 165
3:3–4 155
3:5 165
3:5–15 161
3:6 165
3:10 165
3:16–17 123
3:18–23 156
3:19 165
3:21–23 167
4:1 161
4:1–2 185
4:6 141n36, 161
4:6–7 156
4:7 157
4:8 157
4:8–13 156–158
4:9 157
4:10 155, 157, 165
4:11 157
4:11–13
4:12 157, 163
4:12–13 157

4:13 165
4:14–17 165
4:15 62
4:16 141n36
4:17 53, 53n44,
   54, 55
5:11 71
6 70–72
6:1–11 71, 73
6:5–6 71
6:7–8 71
6:8 71
6:9–11 71
7:7 141n36
8:1 188
8:5–6 179
8:6 180
8:13 61n16
9 159
9:1–6 163
9:6 48n37, 163
9:8–11 163
9:12 163
9:12–17 164
9:13 22
9:18 164
9:19 164
9:22 2
10:23–24 188
10:32–11:1 15
11:1 15, 141n36
11:2 184
11:23 184
11:33 61n16
12:1 66
12:8 179
12:12–27 61n14
12:13 66
15 109–110
15:1–2 109
15:1–9 100
15:1–28 108n13,
   115, 116
15:3 110, 184
15:3–5 144

15:3–8 109, 185
15:3–28 109
15:4 110
15:12–19 109
15:15 127n3
15:20–28 110
15:21–22 115
15:24–25 122
15:24–26 123, 124
15:24–28 123
15:26 119, 122, 124
15:45–49 115
15:54–55 119
15:58 61n16
16:1 84, 92
16:1–2 87
16:1–4 84, 90–93
16:2 96
16:3 87, 92
16:10–11 53n44
16:15 87

2 Corinthians

1–7 149n6
1:1 53n44, 55
1:5 145n46
1:11 61n16
1:12 181
1:19 53n44
2:12–13 9, 51
2:12–7:16 xi
2:13 61n16
2:14 165
2:14–6:13 149n6
3:17–4:6 114n24
4:5 24
4:7 2, 165
4:10–11 145n46
5:16 166
5:16–21 49, 74
5:17 114
5:21 124, 145n47
6:11 64

6:11–13 64
6:13 165
6:16 123
7 64
7:2 9
7:2–4 64, 149n6
7:2–16 51
7:4 64
7:5–7 44
7:7 9
8 95, 149n6
8–9 84, 91–93, 149n6
8:1 92
8:1–5 84
8:3 127n3
8:4 84, 87
8:6 87
8:9 92
8:11 92
8:13–14 96, 97
8:13–15 94–99
8:14 96
8:22–23 61n16
8:23 92
9 149n6
9:2 84
9:4 84
9:5 87
9:6 188
9:6–10 84
9:8 92
9:11 93
9:11–13 92
9:12 87, 93
9:12–14 86n20
9:13 84, 93
9:15 93
10–13 30, 149–152, 149n6
10:1 149
10:2 149
10:3–5 182
10:7 149

10:9–10 150, 160
10:14 150
10:15 150
10:17–18 30
11:5–6 150
11:6 160
11:7–8 150
11:9 53n44
11:11 150
11:12–13 150
11:20–21 150
11:21–23 150, 167
11:23–33 167
11:28 9
11:30 165
12:1 150
12:5 165
12:9–10 165
12:11 150
12:12 150
12:12–14 150
12:14 163
12:14–15 165
12:15–18 150
13:3 150
13:4 165
13:10 149

Galatians

1–2 142
1:10 132
1:13 142
1:13–14 133
1:13–16 138
1:13–2:10 143
1:14 142, 185
1:15–24 142
1:23 142
1:24 142
2 83
2:1–10 83, 142
2:9 83
2:10 83, 87, 90, 91
2:11–14 142

2:11–17 143
2:15–17 131
2:15–21 131, 138, 142
2:18–21 132, 143
2:20 74
3–4 112–14
3:16 114
3:17 113
3:18 113
3:19–26 113
3:22 113
3:23 113
3:25 114
3:28 66
4:4 123
4:5 77
4:7 74
4:12 132, 141n36, 143
4:15 127n3
4:19 5, 62, 165
5:10–11 132
5:11–12 149
5:14 64
6:9–10 83, 87
6:10 70, 101
6:14 132
6:14–16 144

Ephesians

1:5 77
1:8–9 179
1:17 179
1:20–22 123
1:21 123
1:22 125
2:2 123
2:11–22 91
2:19 74
2:19–22 123
2:20 184
3:10 123
4:11–13 184

4:15 125
4:28 83, 87, 90
5:23 125
6:10–17 123
6:12 123, 124

Philippians

1:1 53n44, 55, 164
2 116
2:5–11 158
2:6 95, 115
2:6–11 24, 78,
  115–116, 140,
  185, 188
2:7 115, 123, 140
2:8–9 140
2:9 115, 123
2:10–11 123, 140
2:11 115, 116
2:19 53n44
2:20 95
2:22 54, 62
2:22–23 53n44
3:1 61n16
3:2–16 139, 140
3:4–5 139
3:4–6 155
3:4–16 138
3:5–6 139
3:6 133, 139
3:7–8 139, 140
3:8 139
3:9 139
3:10 139
3:10–11 145n46
3:17 15, 141n36
4:1 61n16
4:9 15, 141n36
4:18 86, 93

Colossians

1:1 53n44, 55
1:1–2 61n16

1:3–8 52
1:7 53, 188
1:7–8 52n42
1:9 179
1:9–10 189
1:12–14 123
1:15 115
1:15–20 52, 115–
  16, 178, 179,
  180, 185, 189
1:16 116, 122
1:16–17 116
1:18 116, 125
1:19 115
1:20 116
1:24 144, 145
1:24–2:5 xi
1:26–27 179
1:28 179
1:29 5, 178
2:1 52, 52n42
2:1–3 177
2:2–3 181
2:3 179
2:4 181
2:8 185
2:8–9 52
2:10 125
2:12–15 189
2:15 122, 123
2:16–23 52
2:18–19 181
2:19 125
2:20–3:11 189
2:20–3:17 67
2:23 181
3:1 123
3:11 66
4:1 96
4:5–6 187
4:7 61n16
4:9 61n16
4:10 48n37, 49
4:12 52, 52n42, 53
4:13 127n3

1 Thessalonians

1:1 53n44, 55
1:5–6 5, 141n36
1:6 15
2 159
2:3 149
2:7 9, 62, 165
2:9 163
2:11 9
2:11–12 9, 62
2:13 5, 9
2:17 10
3:1–2 10
3:1–6 53n44
3:2 55, 61n16
3:5 10
3:6 55
3:8 10
4:3–9 5
4:9 64
4:10–12 64
4:16–17 123
4:19–21 5
5:12 26, 164
5:14 83

2 Thessalonians

1:1 53n44, 55
2:8 123
3:6 184
3:6–12 83, 89

1 Timothy

in toto 109n18
1:2 54
1:3 53n44
1:18 53n44, 54, 55
2:5 21
3:1–13 165
3:4 26, 164
3:5 164
3:12 26, 164
3:16 123, 185

4:12 53n44
4:14 53n44
5:3–16 83
5:8 90
5:17 26, 164
5:17–19 186
6:13 127n3
6:18 83, 88
6:19 88

2 Timothy

in toto 109n18
1:5 55
1:5–6 53n44
2:8 109
2:8–13 109, 116
2:9–14 109
2:11–13 185
3:11 53n44
3:15 53n44, 55
4:9 54
4:11 48n37, 49
4:13 53n44
4:21 53n44, 54

Titus

in toto 109n18
1:5–9 165
1:6 186
3:8 164
3:14 83, 88, 164

Philemon

in toto 72–76
1 53n44, 54, 55,
  72, 73, 74
2 72
3 73
4–7 73
8–16 73
10 62, 74
16 74, 189
17 75

18–19 72
21 75
22 75
23 52n42
24 48n37, 49

Hebrews

2:14–18 77
5:6 21
7:11 21
7:15–17 21
7:20–23 21
8:6 21
9:15 21
10:21 21
11 108n13
12:24 21
13:23 53n44

1 Peter

2:9 22
2:21–23 148
3:18–22 185

2 Peter

1:1 95

3 John

15 59n8

Revelation

12:1–12 108n13
21–22 108n13

**Deuterocanoni-
cal Books**

Sirach

7:10 88
12:3 88
25:1 69
29:12 88

35:2 88
38:24–25 36

Dead Sea Scrolls

CD 108n13
1QM 108n13
1QS 97

Mishnah

Mishnah Avot

1:1 183
2:2 162
2:4 59
4:5–7 162

**Other Ancient
Writings**

1 Clement

4–6 108n13
9–12 108n13
17:1–19:2 108n13
31:1–32:4 108n13

Aristotle

Eudemian Ethics
33n8

*Nicomachean
Ethics*
in toto 33
8 33n8
8.2.5 34
8.3.1–6 36
8.3.8 35
8.5 36
8.12.1–6 69
9 33n8
9.9.10 54
9.10 40

Rhetoric
1.1.1 160n36

Athanasius

*Letter to
Marellinus*
2–8 108n13

Augustus

*Res Gestae Divi
Augusti*
4.1–4 154

Cicero

Brutus
59 160n36
290 160

*De inventione
rhetorica*
1.6 160n36

On Duties
1.150–51 162

On Friendship
5.18 36
6.20 34
9.32 37
13.50 36
19.69 36

*Letters to
Atticus*
17.5–6 34

Dio Chrysostom

Discourses
34.6 160n36

Discourses 1–11
3.86–90 39

Oration 31
in toto 152n13

*Second Tarsic
Discourse*
34.21–23 162

*Inscriptiones
Graecae V.1 1145*

*Laconia et
Messenia*
Line 19 98

Irenaeus

*On the Apostolic
Preaching*
in toto 108n13

Isocrates

To Antipater
4–6 40

John Chrysostom

*Treatise on the
Priesthood*
1:1–3 47

Josephus

*Antiquities of
the Jews*
in toto 108n13
20.34–53 88

Jewish War
108n13

*Life of Flavius
Josephus*
1–2 155
89 155

Letter of Aristeas

228 95
257 95

Origen

First Homily

in toto   108n13

Philo

*On the Special
Laws*

4.231   95

Who Is the Heir?

141–206   95

Plato

Symposium

in toto   35n10

Plutarch

*On Brotherly
Love*

2   63
3   64
5   64
7   69

10   67
12   65
14   65
15   65
16   67, 69
17   70
18   70
20   63, 66

*On Having
Many Friends*

3   34

*How a Man May
Become Aware
of His Progress
in Virtue*

14   35

*How to Tell a
Friend from a
Flatterer*

in toto   39

Parallel Lives

in toto   35

*Sayings of the
Romans*

202.1–3   65n27

*On the Sign of
Socrates*

in toto   97

Pseudo-Phocylides

137   95

Quintilian

*Institutio
oratoria*

12.10.72   160n36

**Sappho and
Alcaeus**

*Greek Lyric:
Sappho and
Alcaeus*

in toto   36

Seneca

*Apocolocyntosis
divi Claudii*

in toto   111

On Benefits

2.17.3–5   97

*Letters to
Lucilius*

3.1–2   38

Strabo

Geography

14.2.5   88

Theophrastus

Characters

in toto   35